The European Center-Right
at the End of the Twentieth Century

The European Center-Right at the End of the Twentieth Century

Edited by Frank L. Wilson

St. Martin's Press
New York

ISBN 0–312–16578–1

Library of Congress Cataloging-in-Publication Data
Wilson, Frank L.
    The European center-right at the end of the twentieth century /
[edited by] Frank L. Wilson
        p. cm.
Includes bibliographical references (p.) and index.
ISBN 0–312–16578–1
1. Political parties—Europe—History—20th century—Congresses.
2. Conservatism—Europe—History—20th century—Congresses.
3. Right and left (Political science)—Congresses.   I. Wilson,
Frank Lee, 1941– .
JN94.A979E8468   1998
324.2'15'09409049—dc21   98–21460
                                                                      CIP

Design by Letra Libre

First edition: November, 1998
10 9 8 7 6 5 4 3 2 1

Contents

INTRODUCTION

The Center-Right
in European Politics

Frank L. Wilson

This collection of chapters on the center-right in Europe has its origins, paradoxically, in a conference on the legacy of the François
Mitterrand years, held in 1995 at Harvard's Center for European
Studies. The final panel reflected on the "state of the left" at the end of
Mitterrand's presidency. The panelists and audience reflected on the social
democratic and socialist parties of Western Europe—nearly all of which
were out of power at the time and many of which seemed unlikely to govern in the near future. As I listened to the discussion it struck me as unusual that academics, including me, would spend so much time and ink on
parties that governed by exception rather than on the center-right parties
that usually dominate politics in Europe.

With the exception of Scandinavia and the newer southern democracies, the center-right has provided government in Western Europe for
most of the postwar period. But we scholars for whatever reasons have
chosen to examine more closely the left and the political extremes of both
the left and right rather than study the center-right parties that have governed. For some of us, our ideological preferences have guided us to the
left; for others, the changes in left-wing parties have been more theoreti-
cally interesting than the less dynamic center-right parties. The result is
large numbers of volumes and articles on left-wing opposition parties and
very few on the center and conservative parties of government.

It was thus at a conference to discuss the left that I thought of providing some balance through a collection of essays on the center-right
in principal West European democracies. The chapters in this volume

were written expressly for this collection. Most were presented initially at panels at the 1996 Conference of Europeanists in Chicago and the 1996 American Political Science Association Annual Meeting in San Francisco.

A New Right?

It is not only the need for balance that motivates our attention to the center-right. Many see the emergence over the past 15 years of a new era of conservativism in advanced democracies.[1] Pundits and politicians alike suggest the demise of the European postwar consensus on mixed economies and social welfare states; many proclaim the emergence of a new neoliberal consensus. With its origins in the thought of conservative economists and social critics, and championed by such conservatives as Margaret Thatcher and Ronald Reagan, neoliberalism reflects the agenda of the right at the end of the twentieth century. It provides an ideological and economic challenge to the mixed economy, interventionist state, and the social welfare programs that had spread through most industrial democracies since the Great Depression of the 1930s. Just as social democracy had become the prevailing paradigm in Western Europe after World War II, some see the neoliberal paradigm as dominant at the end of the century. Its prevalence may well be expected to provide political and electoral benefits to the center-right parties that have advocated it.

There remains much controversy over both the demise of the social democratic consensus and the extent of acceptance for the neoliberal agenda in advanced democracies. This poses broader issues than we can address in this volume. Our essays are efforts to assess the spread of neoliberalism among conservative and center-right parties in Europe. How much of the new agenda has been adopted by these parties? Can they turn widespread, at least at the elite level, acceptance of this new agenda to their political advantage? Broad elite acceptance of new economic and social ideas does not necessarily transform into votes. For example, in much of Western Europe, the success of the postwar social democratic consensus did not mean that the left usually governed. Indeed, in several European countries, it was the center-right parties that built the social welfare states and mixed economies promoted by social democratic principles. Will there be a similar situation now that the agenda seems to be set by the right? Will the ideas of the right permeate the parties of the left in the ways that the social democratic values were accepted by the center-right in the 1940s and 1950s? Will the left implement the center-right's neoliberal policies? We will be examining the political settings in several European countries to see whether center-right parties are able to translate the spread of neoliberal ideas into electoral successes.

What Is the Center-Right?

A central question facing the contributors to this volume was what party or parties constitute the center-right in their countries. In some cases, such as Britain, the answer was easy, but in other countries it was much more difficult. Names are often misleading. For example, the principal center-right party in Portugal is known as the Social Democratic party. Center-right parties often contend that the traditional left/right political spectrum no longer has any meaning—if they accept that such political definitions ever had validity. In several European countries, it is politically unacceptable to be right-wing. As Irwin points out in his chapter on the Netherlands, conservativism often connotes "oldfashioned," "outmoded," "cramped," or even "reactionary." As a result, European parties often deny their conservativism even though most observers would place those parties well on the right. In several major center-right parties—such as the French Gaullists and the former Christian Democrats in Italy—there are strong progressive traditions and factions that see themselves not only as the left-wing of the party but on the left of the entire political spectrum.

Unlike the social democratic left, which is identified with a common historical tradition and ideology, there is no single conservative tradition in contemporary European politics. Indeed, conservativism may refer to a political ideology, a set of values and norms, or simply an incremental, pragmatic method of politics.[2] Even in Britain, where the center-right is dominated by a single Conservative party, that party draws on Whig and Tory traditions. The merger of these two tendencies into a single party is more than a century old, but differences between the two legacies often produce tensions and divisions within the contemporary Conservative party. Elsewhere in Europe, the center-right is fragmented into two or more parties representing one or more traditions or ideologies: classical conservativism, mercantilism, anticommunism, pragmatism, nationalism, Christian democracy, and historical liberalism. These traditions differ from each other within as well as between countries. In most European countries, the remnants of each of these legacies are still present in separate parties or within more inclusive center-right parties. As a result of the different heritages and emphases, the various parties in this volume do not have a common parliamentary group in the European Parliament as do the social democrats. Instead there are four transnational party groups claiming to represent one or another strain of the center-right. One of them, the Portuguese Social Democrats, even sought—unsuccessfully—membership in the socialist European parliamentary group.

This fragmentation of conservative traditions coupled with the reluctance of many center-right parties to accept the conservative label results in some curious names for the parties we will be studying in this volume on the center-right. In France, they are known as the "majority" or even as the "ex-majority" when they are out of office; in Scandinavia, they are defined by what they are not: the "nonsocialist" bloc; in some countries they are the "bourgeois bloc;" in Portugal they are even called "social democrats."

The authors of our country studies have identified the key parties in their separate countries that they believe should be considered members of the broad political family of the center-right. As a result of differences between political settings, there are some inconsistencies in the parties that are included from country to country. For example, in the multiparty systems where broad coalitions of the center-right have played key roles as political partners such as in the Netherlands, Sweden, and Norway, the classical liberal parties have been included in the chapters. In countries where major parties or coalitions dominate the center-right, as in Britain or Germany, smaller liberal parties have not been included here.[3] In general, we have excluded the parties of the far right. They have been covered elsewhere and extensively in recent years as a result of their increased prominence in several European countries.[4]

The Far Right and the European Center-Right

While the parties of the far right are not the object of our study in this volume, they cannot be ignored because of the effects of their presence on and prominence for competing parties on the center-right. One of the key developments in European politics over the past 15 years has been the renewed political presence of the radical right. For nearly 40 years, the defeat of nationalist and fascist causes in World War II discredited and demobilized the far right in most West European countries. The revival of the radical right came quickly in the 1980s and has spread over much of Europe.

Its renewal came with the emergence of issues that the mainstream parties avoided. Over the last two decades, large-scale immigration from third-world countries into once racially homogeneous European countries, the flow of refugees seeking political asylum from conflicts in troubled East European and third-world countries, chronic and serious unemployment, and a concomitant rise of urban blight in the form of increasing crime and drug use brought new anxieties and created new political issues. Sensing the racism and nationalism that underlined these new issues, the parties of the traditional right were hesitant to approach them. When they did address these issues, they advocated moderate solutions that failed to meet the expectations of those mobilized by fears of immigration and its alleged consequences. The mainline parties on both the left and right, to their credit, generally refused to make the connection between unemployment or rising crime rates and the large immigrant populations. But extremist parties were quick to take up the banners of nationalism and racism to blame foreigners for unemployment, crime, and a host of other modern problems. Unfortunately, their calls fell on responsive ears in several countries.

The rise of the extreme right has posed a serious threat to the overall political system and to the center-right parties in particular in several of the countries included in this volume. Other European countries proved more resistant to the far right even though their social conditions and demography did not differ from their neighbors. Our chapters will address the nature of the revival of the radical right in terms of how it affects the political and strategic challenges presented by this movement to the established center-right parties. The focus will be on the effects of this movement on the traditional parties of the center-right rather than on the far right parties themselves. With the partial exception of those in Italy, the parties of the extreme right have been excluded from the main political field of action. But their ghetto position has not kept them from altering electoral alignments and the policy positions of mainline parties on both the right and the left. The questions we will explore in each country include: How serious is the extreme right's electoral threat to the center-right? And to what extent has the radical right affected the policy agendas, programs, and political strategies of the mainline center-right parties?

Center-Right Parties and the Changing Party Systems in Western Democracies

Nearly all observers agree that sweeping changes in party systems are underway in most western democracies.[5] Since the advent of universal suffrage, political parties have been the way of organizing representative democracy. With parties at the core of democracy, their crisis over the last two decades is often seen as a crisis for democracy as a whole. While public confidence in the established parties and voter turnout have declined, the older parties nevertheless shrug off reform efforts from within and with few exceptions successfully resist challenges from new parties and alternative political organizations. This has been true of the parties of the center-right—with the notable exception of the Italian Christian Democrats. As Peter Mair argues, these parties—and those on the left—seem less relevant as representative agencies at the same time that they are achieving greater privileges in terms of money, offices for their members, and status.[6]

Earlier studies indicated that European parties have moved away from the cadre or elite and mass parties described by Maurice Duverger.[7] The "catchall" parties whose development were noted by Otto Kirchheimer also seem less relevant.[8] Today, some talk of a new type of media party based on a professional and expert staff who see electoral politics simply in terms of effective management and public relations. Still others see the emergence of "cartel" parties whose collusion with the state providing key parties of all brands with access to state resources that ensure their collective survival.[9] In the United States, Robert Aldrich has described the emergence of service parties, or parties that stand simply to serve the interests and needs of their candidates in winning elections, candidates who may have other resources to draw on than those offered by their parties.[10]

In the past, European parties have had more of an existence apart from their elected officials, candidates, and their elections. But that is changing in Europe with new patterns in campaign forms, communication and transportation changes, and the growing role of media—and money—in electoral campaigns. The country studies will explore the changing nature of center-right parties and their ability to resist the political party decline that so many scholars identify as a current feature of democratic politics.

Each chapter attempts to locate bases of electoral support for the center-right parties. Changes in society, the economy, and in values have produced changes in the traditional alignment of durable socioeconomic cleavages with parties on a left/right continuum. Broad-based and lasting prosperity coupled with structural shifts in patterns of employment have diluted the class awareness. Religion has become less important in most people's lives and that has diminished some of the effects of religion in structuring the vote. Our authors will look at the changing social bases for center-right parties. They will also explore the political consequences for the center-right parties in the shifts in their electoral bases and the erosion of traditional cleavages.

While there are obvious organizational differences, there are also similarities in how center-right parties structure themselves across countries. Some organizational structures remain from the era when center-right parties were largely the loose coalitions of notables who wanted a party label more than an organization, and other party structures date from the postwar era when conservative parties sought to emulate the better organized social democratic parties. As we shall see, though, the center-right parties have benefited from their lighter organizations, greater flexibility, and lack of constraints from members to adjust to the more candidate-driven campaigns of the 1980s and 1990s.

In most of our countries, the center-right includes more than one party. Our authors look at the relationships among competing center-right parties (where there is such competition) and the alliances that link them together. In most cases, the competing center-right parties differ little in their policy positions. But historical legacies and personal rivalries keep them separate. Our authors look at the nature of their coalitions and how cohesive the center-right is in those settings where separate parties compete.

Despite their different legacies, there is much similarity in the specific policy positions that the center-right parties defend in their different countries. Our authors have explored the presence and impact of neoliberalism on the parties' programs. They also look at how they have addressed new issues such as immigration, moral questions, and the environment. We have tried to devote special attention to the parties' attitudes toward the European Union.

Do Parties Make a Difference?

Nearly two decades ago, as Margaret Thatcher came to power in Britain, Richard Rose posed the question of whether her Conservatives or any other party could make a significant difference on the course of a country's existence.[11] The question remains relevant now at the turn of the century. If a new consensus has emerged based on neoliberal economic and social values and this consensus is accepted by the mainstream parties of the left and right that are likely to dominate politics in European countries, can we expect much change as these parties rotate in and out of power? In addition, intimate international economic interdependency, rapid and improved worldwide communications, and international social and political expectations limit what parties can do in any single country without endangering their country's economic competitiveness or its international image. The inertia of established policies and the bureaucracies that administer them, vested interests of those who benefit from existing policies and practices, and limits on the time and energy on political leaders confronting not only their policymaking tasks but also their need to be reelected, all combine to limit what parties and their leaders can do to change public policy. With these limits in mind, our authors have looked to see how much or how little difference parties can make in the affairs of their countries.

Looking Ahead

In the following chapters, noted scholars will examine the center-right in ten major European democracies: Britain, France, Germany, Greece, Italy, the Netherlands, Norway, Portugal, Spain, and Sweden. We have tried to use a uniform framework to bind together our analyses and to permit cross-national comparisons. But we have recognized that differences between countries do not permit entirely parallel presentations. Each author identifies the most important center-right parties and discusses their social bases, organizations, and political strategies. They will look at the future of the center-right in their countries not only from the standpoint of its electoral fortunes but from the standpoint of its ability to shape and dominate the political agenda.

In a concluding chapter, I will come back to these issues to make some comparative statements. In so doing, we will be able to identify some trends among parties of the center-right and address some of the broader issues of political party change in Europe today. This is an important time to look at the center-right. Its agenda is at the center of policy debates, but its electoral preeminence is far from assured. It is useful to have these country studies of parties that often govern but are also often ignored by scholars.

Notes

1. Desmond S. King, *The New Right: Politics, Markets and Citizenship* (Chicago: The Dorsey Press, 1987). See also Barry Cooper, Allan Kornberg, and William Mishler, eds., *The Resurgence of Conservativism in Anglo-American Democracies* (Durham, North Carolina: Duke University Press, 1988).
2. Suggested by Galen Irwin in chapter six of this volume.
3. For a comprehensive examination of the liberal parties, see E. J. Kirchner, ed., *Liberal Parties in Western Europe* (Cambridge, England: Cambridge University Press, 1988).
4. See for example the two volume study *The Far Right in Western and Eastern Europe,* 2nd ed., ed. by Luciano Cheles, Ronnie Ferguson, and Michalina Vaughn (Harlow, England: Longman, 1995).
5. For a recent summary of challenges facing established parties, see Peter Mair and Gordon Smith, eds., *Understanding Party System Change in Western Europe* (London: Frank Cass, 1990). See also Richard S. Katz and Peter Mair, "Changing Models of Party Organization and Party Democracy," *Party Politics* 1:1 (1995): 5–28.
6. Peter Mair, "Political Parties, Popular Legitimacy and Public Privilege," *West European Politics* 18 (July 1995): 40–57.
7. Maurice Duverger, *Political Parties,* trans. Barbara and Robert North (New York: Wiley, 1954).
8. Otto Kirchheimer, "The Transformation of the European Party Systems," in *Political Parties and Political Development,* ed. Joseph LaPalombara and Myron Weiner (Princeton, NJ: Princeton University Press, 1966).

9. Katz and Mair, "Changing Models of Party Organization and Party Democracy," pp. 5–28.

10. John H. Aldrich, *Why Parties? The Origin and Transformation of Political Parties in America* (Chicago: University of Chicago Press, 1995).

11. Richard Rose, *Do Parties Make a Difference?* 2nd ed. (Chatham, NJ: Chatham House, 1983).

CHAPTER ONE

The British Conservatives: A Dominant Party in Crisis

Jorgen Rasmussen

The Right in Britain

Historical Background and Development

Grassroots partisan organization, as distinct from parliamentary factions, developed in Britain in the second half of the nineteenth century. In 1852 the Conservatives established a central headquarters to coordinate candidature. Then in 1867 they created the first modern party in Britain, linking constituency parties and their members throughout the country. (Their Liberal opponents would not found a mass party organization for another decade.) Despite swings in strength in the subsequent century and a quarter, the Conservatives have been Britain's dominant party.

This success occurred in part because 1867 was a crucial year for another reason: the passage of the second Reform Act. This legislation, enacted by a Conservative Government, expanded the franchise to include industrial workers, making them a majority of the electorate in many factory towns and cities. The Conservatives thus initiated an enduring ability to win substantial support among working-class voters.

The struggle over home rule for Ireland in the 1880s, which split the Liberal party, fundamentally altered the Conservatives as well. To this point the Conservatives had been primarily the party of the landed interests, while the Liberals articulated the views of the commercial and manufacturing elements. Although Ireland was the issue that divided the Liberals, the cleavage drove much of the business interest out of the

Liberals and into the Conservatives. Thus the Conservative party "modernized"; it did not remain simply the instrument through which an increasingly outmoded way of life sought to preserve its dwindling power. The early history of the Conservatives well illustrates the adaptability and pragmatism that made the party more effective and influential than its Liberal opponents.

Although various other right-of-center political groups have existed in Britain, none of them has significantly challenged the Conservatives' control of this portion of the spectrum. The far-right National Front made its greatest effort in 1979, offering more than 300 candidates. But they attracted fewer than 200,000 votes, less than one percent of the total cast. The Liberal Democrats, the current name of the once major Liberal party, do not consider themselves to be even slightly right-of-center.[1] In Britain the right means the Conservative party.

Electoral Support and Bases

The twentieth-century Conservative party has had a broad appeal, having expanded beyond the landed and agricultural interests to embrace commercial interests at whatever level—small business, industrialists, managers. Many professionals, such as doctors and lawyers, have been attracted to the party. In addition, the party has enjoyed greater success than would be anticipated for a right-of-center party in winning support among the working class—both manual and white collar.

A regional analysis of constituency results provides some insight into sources of Conservative strength. All of the British (Northern Ireland excluded) constituencies for each of the 13 general elections since mid-century were assigned to one of three geographical areas and further divided according to whether they were located in major metropolitan areas or in smaller cities and rural areas. The extent to which the Conservative party in the House of Commons over- or under-represented particular areas appears in table 1.1. In 1950, for example, 27 percent of all British constituencies were located in the nonmetropolitan south.[2] Nearly half, 45 percent, of all the Conservatives elected in 1950 won one of the constituencies in this category. Conservatives were overrepresented in "other southern" constituencies by 18 percentage points. The Conservative parliamentary delegation has been skewed disproportionately toward southern nonmetropolitan constituencies for the last half century. In contrast, the party has been persistently and increasingly underrepresented in northern England, Scotland, and Wales, especially in the most urbanized areas.

In Scotland the Conservatives' loss of support has been "nothing short of dramatic."[3] In the 1950s Conservatives actually did somewhat better in

Table 1.1 Regional Deviations in Conservative Representation

A. General elections of the 1950s and 1960s

	1950*	1951	1955	1959	1964	1966
Δ Total seats	+	+	+	+	−	−
Southern urban	−5	−5	−4	−2	−4	−6
Other southern	+18	+16	+15	+14	+18	+21
Other Midlands	0	0	−1	0	+2	+3
Northern & Celtic urban	−4	−4	−3	−3	−7	−7
Other northern & Celtic	−7	−6	−6	−8	−9	−10

B. General elections of the 1970s

	1970	1974 Feb	1974 Oct	1979
Δ Total seats	+	−	−	+
Southern urban	−5	−6	−7	−5
Other southern	+16	+21	+22	+19
Other Midlands	+3	+3	+3	+4
Northern & Celtic urban	−8	−9	−8	−9
Other northern & Celtic	−6	−9	−10	−8

C. General elections of the 1980s and 1990s

	1983	1987	1992
Δ Total seats	+	−	−
Southern urban	−3	−2	−5
Other southern	+16	+19	+22
Other Midlands	+5	+6	+6
Northern & Celtic urban	−11	−13	−13
Other northern & Celtic	−6	−8	−9

Source: Compiled from relevant tables in David Butler and a variety of associates, *The British General Election of 19XX* (London: Macmillan, various dates).
Notes: Southern urban = inner London, southern and Midlands conurbations and major cities.
Other southern includes suburban London.
Northern & Celtic urban = conurbations and major cities in the northwest, Yorkshire, the north, Wales, and Scotland.
*Some columns do not sum to zero because of rounding error.
Demographic change, local government reorganization, and redistricting have affected the allocation of constituencies to one category or another over the period. Classification is quite comparable, but not precisely the same, from one section to another of Table 1.1.

Scottish constituencies than they did in English ones of a similar socioeconomic type. By the start of the 1970s this had reversed and worsened
further before the decade was out, with little subsequent recovery. David
Seawright and John Curtice's analysis suggests that the party blundered in
the mid-1960s by shifting from "Unionist" to "Conservative," seeming to
become Anglicized. The timing of the change was especially ill-advised because the Scottish electorate, in part due to economic problems north of
the border, was moving left. Except for Scotland, Conservative support
does not seem to have experienced notable regional fluctuations in the last
half century, as table 1.1 shows.

The top line in each section of table 1.1 indicates whether the Conservatives gained or lost seats in each general election. The pattern is for
the party to become more representative as its strength in the Commons
expands and to become less so as its strength declines. In October 1974 the
proportion of the Conservative parliamentary party representing southern
nonmetropolitan constituencies was 22 percentage points greater than was
the share of seats of that type among all British constituencies. As the Conservatives gained seats in both of the next two elections, that disparity declined to 16 percentage points, only to return once again to 22 points as
the party lost seats in the next 2 elections.

When Conservative underrepresentation in northern and Celtic urban
areas was at its lowest toward the close of the 1950s, the party had increased
its strength in the Commons in four consecutive elections. In 1970, however, the Conservatives' gain in total seats failed to make the party any less
unrepresentative of northern and Celtic urban areas. Nor did its total gains
in 1979 and, especially, in 1983 help. Conservative losses in the next two
elections, starting from a notably skewed distribution of seats, served to
drive unrepresentativeness in these areas to a new depth.

Summing the deviations (regardless of signs) for 1992 in table 1.1 totals
55 percentage points, the largest gap for any of the 13 general elections.
The Conservatives long have claimed to be the party of the entire country, and have denounced Labour as a sectional party devoted to the interests of only some classes. The skewed distribution of Conservative
legislative strength undermines such a claim and may well impede the
party's ability to formulate policy with broad appeal.

A socioeconomic classification of constituencies provides further insight into the bases of Conservative support. A factor analysis in 1970 of
40 indicators of demographic type yielded 6 "families" of constituencies.[4]
As can be seen from table 1.2, during the 1970s Conservative representation in the Commons derived disproportionately from 3 of these families.

Conservative strength in suburban, rural, and seaside resort seats hardly
was surprising. What was notable was the party's dominance in growth

Table 1.2 Deviations in Conservative Representation by Socioeconomic Constituency Type

	All Brit. Seats		1974 Feb. Conservative			1974 Oct. Conservative			1979 Conservative		
	#	%	#	%	dev. pp*	#	%	dev. pp*	#	%	dev. pp*
Suburban & service	105	17	93	17	+14	90	32	+15	98	29	+12
Rural & resorts	109	17	88	17	+13	84	30	+13	96	28	+11
Growth	123	20	92	20	+11	85	31	+11	110	32	+12
Stable industrial	159	26	13	26	−22	8	3	−23	21	6	−20
Council housing	67	11	3	11	−10	2	1	−10	4	1	−10
Inner metro	60	10	8	10	−7	8	3	−7	10	3	−7
Total	623		297			277			339		

Notes: *Some columns do not sum to zero because of rounding error.

areas.[5] With nearly a third of the Conservative delegation in the Commons sitting for growth areas, the party had some incentive not to remain content to represent its traditional clientele, but to articulate as well the interests of more modernizing elements in the British economy. A majority of these growth areas were located in the Midlands, which helps to explain the party's success (indicated in table 1.1) in holding its own in this part of England.[6]

Similar analysis for the 1992 general election suggests that the pattern of Conservative strength indicated in table 1.2 did not change notably in the 1980s and early 1990s.[7] A bit of a shift from rural and resort constituencies to suburban ones is about all that might have occurred. Any such shift was too slight to transform the nature of the Conservatives' delegation in the Commons.

On the eve of the Thatcher era, then, the Conservatives were a party based on support in southern, nonmetropolitan areas, especially suburbs, service centers, rural areas, and seaside resorts. Helping to offset the traditionalist influence of such areas was notable additional strength in Midlands growth areas. Any change during the Thatcher era in the bases of support is unlikely to have been sufficient to alter this description. Change was more notable in an area of party weakness. The party always has been weak in northern and Celtic areas, especially in urban constituencies. Under Thatcher this became even more true.[8]

Party Organization and Social Composition

The national organization the Conservatives founded in 1867 did not remain a loosely linked cadre party, but developed into an integrated mass membership party. At its height, shortly after the party's return to power in the early 1950s, the Conservatives had nearly 3 million dues-paying members. Since 1960, however, the party has lost about 64,000 members a year and by the turn of the century may fall below 100,000.[9]

Past Conservative success in recruiting members is rather puzzling given the party's lack of concern with internal democracy. To what extent the antidemocratic power structure portrayed in Robert McKenzie's classic study *British Political Parties* must be qualified is a matter of controversy.[10] Plainly, however, the Conservatives never have sought to give members any control over party policy and tactics. The Conservative Leader, not an organ of the mass party as is true for Labour, personally controls headquarters. The Leader, assisted by his or her personally appointed staff, decides matters of party strategy and finances. The Conservative party annual conference of delegates from the various constituency parties is not granted the power specifically given its Labour counterpart to determine party policy. At times Conservative leaders have simply ignored the resolutions passed at conferences.

Party members' most significant power is selecting candidates. A local constituency party seeking a new candidate may ask headquarters to suggest some possibilities. Individuals wishing to be considered may apply, however, directly to the constituency party. Although the constituency party is supposed to seek headquarters' endorsement for anyone not on a centrally approved list, it does not always do so. Such failures rarely are punished because all local parties tenaciously defend the right to select whomever they wish as their candidate. While central headquarters has a role in candidate selection, the bulk of the power lies with the constituency party. Here, as in other matters of procedure and policy, consistent implementation is hampered by loose articulation.[11]

The electoral importance of power to select a party's candidates is obvious. More important, however, is the long-term impact on the nature of the party. If constituency parties consistently select free-market ideologues in preference to social-market moderates, the bulk of the Conservatives MPs will in time shift to the right. Not only are MPs able to influence party policy, but they are the pool from which party leaders are drawn, and they themselves elect the party's Leader.

David Butler and Michael Pinto-Duschinsky have argued that reform of the party after its 1945 defeat failed to broaden its social composition. They found that Conservative MPs and their leaders differed little in occupational and educational background in the mid-1970s from what they had been half a century earlier. The proportion coming from aristocratic families had declined and the average ability had increased, but the party was no more diversified than it had been—still dominated by upper-middle-class men.

While granting that members of the social elite can hold liberal policy views, Butler and Pinto-Duschinsky believed that the party's unrepresentativeness hurt it (and British politics generally) for three reasons. First, class was a significant influence on voting behavior; being regarded as elitist obviously must cost a party votes. Second, many issues had become valence issues, forcing the parties to appeal on grounds of being able to perform better. Convincing the public they could do so was difficult for the Conservatives when none of their leaders had any personal experience of ordinary people's lives. Finally, even should the party choose as its Leader someone not of the social elite, he or she was pressured to become like the upper-middle-class people who, given the party's unrepresentativeness, would be their chief colleagues.[12]

Whether Butler and Pinto-Duschinsky's concern has remained valid through the period of Thatcherism can be ascertained by comparing the social background of its MPs at three elections (1951, 1979, and 1992) returning very similar numbers of Conservatives.[13] Table 1.3 suggests little change between the first pair of elections, despite the interval being twice as long as that between the second pair. Only during the Thatcher era does even a slight change occur.

The presence of women among Conservative MPs and candidates did increase, but failed to make either group representative.[14] Section B of table 1.3 shows that the Butler and Duschinsky finding of growing average ability among Conservative MPs (at least as measured by educational attainment) continued. The proportion of MPs (of candidates, as well) not having gone beyond secondary school was halved from 1951 to 1992 while the proportion with a university education rose somewhat. More indicative of any change in social elite image is the decline of Old Etonians—perceptible in 1979 but not clearly a trend until 1992. Their presence also was halved among both MPs and all candidates over the entire period. The figures on public school (in fact, elite private school) educational background suggest the end of an era. Conservative MPs and candidates were just as likely to have been educated in the public schools in 1979 as they had been over a quarter of a century earlier. A little over a decade later, however, the proportion had declined sufficiently that for the first time a slight majority of Conservative candidates were educated in the state school system—most did not go to public schools.

The benefit of coming from a socially elite background, however, persisted as the first and second columns for each of the three elections show. In every instance the proportion of MPs from an elite educational background (and education at any university does make one elite) is greater than is the proportion of candidates. This means that those with the more elite background are more likely to be adopted for the more desirable seats. What activists in such areas want continues to be a white man of the proper background.

Section C of table 1.3 suggests that although certain occupational backgrounds are preferred, employment does not seem to have the same social cachet as education. The proportion of each category among MPs differs little from that for all candidates. As was true for education, occupational background alters little over the entire 40-year period, and what shift does occur comes during the Thatcher era. Not even slight progress was made in obtaining working-class candidates or MPs. Business rose slightly to become the leading source of MPs and candidates, while the professions slipped back.

Butler and Pinto-Duschinsky's concern about unrepresentativeness goes beyond MPs to focus on party officers. They noted that at the end of

Table 1.3 Social Background of Conservative MPs

	1951		1979		1992	
	% MPs	% Candidates	% MPs	% Candidates	% MPs	% Candidates
A. Gender						
Women	2	4	2	5	6	9
B. Education						
No more than secondary	13	19	8	10	6	9
Eton	24	16	18	10	10	7
Public school	75	59	73	61	62	49
Oxbridge	52	22	49	38	45	31
All universities	65	53	68	60	73	68
C. Occupation**						
Professional	40	38	40	41	32	30
Business	35	31	33	32	37	39
Miscellaneous	21	16	19	15	19	18
Teachers	2	4	5	7	7	7
Clerical	3	8	2	2	4	5
Workers	*	2	1	2	1	1

Sources: Calculated from Butler and a variety of associates for 1951, pp. 35–43; for 1979, pp. 278–289; and for 1992, pp. 211–230.

Notes: * = less than 0.5

**Some columns do not sum to zero because of rounding error.

Teachers includes all levels.

Miscellaneous includes farmers, housewives, journalists, private means, and politicians.

Clerical: 1951 combines "Business: commerce: clerical" and "miscellaneous white collar." 1979 and 1992 combines :Business: management/clerical" and "miscellaneous white collar."

the 1960s, while Conservative candidates were twice as likely to come from the professions than were the chairmen of local constituency parties (47 percent to 24 percent), constituency chairmen were twice as likely to come from business backgrounds as were MPs (66 percent to 35 percent). Here again the party was dominated by middle-class men.

Recent nonacademic comment has suggested a possible change during the Thatcher era. Julian Critchley, a Conservative MP who retired from Parliament at the 1997 election, expressed the view most bluntly. In trying to explain why his party was headed for electoral disaster, he warned that "what is becoming increasingly plain is the change of character that is taking place among Conservative MPs. The ballast is now made up of bounders, whose prime objective seems to be the making of money via public relations."[15] He bemoaned the fact that not only have the upper classes long since deserted politics, but so have the educated upper-middle class, in particular the men. As a result, "the majority of those who serve on the selection committees of Tory associations have never picked anyone for anything in their lives" and are easily swayed by the slick appeal of PR types. (He implied, with more than a hint of gender bias, that most of the selectors were easily charmed women.)

A more recent study found that the typical Conservative party member proved to be retired (two-thirds over 55) and not well educated (over half left school at age 16 or younger).[16] Members were not wealthy (nearly half had a household income of £15,000 or less) and did not run businesses (only an eighth were petty bourgeoisie). In contrast to Butler and Pinto-Duschinsky, the study's findings did not suggest that local businessmen dominated constituency parties. The petty bourgeois minority was no more activist than were other members, and women were slightly more active than men.

Those usually considered the pillars of the local community had come to have little to do with the Conservative party; the genteel Conservative MP of the past was being replaced in the Thatcher era by the self-made moneygrubber. Such a change was facilitated by the rise among the electorate of "Essex man." Essex man is a shorthand label for working class— rather more white collar than skilled manual—voters who became very dedicated supporters of Thatcher early on and have not departed from their convictions. Such voters were particularly prominent in a group of five counties north of London where the Conservative vote held up rather better in both 1987 and 1992 than would have been anticipated.[17] Candidates of unpretentious background, in contrast to the more patrician Conservatives of the past, were an important element in obtaining such support. The Tory old guard's complaint about gauche candidates may be a symptom of the party's greater representativeness.

Thatcher did not order a change in the party's social composition. Nonetheless, a shift occurred during her leadership and was further encouraged by John Major's emphasis on classlessness. (It is not without significance that Major is the third successive Conservative Leader from a socially undistinguished background.) Thatcher was contemptuous of the "wets," the more moderate, less fervently dogmatic Conservative MPs. The wets and the more socially prestigious Conservative MPs tended to overlap a good deal. To a considerable extent Thatcher's management of her Cabinet during the 1980s was a process of ridding it of the well-bred and adding the self-made. Butler and Pinto-Duschinsky's expectations proved mistaken: Thatcher was not molded as Leader by associating with the traditional party elite; she dispensed with them as quickly as she could and set a tone for a social reorientation of the party. The long-term effect of "Thatcherism" may be at least as great upon the nature of the Conservative party as upon the values of the British people.

Factions and Tendencies

As the only significant right-of-center party in Britain, the Conservative party spans a considerable distance on the political spectrum. The various political orientations that it encompasses can be placed into several categories.[18] The most fundamental contrast, however, is between the Tory and the Whig traditions, which to a considerable extent correspond to the landed and the commercial interests mentioned above. Tories are especially concerned with social discipline and authority, while Whigs are more concerned with economic efficiency and the creation of wealth. Tories tend to be motivated by, as Philip Norton and Arthur Aughey express it, "compassion and . . . concern for the moral as well as the economic wellbeing of the people," while Whigs give priority to progress over social harmony.

Two of the four types of Tories Norton and Aughey distinguish deserve emphasis: those motivated by noblesse oblige and those by an updated form of paternalism, whom they label "progressive Tories." These two types are the exponents of One-Nation Conservatism. This strand of Conservatism is attributed to the party's late-nineteenth-century Leader Benjamin Disraeli. One-Nation Tories proclaim that all British (originally English) belong, regardless of social station, to the same national community. Therefore, a paternalistic government must provide for the basic needs of all, and everyone can take pride in the glories of the Empire (later Commonwealth).

The Whig tradition, which derives more from self-made men than from patricians, frowns on dependency and thinks that everyone should accept responsibility for themselves. The Whig tradition tended to dominate the

Conservative party between World Wars I and II. The party's typical attitude was that little could be done about the economic problems associated with the worldwide depression. Certainly the ordinary person should not expect the government to insulate them from the necessary workings of the laws of economics. Any interference with these through extensive social welfare programs would only make matters worse. The Conservatives' electoral disaster in 1945 helped to swing leadership of the party to One-Nation Tories. The fissure in the party did not disappear, however, but merely remained dormant for three decades.

Policy and Ideology

Neoliberalism and the Decay of Consensus

In the mid-1970s the advent of a new Leader drawn from the Whig, not the Tory, tradition revivified the party's basic cleavage. Ironically, Margaret Thatcher was elected Leader not so much because Conservative MPs consciously wished to reorient the party, but because they personally disliked the aloofness of then Leader Edward Heath. The party's loss of three of the four general elections in which Heath led the Conservatives made him vulnerable. Initially, Thatcher was merely a stalking horse; a sacrificial lamb who would enable a party heavyweight to topple a Heath damaged by the preliminary skirmish. Her daring won sufficient support, however, to continue the challenge and be chosen his successor.

Although temperamentally opposed to consensus, Thatcher did not arrive in office with an ideologically based program of policy reforms when the Conservatives won in 1979; this program emerged only gradually during her decade in power.[19] The Conservatives traditionally have maintained that they, unlike the Labour party, do not have an ideology; they are too practical for that. The policies they advocate derive not from an integrated worldview, but simply emerge from general attitudes or convictions: for example, that evolutionary, organic change is preferable to root and branch reform. Whether Thatcherism came to be an ideology is a matter of controversy.

Her efforts during the 1980s to implement her beliefs reoriented the party. Her core concern was that government should be downsized. This required improved efficiency, so that fewer civil servants would be needed, and a diminished role for the government—curtailing its scope to fewer activities. A second closely related objective was to extract the government from business. One prong of this effort was competitive tendering. Rather than having certain governmental activities (as routine as janitorial services in public buildings, but going as far as operating the prisons) automatically performed by government employees, the contract to provide the service would be open to bid. If a private firm offered to perform the function at a lower cost than government personnel could, it would be hired to do so. The other prong was to sell much of government-owned enterprises—not only those that Labour had taken into public ownership in the late 1940s, but including even the water supply. "Privatizing" appealed to Thatcher not only because it downsized government, but because selling shares to the public strengthened property-owning democracy. When more people had a stake in society, more would be immune to the appeals of socialism and dependency on the government.

A third fundamental Thatcher goal was to enable the market to perform its task as an instrument for setting society's priorities. The unseen hand of competing market forces should make such decisions, not the all too obvious hand of politicians and Whitehall mandarins. Thatcher was not pro-business. She was unwilling to continue the corporatism of her predecessor, Edward Heath, and to bail out economically hard-pressed businesses with subsidies. Government should not intervene directly in enterprise. Its fiscal and monetary actions would influence economic conditions, but so long as government announced its plans well in advance, business should be left to fend for itself. Those unable to operate efficiently enough to make a profit should go bust; the demise of weak enterprises would strengthen the economy's performance in the long run. Government should intervene only to protect the working of the market. Therefore, trade unions, which had grown so powerful they could extort wage increases in excess of productivity gains, had to be brought to heel.

The fundamental objective of these policies was to break the dependency culture. The basic theme, the central value of Thatcherism, was personal responsibility. While the government might provide some benefits—and she herself proclaimed in the 1987 election campaign that "The National Health Service is safe in our hands"—people should think first about taking care of themselves. Perhaps some political figure can be found elsewhere who challenged the postwar social democratic consensus prior to Thatcher. But her efforts in Britain during the 1980s to beat a retreat from the mixed economy and put much greater emphasis on the working of the market along with shifting the welfare state from elaborate provision of benefits to a minimal safety net clearly made her the best known exponent of neoliberalism. If the postwar social democratic consensus in Western democracies is giving way to a neoliberal orientation, the instigators of that sea change were the British Conservatives under Thatcher.

Movement toward a new consensus is especially noticeable in Britain. Having lost four elections in a row to the Conservatives, the Labour party became desperate for victory. Since fighting Thatcherism had failed to work, Labour decided to embrace much of it—trade unions would *not* be restored to power, enterprises sold to the private investors would *not* be taken back into government ownership, spending would *not* be increased, taxes would *not* go up. Labour Leader Tony Blair became known to disillusioned leftwingers as "Tony Blur" and they referred to his policies as "Tory Lite." The image "new Labour" projected to the electorate is ample evidence that a decade of Thatcherism has shifted the terms of political debate in Britain.

Few dramatic shifts or discontinuities in policy can be expected, therefore, from Labour's 1997 electoral victory. Constitutional reform, however, is the exception. The Conservatives under Major had been unwilling even to consider the possibility. In contrast, Labour and the Liberal Democrats set up at the end of October 1996 a joint committee to devise a mutually acceptable program to alter the power and membership of the House of Lords, establish a bill of rights, and devolve some power to the regions, especially Scotland and Wales. Change in the structure of the British political system had come to be predicated on a Conservative fall from power. The prospect of such constitutional changes, however, hardly were major vote winners.

If most of what Labour was offering was warmed-over Thatcherite policies, why did not the electorate prefer the Conservative original rather than the Labour substitute? Why, if a neoliberal consensus had replaced the old social democratic one, was the Conservative party floundering in the polls for months prior to the 1997 election?

Norton and Aughey foresaw at Thatcherism's origins a danger that her leadership might alienate the party "from a crucial element of its own tradition. That element is the avoidance of apparent dogmatism and the narrow pursuit of an abstract goal." *How* something is done, the style of governance, matters as much as *what* is done. If one appears to be a dogmatic ideologue, then protestations about one's stewardship of the health service are unlikely to be believed. An attempt to improve efficiency and constrain costs by introducing an "internal market" in the health service is likely to be perceived as a threat to privatize it. Any new Labour Government would face the same problem of burgeoning expenses, but any action it might take would not automatically be regarded with suspicion. In vain the Conservatives protested that they had in the past, and would in the future, increase spending on the health service well in excess of the rate of inflation; by the winter of 1996 the health service was widely perceived to be in crisis. A new Labour Government, especially one pledged not to raise taxes, hardly could spend more on health. Its continuity in policy, however, was likely to be perceived more favorably.

The Conservatives' Mix of Policy

The Manifestos.   In Britain official party policy is what the election manifesto says it is. The electorate is said to have given the party that wins the election a mandate to implement the proposals in its manifesto. Conversely, given the absence of impediments in Britain to the party in power, it must justify any failure to deliver on a manifesto commitment.

Control over drafting the manifesto was one of the key struggles during Labour's civil war of the 1980s. In contrast, the Conservative Leader's authority is unchallenged. The party elite will be consulted, but rank-and-file MPs, to say nothing of the mass party or its officers, will have little, if any, input. Should the elite disagree as to whether a particular policy is included or excluded, no vote is taken; the Leader decides. Table 1.4 indicates the most common topics in these Conservative electoral appeals for about half of the twentieth century.[20] Ten topics were mentioned in at least 5 percent of a manifesto's sentences for three or more of the 15 general elections from 1924 through 1979.

Perhaps the most striking aspect of table 1.4 is the evidence of the need the Conservatives have felt to include social services in their election appeals. Surely Labour has the edge on this issue. Yet in *every* election (except for 1931) for over a half century the Conservatives devoted at least 5 percent of

Table 1.4   Topics Receiving the Most Emphasis in Conservative Manifestos, 1924–1979

	1924–1945 (5 elections)	1950–1979 (10 elections)
Social services	4	10
Internationalism	1	8
Empire/special foreign relationships	5	2
Enterprise	1	7
Incentives	0	4
Regulation	0	4
Economic stability	3	2
Regionalism	0	4
Agriculture	4	0
Government performance	2	3

Source: Ian Budge and Dennis Farlie, *Explaining and Predicting Elections* (London: Allen & Unwin, 1983), p. 135.

Note: To be counted for a particular election a topic had to be mentioned in at least 5 percent of the sentences in the manifesto. Only those topics which met that criterion in at least 3 of the 15 general elections are included in the table.

their manifesto to the topic. In fact, in 11 elections they gave it more than a tenth of their attention. The emphasis of social services might make the Conservatives appear to be proponents of welfare capitalism or the social market economy. To the contrary, note how the more recent stress on enterprise, incentives, and regulation characterize the Conservatives as more preoccupied with traditional capitalist concerns in the second half of the century than they were earlier. Interestingly, although Keynesianism won wide acceptance only after World War II, Conservative manifestos since 1950 were less likely (only 20 percent of the elections) than they had been earlier (60 percent of the elections) to emphasize economic stability.

Beyond social services and capitalist themes, foreign affairs has been another major element in Conservative electoral appeals. Not surprisingly, the Empire was more emphasized in the first half of the century. A recent decline in such concerns was more than offset by a rise in emphasis on internationalism. Dedication to the Empire/Commonwealth has long given Conservatives broad policy horizons. Interest in world affairs does not mean, however, that Conservatives have been proponents of regional integration. An analogy to American Midwest isolationism can be found among the "Little Englanders," prominent in—although not confined to—the Conservative party. Cooperative associations are the Conservatives' preferred structure for international bodies. As the European Union has moved toward a common currency and a common security policy, vociferous opponents in the Conservative party have demanded that British sovereignty be protected from continental "federalists." Such concerns complement the Conservatives' traditional claim to be the most patriotic party and their long-standing defense of a strong central government.

The new attention to devolving power within the United Kingdom, therefore, does not indicate a recent evolution in the party's stance. The rise of Scottish and Welsh nationalism, beginning in the late 1960s, compelled the Conservatives to articulate, as had not been essential before, their strong commitment to a *United* Kingdom precluding any element of federalism.

Finally, shifts in manifesto coverage suggest the party's abandonment of a traditional clientele group—farmers. Virtually all of the pre-1950 manifestos stressed agriculture, while none of them for the 10 subsequent elections accorded that topic as much as 5 percent of the total sentences.

Contrasting Conservative manifestos with American Republican party platforms accentuates the British party's distinctive mix of electoral appeals. Of the five topics to which the Conservatives devoted the largest mean percentage of sentences in their manifestos from 1924 through 1979 only two were among the top five in Republican platforms from 1920 through 1972. Both parties stressed government performance, with Republican platforms giving the topic even more space than did Conservative manifestos. While both emphasized social services, the Conservatives accorded it three times as much attention as did the Republicans.

The other chief concerns of the two parties diverged even more. The three remaining of the top five Republican topics were agriculture, the military, and freedom—none of these were among the Conservatives' top five. On the other hand the Conservatives emphasized enterprise, economic stability, and internationalism, giving them half again to twice as much attention as they received in Republican platforms. The evidence from the manifestos suggests that while the Conservatives clearly resemble the stereotype of what a right-of-center party is likely to offer to the electorate, yet their policy mix has been distinctive, including some elements not anticipated. The party has stressed enterprise, incentives, and regulation even more than it did earlier in the century. But it also has been a party of considerable international concerns and one that has given top priority to taking positions on social services. And it has emphasized economic stability. Finally the party has been adaptable. As world conditions changed, it shifted priorities from the Empire to internationalism. The Conservative party did not remain wedded to its traditional clientele, but deemphasized agriculture.

Election Addresses. Although the manifesto is the official statement of the party's program, the voters may well think that party policy is what the candidates say. Therefore, the contents of election addresses, the leaflet that the post office delivers without charge for each candidate during the course of the campaign, should be examined. Comparing addresses for 1951 (the year of the party's return to power after World War II), October 1974 (the last election before Thatcher became Leader), 1979 (the first election when she was Leader), and 1987 (the last election before she left office) helps to discover any shifts in issues emphasized by Conservative candidates.[21] To make the analysis manageable, only those issues mentioned in at least 64 percent of the sample are included in table 1.5.

Economic issues have received persistent attention from Conservative candidates. That candidates for the right-of-center party should be concerned about inflation is not surprising, but note that even they cannot ignore unemployment. Social issues also have been prevalent in Conservative election addresses, with a bit of a tendency for those in earlier elections to be more interested in providing social benefits. Nonetheless, in 1987 Conservative candidates clearly picked up on Thatcher's concern to reassure the voters that her party would not weaken health care. The frequent reference in 1987 to the sale of public housing to its occupants (surprisingly mentioned just as often more than a decade earlier) is worth noting. During

Table 1.5 Issues Most Often Mentioned in Conservative Election Addresses

	1951	1974	1979	1987
A. Economic				
Inflation		79	83	64
Un- or full employment	69		86	78
Taxes			88	
Property taxes		78		
Increased production	69			
Public ownership		74		
B. Social				
Pensions	66	83		
National Health Service				78
Increased public housing	76			
Sell public housing		69		70
Help first-time buyers		65		
Mortgages		82		
Law and order			87	74
Trade union reform			71	
C. Foreign				
Commonwealth and Empire	64			
Rearmament	72			
Nuclear defense				80
D. Political				
Socialist extravagance	65			
Labour's performance			67	
Need for a government of national unity		70		

Source: Butler and a variety of associates, *The British General Election of 19XX,* 1951, pp. 55–56; 1974, pp. 235–236; 1979, pp. 298–301; and 1987, pp. 222–226.

the 1980s the Conservatives managed to obtain more support from the skilled manual working class than did Labour, which would seem to be the natural recipient of its votes. Some public housing in Britain is of desirable quality; Conservative legislation required local government to permit public housing tenants to buy their residence on very favorable terms. Some have argued that many prosperous working families, especially the wives and mothers, voted Conservative out of gratitude for being enabled to own a home of their own.

Section C of table 1.5 indicates how seldom foreign affairs matter in British elections. Party leaders may emphasize international affairs in the manifesto's program, but legislative candidates seldom try to win votes with such appeals. In 1979 more than three quarters of the sample of addresses made no reference to international matters, and in 1974 virtually none did (no mention in 95 percent). The prominence of the nuclear weapons issue in 1987 was part of the Conservative effort to swing sentiment against Labour Leader Neil Kinnock for his past association with the Campaign for Nuclear Disarmament. Only in such an exceptional case do election addresses echo the manifesto's stress on internationalism.

Some other omissions in table 1.5 are of interest. Only in 1974 did a substantial proportion of Conservative candidates refer to government ownership of business. In 1951, when the Conservatives were trying to wrest power from a Labour Government that had taken many enterprises into government ownership, less than half of the sample of addresses mentioned the need to end such action. In 1979, on the eve of the Thatcher revolution, only 6 percent of the sample discussed selling nationalized enterprises back to private owners. Even in 1987, with Thatcher's program of sales well underway, only a seventh of the Conservative candidates referred to the policy. Conservative MPs might accept her views about downsizing the government and removing it from business, but apparently few candidates felt that the process would excite the public sufficiently to win votes.

Although logic need not prevent a party on the right from being environmentally friendly, in point of fact that issue received little attention from Conservative candidates until 1987, and even then only a fifth referred to it. Turning to another issue of recent political prominence in Europe, right-wing Continental parties increasingly have sought votes by attacking immigrants. Conservative election addresses are instructive on this matter because they show how influential the party Leader can be. In 1974 only a tenth of the sample of addresses so much as mentioned immigration, and in 1987 even fewer did so. In 1979, however, fully a quarter of the addresses included the issue. This surely was due to Thatcher's advocacy of controls to reduce the number of entrants into Britain. The year before the election she had gone so far as to say that "people can feel rather swamped" by the inflow of immigrants. Lacking such encouragement from the top, however, Conservative candidates apparently did not regard immigrant/ethnic bashing as a vote winner. On the other hand, even fewer of them—only 3 percent in 1987—saw any reason to mention anything about race relations in their address. Given the virulence of much of the right on the Continent, perhaps such silence should be considered a positive stance.[22]

Finally, given the emergence of European integration as a possible seismic issue that might cleave the party for a generation, what attention have

Conservative addresses accorded to it? In 1974 a quarter of the Conservative candidates mentioned their support of the European Economic Community. Five years later only an eighth bothered to do so.[23] By 1987, having witnessed their Leader savage the European Community with her handbag for a few years, most Conservative candidates decided to keep their head below the parapet—only 3 percent referred to the EEC. Apparently, at this point the process of European integration was not seen by Conservative candidates as posing a threat to British sovereignty.

Thus while the issues most often mentioned in Conservative election addresses do respond to events and the current enthusiasms of the party Leader, what seems most striking is the relative continuity of concerns. There is little evidence to suggest that Thatcher dramatically shifted the policy views of Conservative candidates in any enduring fashion. The emphasis on law and order in the most recent elections might be regarded as indicating a shift to the right, but Blair's Labour party has sought to claim that it is the true party of law and order. In any event the Conservatives have not used the issue as a cover for anti-ethnic sentiment. Although the addresses and the manifestos differ in the emphasis given to internationalism, both give considerably more attention than would be anticipated to social services and both show similar concern with equivalent capitalist themes.

The Conservatives and Power: Dominance and Adaptability

The Party of Government

In the general election of 1900 the Conservatives won more than half of the vote (a feat not to be duplicated by any party for a third of a century) and three-fifths of the seats in the House of Commons. In the following 45 years they would be out of power for only 13. At the end of World War II, however, the party appeared debilitated. Identified with appeasement of Hitler prior to World War II and with the economic hardships suffered by ordinary Britons in the 1930s, the Conservatives in 1945 suffered their worse electoral defeat in 40 years.

The party quickly sought to enhance its appeal by revising its policies and modifying its organization. The central organization, which virtually had been closed down during World War II, was resuscitated and expanded. Middle-class candidates of greater appeal to a society increasingly concerned with equality were recruited to stand for Parliament. On policy the Conservatives accepted a greater role for the government in economics and social benefits. The party might alter some of the details of Labour's new National Health Service ("socialized medicine"), but would not abolish it. Nor would it return to private ownership the great bulk of the enterprises that Labour had transformed into government-owned operations.

The key figure in redirecting the party to accept the emerging social democratic consensus was Richard A. Butler, an exponent of the One-Nation stream of Conservatism. Under his direction, the party issued the *Industrial Charter*, termed by his biographer "the most memorable concession a free enterprise Party ever made to the spirit of Keynesian economics."[24] The Conservatives made clear that they could be returned to power without people having to fear a return to the laissez faire of the 1930s.

Butler was a key figure in shaping the nature of British politics for a third of a century after World War II. Toward the close of Labour's period in office immediately after World War II, Hugh Gaitskell became Chancellor of the Exchequer. When the Conservatives returned to power, Butler acquired this position. The similarity of their economic policies lead to the coining of the word "Butskellism," the label for the new cross-party consensus on the mixed economy and the welfare state. The Conservatives would remain committed to this policy orientation for nearly three decades.

As a result of its adaptability, the party made one of the most remarkable recoveries in political history; only six years after its disastrous defeat the party was back in power and held office for 13 years without a break. The 45 years following the Conservatives' return to office in 1951 in fact duplicated their record at the start of the century: they were out of power for only 11 years. From 1950 through 1992 the Conservatives' share of vote, as figure 1.1 shows, ranged from 36 to just under 50 percent, averaging more than two-fifths. What is especially striking about figure 1.1 is the relative stability of support.

From 1979 to 1997 the party won four consecutive elections for an uninterrupted 18 years in power, a twentieth-century record for unbroken longevity. A long period in office may produce aloof arrogance toward public opinion and deplete a party's store of useful policies and ideas. Although only one of the 21 members of Thatcher's first Cabinet still was in the Cabinet in 1996 (and his service had not been unbroken), keeping a party fresh for nearly two decades is difficult. In the fall of 1995 more than two-thirds of Gallup's respondents agreed that "the Government is tired and stale and has run out of steam."

Challengers and/or Allies

Since the British party system is less fragmented than the typical European one, the Conservatives do not have to worry about fending off challengers for their core clientele. The less fortunate aspect of their position is that

Figure 1.1 Conservative Percentage of the Vote in Recent General Elections

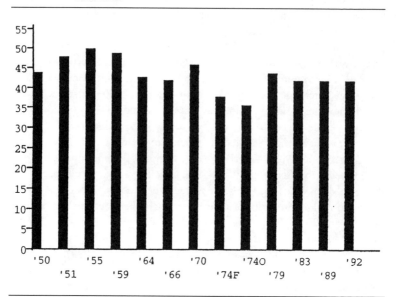

they must seek power entirely on their own—they cannot hope to hold office with the support of a junior partner. In February 1974, when the Conservatives won more votes than did Labour but four fewer seats, Prime Minister Edward Heath sought support from the Liberal party. When that was refused, he resigned and Labour took office. On the other hand, for about a year and a half during 1977–78 the Liberals did help a minority Labour Government remain in office.

During the 1980s the Liberals and the Social Democratic Party (a group of moderates who had broken away from Labour) formed the Alliance and hoped to replace Labour as the main opponents to the Conservatives. The Alliance was coy about its actions should neither the Conservatives nor Labour manage to win a majority of seats in the Commons, which seemed possible in both 1987 and 1992. Eventually, however, the Liberal Democrats (the new party that emerged from the Alliance) decided to abandon the tactics of equidistance. While willing to negotiate an arrangement with a minority Labour Government, they would not support a minority Conservative Government in power.

The only additional support that the Conservatives can seek is the handful of Protestant representatives (Ulster Unionists) from Northern Ireland. Given their fear that the Conservatives might try to resolve the long-running religious conflict by concessions to the Catholic Irish nationalists, the Ulster Unionists are an unlikely source of additional parliamentary support. Coalition strategies, therefore, are of only limited relevance to the Conservatives. They have had little need or opportunity to engage in Byzantine activities to maintain their hold on power.

Conservative Prospects

1945 All Over Again?

As the end of the century neared, the Conservatives were a party in disarray. Virtually every element in British society seemed opposed to them, as table 1.6 shows. Not only did unskilled manual workers (DE) overwhelmingly support Labour, but the skilled manuals (C2), who on balance supported the Conservatives during the 1980s, had returned "home" to give Labour a 35 percentage point lead in voting intention.[25] White-collar workers (C1), who were two to one Conservative in the 1992 election, now favored Labour. Only top social groups (AB: professionals, managers, and the like) just barely preferred the Conservatives to Labour. Not only did union members favor Labour, but so did nonmembers. Not only did the unemployed favor Labour, but so did those working full-time. Not only did tenants in public housing favor Labour, but so did owners. Not only did young people favor Labour, but so did the middle aged and the elderly.

Even more remarkable is how similar the shift to Labour was across all elements of British society. Although Labour's support was greater among men than among women, the shift to Labour since the 1992 election was almost exactly the same regardless of gender. Whether the electorate was classified by the standard social class categories, by 10-year age intervals, by housing tenure, by union membership, or by employment, the shift to Labour ranged from 24 to 38 percentage points. Segments of society had not deserted; everyone had.

Rarely can the decline of a party be dated as precisely as can the Conservatives' collapse. Following the 1992 general election, for the remainder of the spring and on through the summer, more than 40 percent of respondents told Gallup that they supported the Conservatives. In fact, in the first week of September slightly more (43 percent) favored the Conservatives than had voted for them four months earlier. Then came Black Wednesday, September 16. Britain was forced by a run on the pound in international currency markets to pull out of the European Union's Exchange Rate Mechanism (ERM). A Gallup poll the following week found that the Conservatives had dropped six percentage

Table 1.6 Support for Leading Parties, Third Quarter 1996, and Change since General Election of 1992

	Lab Lead over Cons*	Change**
Gender		
Men	27	31
Women	22	32
Social Class		
AB	−2	35
C1	10	37
C2	35	34
DE	50	32
Age		
18–24	39	36
25–34	33	36
35–44	30	34
45–54	22	38
55–64	19	28
65 & over	10	24
Unions		
Member	45	30
Non-member	19	32
Employment		
Working full-time	25	36
Unemployed	52	26
Housing		
Owners†	4	30
Council tenants	60	29

Source: Market & Opinion Research International (MORI), *British Public Opinion* XIX (October, 1996), no. 8, p. 4.

Notes: *Negative number indicates Conservative lead.

**e.g., The Conservatives' lead among men was 4 percentage points in 1992. Labour lead by 27 points in 1996. The total change was 31 points in Labour's favor.

†Excludes those still paying on mortgage

points to only 37 percent support, while Labour had gained three and a half points to move into the lead at 44 percent. Never in the next four years did support for the Conservatives rise that "high" again. By 1996 the Conservatives were below 30 percent in Gallup's polls, trailing Labour by about 30 percentage points.

Voting intention is only one measure of the magnitude of disaster Black Wednesday produced. The week before, 47 percent had been *satisfied* with the job that Major was doing as Prime Minister; in early October 65 percent were *dissatisfied*. Only in two months during the next four years did satisfaction with Major surpass 28 percent and never did he get closer than 14 percentage points below his former level of approval. The Government's record already had been unpopular—little more than a quarter approved it at the start of September. Following Black Wednesday approval dwindled to only a sixth and never again did as "many" as a fifth endorse it. In short, not only were the Conservatives unable to regain the level of support and endorsement they had possessed prior to Black Wednesday, they generally could not even maintain the immediately ensuing reduced level of approval. After Black Wednesday virtually everything was downhill.

Some will protest that surely not one person in a hundred could tell you what ERM stood for, much less whether it made any difference if Britain were in or out. No doubt, but the Conservative Government had made the linkage of the pound to the rock-stable deutsche mark by means of ERM its principal weapon in combating inflation. Membership in the ERM "had been the central tenet of Conservative policy, affirmed in the boldest and most uncompromising terms by the Chancellor and the Prime Minister in speech after speech. . . . Withdrawal from the ERM was a stunning blow to the credibility of Major and Lamont."[26] Collapse of the policy made the Conservatives appear incompetent, and undermined one of the party's strongest traditional appeals to the voters. While the Conservatives offer voters a policy program, their appeal stresses the quality of personnel they provide. Breeding, training, and experience—characteristics they claim their Labour opponents lack—supposedly make them the party of government. Like the Radical party in Third Republic France, they pose as the source for the *ministrables*. Black Wednesday made such claims incredible to even the most deferential voter. To utilize a British cliché: that lot can't even run a whelk stall.[27]

The Conservatives' emphasis on their ability to govern makes worth examining the level of confidence the public held in the party during the Thatcher era and its relation to support. On 16 occasions Gallup asked respondents to what extent they thought the Conservatives could "deal wisely with Britain's problems." The results are plotted in figure 1.2 against the proportion saying they would vote Conservative. The relation is striking ($R^2 = .64$). For every 4 percentage point change in the proportion having very great or considerable confidence in Conservative politicians, voting preference for the Conservatives shifted 3 percentage points.

The relation exists at the relative level as well as the absolute one. The proportion expressing very great or considerable confidence in Labour politicians was subtracted from the proportion according confidence to Conservative ones to produce a confidence margin. This margin was plotted in figure 1.3 against the Conservatives' lead in voter preference. Not only is

Figure 1.2 The Impact of Confidence in the Conservatives on Intended Vote for the Conseratives, 1981–1995

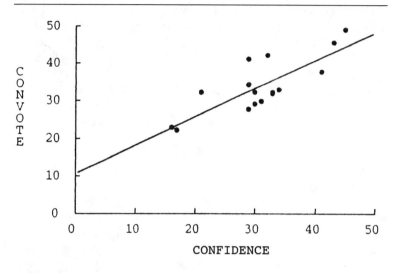

CONVOTE=10.646+0.749*CONFID

Source: Gallup Political and Economic Index, various issues courtesy of Robert Wybrow of Gallup.
Note: Gallup asked respondents, "On the whole, how much confidence do you have in Conservative politicians to deal wisely with Britain's problems—very great, considerable, little or very little?"

the relation equally strong (R^2 = .65), but relative confidence translates into relative voter preference at almost parity, that is, for every five-point shift in difference in confidence between Conservative and Labour politicians, the gap in voter preference between the parties altered by four and a half points.

Interestingly, confidence in Conservative politicians did not collapse as immediately after Black Wednesday as did voting support. When Gallup posed the confidence question late in October 1992, a third still expressed very great or considerable confidence—just as had been true in October 1990 and July 1992, the two immediately previous usages of the question. When next Gallup inquired, in May 1993, however, only a fifth expressed confidence—considerably fewer than did so in Labour politicians. Thus it appears that the continuing factional warfare touched off by Black Wednesday, more than the event itself, destroyed confidence.

While competence has long been a major theme in the Conservatives' appeal to the electorate, it was only one factor in the party's success. How

Figure 1.3 Relation between Relative Confidence in the Conservatives and Conservative Lead Over Labour in Voter Preference

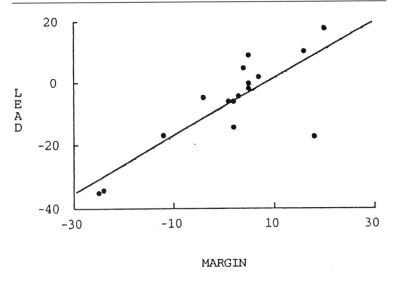

MARGIN

LEAD=-7.601+0.918*MARGIN

Source: Gallup Political and Economic Index, various issues courtesy of Robert Wybrow of Gallup.
Note: Gallup's question as for Figure 1.2.

could the inherent elitism in such a boast be made palatable to the ordinary person? By appearing to be a caring elite—*noblesse oblige,* the motto of the One-Nation Tory. The Conservatives suffered electoral disaster in 1945 because too many voters perceived them to be too little caring. Conservative Governments of the 1920s and 1930s appeared callous, appeared to have abandoned the One-Nation tradition. When the Prince of Wales, while touring economically depressed areas, said, "Something must be done," the Conservatives were outraged—the heir to the throne had criticized their running of the country. The reorientation of the party in the late 1940s was intended to disabuse the public of its negative perception and to regain for the party a caring image. As we have seen, that effort was highly successful. With the rise of Thatcher, however, the One-Nation tradition was shouldered aside.

The importance of a caring image in generating support for the Conservatives can be examined with a question that Gallup posed 17 times during the Thatcher era. Respondents were asked about the concern the Conservatives possessed "for the interests of people like you." The proportion thinking the party was becoming more concerned is plotted against voter preference for the Conservatives in figure 1.4. The linkage is substantial ($R^2 = .72$). Furthermore, the relation is multiplicative. For every 4 percentage-point shift in the proportion thinking the Conservatives are becoming more concerned, support for the party changes by 7 percentage points.

Only once during 13 surveys while Thatcher was Prime Minister did as many as 17 percent think the Conservatives were becoming more concerned, and even then slightly more than half thought they were becoming less concerned. The first time the question was asked (not until July 1992) after Major became Prime Minister, only 17 percent perceived greater concern, those feeling less concern were fewer than a third. Gallup did not use the question again until almost half a year after

Figure 1.4 Influence of Perceived Conservative Concern on Intended Vote for the Conservatives, 1981–1994

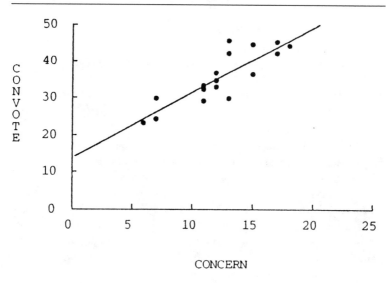

CONVOTE=13.438+1.781*CONCERN

Source: *Gallup Political and Economic Index,* various issues courtesy of Robert Wybrow of Gallup.
Note: Gallup asked respondents: "Do you think the Conservative party is becoming more concerned for the interests of people like yourself, less concerned, or is there no change?"

Black Wednesday. On both that occasion and the remaining two instances the Conservatives' reputation for concern under Major was no better or even worse than it had been when Thatcher was in power. So much for Major's declared intention to create a classless nation at ease with itself.

Additional evidence of how widely the Conservatives are perceived as callous can be gained from two other survey questions. On 24 occasions from 1983 to 1993 Gallup asked whether the "Conservatives don't care what hardships their policies cause." Never did a majority fail to agree with this statement and usually substantially more endorsed it (58 to 71 percent agreed). Support was quite similar for the statement that "The Conservatives look after the interests of the rich, not ordinary people" (those agreeing ranged from 59 percent to 76 percent). In vain did Thatcher in the 1987 election campaign proclaim, "The National Health Service is safe in our hands." In vain did the Conservative 1992 election manifesto announce that, after allowing for inflation, spending on the NHS went up from 1979 to 1992 by 55 percent. People simply do not believe it. Paternalism is offensive to some; the Conservatives would be happy to be credited with having it. Thatcher wanted to destroy the dependency culture. All that she seems to have achieved is to convince much of the electorate that the Conservatives are heartless. The One-Nation appeal that gained the Conservatives support across class divisions and won elections for them is now fighting a defensive rearguard action within the party.

To make matters worse, in the last few years the Conservatives appear to have fallen so far from *noblesse oblige* that they regard public office not as a chance for service but for personal enrichment. In some preliminary work on comparative corruption a number of years ago, Anthony King argued that in Britain political scandals were usually about sex (hetero or homo, as the case might be), while in the United States corruption was more a matter of venality. This appears to have changed, as instances become public of British MPs accepting expensive vacations for services, and offering to submit inquiries during the House of Commons' question time for a stated per question fee. Such behavior appears to be disproportionately prevalent among Conservative MPs.

On 12 occasions from 1994 to 1996 Gallup asked whether respondents agreed that "The Conservatives these days give the impression of being very sleazy and disreputable." Never once did a majority fail to agree with the statement and in one instance three-quarters agreed. While the public has little regard for MPs generally,[28] the perception of sleaze did not tar all politicians. Only a tenth to a quarter regarded Labour as sleazy and disreputable. All of these perceptions—competency, caring, corruption—come together in a query that Gallup has employed only sparingly: fitness to govern. In 1989 fewer than half were willing to accord Labour that status while more than half felt the Conservatives possessed it. By the spring of 1990, as Neil Kinnock seemed to have controlled Labour's left wing and the Conservatives under Thatcher were pressing ahead with the hated poll tax, the Conservatives no longer had majority endorsement, while more than three-fifths now granted it to Labour. By 1995 little more than a quarter judged the Conservatives, who had run the country for 16 consecutive years, fit to do so. Although this perception improved in 1996, less than two-fifths thought the Conservatives fit to govern while more than three-fifths thought that Labour was. Such is the devotion which Thatcher inspired during her decade and a half of leading the party that even more than five years after her departure, the Whig tradition she embodied continued to battle the Tory outlook. Whiteley and his associates attribute the Conservatives' long-term decline in number of members and party activism to Thatcher's impact. They charge that she so alienated progressive Conservatives that many were either driven into passive membership or out of the party entirely. Thus she seriously damaged the health of Conservative local party organization. Furthermore, as discussed above, her impact on the Conservatives' legislative delegation was to make it more a party of self-made men to whom *noblesse oblige* was of little relevance. Thus the Tory-Whig fissure was particularly acute in the mid-1990s and seemed to be driving the party to electoral disaster, just as it had a half century earlier. Serious as this fissure was, equally perilous was the cleavage over Europe. Not only did the exit from the ERM make Conservative leaders appear incompetent, but, as Wilks points out, it also "re-opened the dispute about Europe and the Maastricht Treaty within the Conservative party."[29] This debate fatally undermined John Major's leadership during his final term as Prime Minister.

The Corn Laws All Over Again?

The opening pages of this study recounted how the Conservatives benefited from a major split in the Liberal party toward the close of the nineteenth century. In the middle of that century it had been the Liberals who had benefited from a Conservative split. In 1846 Prime Minister Robert Peel split the Conservatives over the issue of repeal of the corn laws (tariffs on imported wheat). For the next 28 years the Conservatives held power for less than four. At the close of the twentieth century anyone with a sense of history must wonder whether John Major (abetted by his Chancellor of the Exchequer Kenneth Clarke) had managed to do the same thing over European Union, Maastricht, and the single currency.

The 1997 election was an unparalleled disaster for the Conservatives, worse even than the rout of 1945. Only once in the twentieth century—way back in 1906—had they won fewer seats than they did in 1997. Never before in the century had their share of the vote fallen below 35 percent; in 1997 it dropped well below 30 percent. More Conservative government ministers lost their seats in the House of Commons than ever before. And the party was wiped out in Wales and Scotland; for the first time in its history it won seats only in England.

A defeat of this magnitude cannot be explained by the old cliche that the electorate thought it was time for a change. Nor can the aura of minor corruption that tarnished the party account for a major shift in votes. The explanation lies in the Conservatives' squandering of their reputation for competence and destroying their image of unity. In contrast to the Labour party, whose fractious image suggested an inability to run its own affairs, much less those of the nation, the Conservatives knew how to resolve disagreements. An event like the SDP breakaway from Labour in the early 1980s never could occur in the Conservative party.

By the end of the 1980s, however, the parties' images were converging. Shortly before the 1992 election Gallup polls showed that about as many respondents (around half) were likely to perceive Labour as a united party as thought that the Conservatives were. Although a decline from the past, this equal assessment was better than what followed. Prior to the 1997 election, while around three-fifths believed that Labour was united, only about a sixth regarded the Conservatives that way. Obligingly, the Conservatives during the 1997 election campaign proved to the voters that this assessment was correct. Over two-fifths of its candidates defied the Prime Minister, their party leader, on the issue of the European Union's single currency. John Major declared that Britain should await further negotiations before announcing whether it would join. The Euro-skeptic rebels proclaimed in one way or another that they never would support British entry into a single currency. So besieged was Major that he had to concede that if he were returned for another term as Prime Minister, he would allow his party a free vote at the end of the House of Commons' debate on whether to join.

As for competency, in the run up to the 1992 election (winter to early spring), five consecutive Gallup polls showed that about as many people (a third) thought that the Conservatives were the party that could best handle what they (the respondents) regarded as Britain's most urgent problem as believed that Labour would do best. During the same period prior to the 1997 election nearly half thought that Labour would do best while only a quarter thought the Conservatives would. An incompetent, divided party that has been in office for nearly two decades and looks sleazy to boot—is it any wonder that it suffered its worst defeat of the twentieth century, if not of all time?

The irony is that Conservative policies *weren't* rejected; Tony Blair's New Labour had to embrace most of them in order to win its landslide victory. New Labour would not take back into public ownership anything that the Conservatives had privatized, and might even sell a few government enterprises itself. Little, if any, of the restrictions the Conservatives had imposed on the trade unions would be repealed. Even Labour's promise to give unions a statutory right to collective bargaining (granted to American unions about two-thirds of a century ago when Franklin Roosevelt was president) was beginning to look uncertain. Labour had claimed that it would revitalize the National Health Service, but where would the money be found when the party had promised not to raise taxes and to keep spending within the projected limits drawn up by the departing Conservatives? By both rhetoric and action Labour had shown that it was as willing as the Conservatives to violate civil liberties to prove that it was strong on law and order. The Conservatives had lost the election, but Conservatism, indeed, even Thatcherism, appeared to have triumphed.

Thus as the Conservatives seek to regroup at the turn of the century they face a different situation from that encountered by their predecessors at the middle of the century. Then, the party had to transform its policies to make itself electable. Now its policies are so attractive to British voters that its opponents have stolen them in order to win. Therefore, one might say, the task ahead should be easy—just stop the infighting. That is easier said than done, however. On the night of the election, even before all the results had been announced, on the center-left groups in the party issued a press released blaming the right wing for the massive defeat. The next day one of the grandees of the right returned fire. Major's announcement that he would retire as party leader meant that the party would have another opportunity to display its divisions in a bloody leadership election. Even during the election campaign some potential successors had seemed more interested in jockeying for post-election position within the party than trying to win an election they already deemed lost. A leadership election that was no more than a clash of personalities would not need to be particularly divisive. The Conservative contest, however, would be a struggle over policy and the future orientation of the party.

As soon as Major declared his departure, Kenneth Clarke, the Cabinet's most vociferous advocate of close relations with Europe, announced his candidacy to lead the party. On June 19, 1997, the Conservatives chose as their new Leader 36-year old William Hague over the more experienced 56-year old Clarke. Thus the party signaled its willingness to remain out of power for 10 to 15 years and its continuing determination to oppose closer integration with the European Union. As noted previously, Europe is a perilous issue for the Conservatives. The single currency does not lend itself to compromise—either Britain joins or it doesn't. Since Labour seems unlikely to decide that Britain should enter with the first wave of members, the issue may remain unresolved by the time of the next general election and play havoc once again with Conservative unity. Even should the issue of the single currency be resolved, Britain's relations with Europe can easily spawn a host of other questions to bedevil the Conservatives. Those in the party who see the single currency as a threat to British sovereignty are hardly likely to be amenable to the second pillar of Maastricht—movement toward a common foreign and defense policy for Europe—or to greater use of qualified majority voting in the Council of Minister's decision making.

And even were the party to settle its differences on Europe and become either pro-Europe or Euro-skeptic, unity would not be restored. There would remain the fundamental division between the Disraelian One-Nation Tories and the Thatcherite Whigs. The feeling that Labour's victory—having been constructed on a foundation of acceptance of the main elements of 18 years of Conservative rule—will leave many in the party with the feeling that party need do nothing to revive itself. The Thatcher/Major regime in effect reversed R. A. Butler's transformation of the party. As a result, the battles of mid-century must be fought again at the same time that those over Europe are being waged. Such a double burden suggests that the early years of the twenty-first century are more like to see the British Conservatives replaying events of the mid-nineteenth-century than of the mid-twentieth.

NOTES

1. Cooperating in various European organizations with continental liberal parties often is difficult for the British Liberals because the former are so much more conservative, especially on economic matters.
2. Nonmetropolitan is not synonymous with rural. Urban includes only conurbations and major cities. Seats not of that type, including those in small cities and towns, are labeled nonmetropolitan.
3. David Seawright and John Curtice, "The Decline of the Scottish Conservative and Unionist Party, 1950–92: Religion, Ideology or Economics?" *Contemporary Record* 9 (Autumn 1995): 319.
4. They were: (1) suburbs and service centers, (2) rural areas and seaside resorts, (3) growth areas, (4) stable industrial areas, (5) areas dominated by council housing, and (6) metropolitan inner areas. Richard Webber, *Parliamentary Constituencies: A Socio-economic Classification,* Occasional Paper 13 (London: Office of Population Censuses and Surveys, 1978).

5. Even at its most successful during this period—October 1974—Labour was unable to win as many as a third of these constituencies.

6. Not every Midlands constituency was a growth area—a number fell in the stable industrial family. In that case Labour was the usual victor.

7. Unfortunately, Webber did not repeat his analysis after the boundaries were changed again prior to the 1983 general election. Nearly a quarter of the constituencies were not altered drastically—10 percent or less change in the electorate from 1979 to 1983. *The BBC/ITN Guide to the New Parliamentary Constituencies* (Chichester: Parliamentary Research Services, 1983).

8. Since Webber's typology is applicable to less than a quarter of the constituencies in 1992, conclusions must be tentative. Nonetheless, in local authority housing seats the Conservatives seem to have weakened further. About two-thirds of the constituencies in this "family" are Scottish seats.

9. David Butler and Gareth Butler, *British Political Facts 1900–85,* 6th ed. (New York: St. Martin's, 1986), p. 139, and Paul Whiteley, Patrick Seyd, and Jeremy Richardson, *True Blues: The Politics of Conservative Party Membership* (Oxford: Clarendon Press, 1994), p. 222. Until the late 1990s the Conservatives always had more members than Labour had direct ones. Only Labour's direct members are comparable, since only they join a local party rather than being affiliated by their trade union. The number of Labour direct members peaked at the same time as did Conservative membership, but never totaled higher than slightly over one million. A drive to recruit direct members took Labour over 400,000 by 1997.

10. See the summary of views in Whiteley et al., *True Blues,* pp. 28–39.

11. The party's Standing Advisory Committee on Candidates, "Notes on Procedure for the Selection and Adoption of Conservative Parliamentary Candidates in England, Wales and Northern Ireland," (London: Conservative Central Office, 1994), p. 6, comments rather plaintively, "From time to time the Party has passed resolutions urging the need for more women and more candidates with varied backgrounds and Selection Committees should endeavor to include them in short lists." A clarification at the end (p. 7) explains, "Throughout this booklet reference to 'he' should be read as 'he or she.' Increasing numbers of women are becoming Candidates and Chairmen [*sic*]—a trend we wish to encourage!" But since headquarters can only "encourage," the Conservatives have lagged behind Labour in selecting women as candidates in winnable seats and the proportion of MPs who are female is considerably higher in the Labour party.

12. David Butler and Michael Pinto-Duschinsky, "The Conservative Elite, 1918–78: Does Unrepresentativeness Matter?" in *Conservative Party Politics,* ed. Zig Leyton-Henry (London: Macmillan, 1980), pp. 186–209.

13. The first election marked the party's return to power for the first time after World War II. The second, more than a quarter of a century later, brought Thatcher to power. The third was the first election after her loss of power.

14. Not surprisingly "ethnics" were even more thin on the ground. In 1992 the party had eight black or Asian candidates. One of the latter won to become the first Asian Conservative MP since early in the century. The party never has had a black MP. The Conservatives offered no black or Asian candidates in 1951 and only two in 1979 (both unsuccessful). Pippa Norris, et al., "Race and Parliamentary Representation," in *British Parties and Elections Yearbook 1992,* ed. Pippa Norris, et al. (Hemel Hampstead: Harvester Wheatsheaf, 1992), p. 93.

15. Julian Critchley, "Flight of the Tory Men," *The Times,* October 28, 1995. The irony is that Critchley's social background is not elite; he labels himself in his youth a bounder. But he was a bounder who sought fame rather than riches. See Julian Critchley, *A Bag of Boiled Sweets: An Autobiography* (London: Faber and Faber, 1994).

16. Whiteley, et al., *True Blues,* pp. 42–45, 106.

17. John Curtice and Michael Steed, "Appendix 2: The Results Analysed," in *The British General Election of 1992,* ed. David Butler and Dennis Kavanagh (New York: St. Martin's, 1992), pp. 329–31.

18. See Philip Norton and Arthur Aughey, *Conservatives and Conservatism* (London: Temple Smith, 1981), pp. 53–89, and Whiteley, et al., *True Blues,* pp. 127–32.

19. Jorgen Rasmussen, "Margaret Thatcher and the Transformation of British Politics," in *Margaret Thatcher: Prime Minister Indomitable,* ed. Juliet Thompson and Wayne Thompson (Boulder, CO: Westview Press, 1994), pp. 39–52, and Hugo Young, *One of Us* (final ed.; London: Pan Books, 1993), Chapter 11.

20. The Manifestos Project, based at the University of Essex, has collected and analyzed election programs for many parties in various democracies over a considerable period of time. The discussion in this survey draws on the report in Ian Budge and Dennis Farlie, *Explaining and Predicting Elections* (London: Allen & Unwin, 1983).

21. The Nuffield election studies by David Butler and a variety of associates, *The British General Election of 19XX* (London: Macmillan, various dates) have regularly analyzed a sample of these addresses. For 1951 and 1974 the Nuffield studies used a one-fourth sample for 1979 and in 1987 a one-sixth one. The rise of the personal computer and targeted electoral mailings eventually made analysis of election addresses misleading. Therefore, the traditional summary table was omitted from the volume on the 1992 election.

22. Note, however, that Budge and Farlie (pp. 209–10) in seeking to predict election results in 23 democracies over a period of about a third of a century rate the Conservatives' restrictive immigration policy as the issue that augmented their "basic vote" the most in both the 1964 and 1970 general elections.

23. One percent—only one address in a sample of slightly more than 100—favored threatening to withdraw.

24. Anthony Howard, *RAB: The Life of R. A. Butler* (London: Jonathan Cape, 1987), p. 155.

25. This discussion uses Market & Opinion Research International's aggregate polling results for the third quarter of 1996, *British Public Opinion* 14 (October 1996): 4.

26. Steven Wilks, "Economic Policy," in *Developments in British Politics 4,* ed. Patrick Dunleavy, et al. (New York: St. Martin's, 1993), p. 221.

27. In Budge and Farlie's analysis the "issue" of Government record and prospects had the second largest absolute (ignoring positive or negative signs) impact on Conservative electoral fortunes for the period 1950 through 1979. The "issue" having the greatest effect was voter reaction to leaders' qualities. The only time this reduced the Conservatives' "basic vote" was in the two elections of 1974 when Ted Heath was perceived as a "confrontationalist maladroit Prime Minister."

28. A MORI poll late in 1995 found that the public had less respect for MPs than for real estate agents and, the unkindest cut of all, no more respect for MPs than for journalists.

29. Steven Wilks, "Economic Policy," in *Developments in British Politics 4,* p. 222.

CHAPTER TWO

The French Right in Search of Itself

Frank L. Wilson

In France, the country of The Revolution, political parties have traditionally scorned the label of "conservative," or "right," or even "center-right." Indeed, many of the parties with the most radical sounding titles have been parties more committed to the values and policies identified with the right than with the left. Until the Fifth Republic (1958-present), the French center-right was characterized by its internal divisions, transient groupings, extreme individualism, basis in local politics, lack of formal organizations, and uncertainty about its own ability to compete in democratic politics.[1] Nevertheless, the center-right governed far more often than it found itself in opposition to a left-wing government. With only brief intervals during the *Cartel des Gauches* in the 1920s, the Popular Front in the 1930s, and the Tripartism immediately after World War II, the center-right dominated French politics.

That pattern of center-right political dominance continued under the Fifth Republic. However, it is a substantially different political movement compared to the center-right in the past. Many of the historical features of French conservative parties have disappeared: the center-right has acquired new unity, confidence, and organizational strength. At the end of the twentieth century, the center-right remains the key political force in France. It no longer enjoys the hegemonic dominance that characterized the first 20 years of the Fifth Republic. It now rotates in and out of power with the left. But the center-right is now endowed with the institutions, cohesion, and leadership needed to confront a stronger left than that faced by conservatives and centrists during most of the twentieth century.

The center-right's cohesion and organizational strength are periodically challenged. As the 1990s come to a close, the parties of the right are in crisis. The premature—and unnecessary—elections of May-June 1997 resulted not only in the center-right's loss of power but new divisions within and between the two major groupings on the right. Struggles over leadership, doctrine, and strategy have weakened the right more than at any time since the mid-1970s. In addition, the center-right faces a critical challenge from the radical right. But the center-right's political base and organization are sturdy enough to keep it the most important political movement in contemporary France.

The French Center-Right at the Polls

The contemporary center-right as represented in the Gaullist Rally for the Republic (RPR) and the Giscardian Union for French Democracy (UDF) has maintained its hold upon traditional bases of electoral strength and built an appeal that attracts new categories of voters. The result is a broad electoral coalition that makes the center-right the predominant, at times hegemonic, political force in Fifth Republic France. From 1958 to 1981, the center-right dominated national politics. Since 1981, it has rotated in power with the Socialists.

This electoral strength is based on the broad appeal of the RPR and UDF to French voters of many social backgrounds.[2] The center-right has strong electoral support drawn from across most social classes. Although it is particularly strong in the middle classes and among farmers, it has also drawn significant support from the traditional working class (see table 2.1). Center-right parties tend to be more successful in attracting the vote of the more faithful Catholics as opposed to those with few religious ties (table 2.2). This effect continues even as religiosity has declined in France.[3] The electoral appeal of the RPR and UDF has not been affected since the parties have succeeded in extending their appeal to nonpractitioners. Indeed, current social trends seem to offset each other in France: the decline of religious commitment which might give an advantage to the left is balanced by a reduction in the political salience of social class which might help the right. The result today is that both right and left have broader electoral appeals across traditional social cleavages than has historically been the case.

Despite the broadened electoral base, it is still accurate to see the center-right as having a political base among the middle classes and more religious voters in France. Recent electoral studies show that the French voters' electoral behavior remains rooted in social class and religious cleavages. There is some disagreement over which of these is most important. Some contend that "Religion and class reliably shape preferences, with the

Table 2.1 Socioeconomic Background and Voter Preference, 1997

	Far Left	Communists	Socialists	Center-Right	Ecologists	Far Right
	Percentage of each occupation voting for:					
All voters	2.5	10	26	31	7	15
By occupation:						
Farmers	0	3	29	54	0	4
Small business	0	8	15	30	8	26
Professionals and business	5	7	29	30	13	4
White-collar	3	10	31	23	10	14
Blue-collar	2	15	28	19	8	24
No profession and retired	0	6	17	44	12	12

Source: "Le Profil des électeurs au premier tour des élections législatatives," *Revue Française de Science Politique* 49 (June–August 1997): 464.

Table 2.2 Religion and Voter Preference in France, 1997

	Far Left	Communists	Socialists	Center-Right	Ecologists	Far Right
	Percentage Voting on the First Ballot of the 1997 National Assembly Election for:					
All voters	2.5	10	26	31	7	15
By religious commitment:						
Practicing Catholic	0	2	14	58	6	7
Occasional Catholic	5	4	22	43	6	12
Nonpracticing Catholic	0	11	28	27	7	18
Other religions	0	11	32	29	7	18
No religion	5	20	32	12	9	17

Source: "Le Profil des électeurs au premier tour des élections législatatives," *Revue Française de Science Politique* 49 (June–August 1997): 464.

former more important than the latter."[4] For others, it is the left–right division, rooted in lasting social and religious differences but distinct from these social roots, that has become the key to the structuring of French voting.[5] In spite of such differences, there is broad agreement on the cumulative effect of socioeconomic cleavages in French electoral behavior. Roy Pierce's recent study of presidential elections demonstrates the much greater effect of religion and class in polarizing the electorate and in shaping electoral coalitions in France compared to the United States.[6] In addition, voter identification with broad political families, such as right and left, provide meaningful and durable anchors for voting choices.[7]

Some evidence suggests that there is now a significant degree of voter volatility in France. A small but important group of voters are willing to shift back and forth between the right and left at election times. The movement of these swing voters toward or away from the center-right parties seems to be a key factor in electoral success in recent French national elections.[8]

While the distinctions between voters supporting parties of the left and right are fairly clear, there are few differences in the attitudes and socioeconomic backgrounds of voters for the different parties of the center-right.[9] Some contend that the UDF is more "centrist," more liberal on civil rights, more favorable to European integration, and so on than is the RPR. The RPR is seen as more nationalistic, more committed to executive rule, and more interventionist in economic matters than is the UDF. But these differences are slight and do not derive from different electorates. Center-right voters seem equally willing to support candidates from the Gaullist RPR or the various branches of the UDF. When there are different candidates from these parties on the first ballot, similar groups of voters support their different candidates based more on personality than on their own issue preferences or issue differences between the center-right candidates. Except where personal rivalries between Gaullist or UDF candidates have become heated, there are few problems in persuading center-right voters to support the remaining candidate on the second ballot when their preferred candidate has been eliminated.

The center-right has faced a serious electoral challenge from the far right during the last fifteen years. From 1958 to the mid-1980s, the Gaullists and other moderate center-right parties could count on support from voters attached to the values of the far right because there was no viable alternative party to represent their more extremist views. This changed with the emergence of Jean-Marie Le Pen's National Front (FN).[10] Drawing on popular mistrust of both the left and center-right mainstream parties and especially on popular resentment of immigrants, the FN quickly established a strong electoral base. The FN's major challenge to the center-right is for those voters who in the past had voted for the center-right simply because there was no far right option. Later in this chapter I will return to the center-right's response to the threat from the far right.

Evidence of a shift in public attitudes toward traditional free-enterprise liberalism and limited government is uncertain in France. Since the mid-

1980s, French governments of the left and right have acted on the premises of more limited social and economic roles for government. In the mid-1980s, the center-right moved away from its commitment to state economic management and adopted some elements of the neoliberal agenda of Margaret Thatcher and Ronald Reagan. However, many on the center-right, and especially in the RPR, harbored statist and Jacobin values. They were nervous about these neoliberal policies. Some party leaders and political analysts interpreted the center-right's defeat in the 1988 presidential and legislative elections as signs of popular dissatisfaction with the neoliberal agenda the RPR and UDF had attempted to enact.

In the mid-1990s, pressure for reductions in the state's role in society came more from the European Union than from internal French politics. As an easy means of "leveling the playing field," the EU opposed national government ownership or subsidization of enterprises and advocated reduced state economic regulation. The urgency of the Maastricht criteria for participation in the single European currency added new momentum to moves to curtail government expenditures by reducing public employment and cutting back on social welfare benefits. This kind of "neoliberalism" was pragmatic and utilitarian rather than ideological and drew support—although with varying degrees of enthusiasm—from parties on both sides of the political spectrum.

However, public support was much less than elite acceptance of these reductions. There remains considerable popular support for a large public sector and for generous social welfare programs. There is broad sympathy from many points on the French political spectrum supporting state activities to protect the *exclus:* those excluded from the current economy and society by long-term unemployment, disabilities, illnesses, and so on whose needs can only be met by a munificent state.[11] Public-opinion polls at the end of 1996 showed that two-thirds of French voters wanted the state to be more involved rather than less involved with society and the economy.[12] Further evidence of public backing for an interventionist state is found not only in abstract public-opinion polls but in popular alignments in recent strikes by public sector employees. For example, the public sector strikes at the end of 1995 attracted broad popular support despite their length, the public's inconveniences, and economic costs. Indeed, the French center-right's defeat in the 1997 elections demonstrated in no uncertain terms the voters' lack of support for state economic austerity in times of record high unemployment and economic insecurity. The French are loath to give up the heavily subsidized public transportation services, medical programs, social programs, and state retirement benefits. They expect the government to play the major role in overcoming the high unemployment rates that have plagued France over the past decade. The new liberal consensus that seems to dominate British or American politics is much less well-accepted by French citizens.

The electoral base for the French center-right is uncertain at the end of the century. Its strength since World War II and especially during the Fifth Republic was based on its ability to absorb the vote of those who might be tempted to vote for far right parties. Now, an electorally attractive movement on the far right has lured voters away. Social trends have weakened the traditional cues to partisan choice: religion and class. Public interest in the new issues of limited government and neoliberalism is limited. An important bloc of voters swings between left and center-right from one election to the next. Despite a landslide victory in the 1993 National Assembly election and a solid win in the 1995 presidential election,[13] the center-right's hold on the electorate in France remains tenuous, as was shown graphically in the center-right's defeat in the 1997 National Assembly election.

The Parties of the Center-Right in France

Since 1962, two major groups have made up the center-right: the Gaullists (now known as the *Rassemblement pour la République*—RPR) and the *Union pour la Démocratie Française* (UDF). Compared to the complexity and fragmentation of the right during the Third (1870–1940) and Fourth (1946–1958) Republics, this is a far simpler and more unified right than republican France has experienced in the past.

The Gaullists

The Rally for the Republic (RPR) is the latest name for the party embodying Gaullist traditions. It was first organized in 1958 as the *Union pour la Nouvelle République* (UNR). Until 1981, the Gaullist party was the dominant political force in France. For 15 years the president of the republic was a Gaullist; all the prime ministers from 1958–1976 were Gaullists; the party had the largest parliamentary group in the National Assembly until 1981; and from 1968–1973, the Gaullist party alone held a majority in the National Assembly—the first time in French democratic history that a single party had controlled a parliamentary majority. The party suffered decline in the 1970s and early 1980s but has steadily rebuilt its organization and electoral base in the last decade so that by the early 1990s, the RPR was the preeminent party in France. But its standing was precarious, as seen in the 1997 election defeat and subsequent squabbling within the party and with its UDF allies.

Originally designed as a means of providing supporters of Charles de Gaulle with a political movement,[14] the Gaullist party was not expected to survive the general's retirement. However, from the beginning, de Gaulle stayed aloof from the party, allowing it to develop its own structures and leadership. The UNR soon became the tool for organizing public support for the party and its leader. While still prime minister under de Gaulle, Georges Pompidou shaped the Gaullist party into an effective means of mobilizing his personal supporters.[15] A decade later, Jacques Chirac took leadership of a faltering party and turned it into a powerful political machine (under a new name, the RPR) that has supported his political ambitions for over two decades. In return, Gaullism owes its current status, both its strength prior to 1997 and its weakness thereafter, to Chirac.[16]

The RPR stands for a vaguely defined Gaullist legacy: institutions, national independence, economic modernization, and participation. It embodies the Jacobin tradition of a strong, central government with important powers over society. Above all Gaullists are loyal to the political institutions of the Fifth Republic as established by Charles de Gaulle. They support maintaining a distinctive and autonomous role in world politics. In pursuit of French *grandeur,* Gaullists advocate French independence in diplomatic and military affairs. De Gaulle and many old-time Gaullists were suspicious of European integration. In the effort to assert French independence, de Gaulle and his immediate successors often sought ways to show their differences with the United States. De Gaulle and his successors recognized that French independence was contingent upon a strong economy. Unlike traditional conservatives who avoided economic intervention, the Gaullists are *dirigistes* who have had "the State in their blood."[17] Gaullists also promote a populist theme of public involvement that extends from de Gaulle's notions of "association and participation" to Chirac's 1995 campaign rhetoric promising help to those not sharing in the benefits of a growing European economy.

Despite its electoral base in historical areas of conservative strength and its occasional nationalist ventures, the RPR is not a traditional French conservative party. Gaullist governments achieved many of the changes that adapted France to a modern world. They brought France into the European Community and contributed to the expansion of that body. It was under de Gaulle that France completed decolonization. Gaullist governments enacted major university reforms and agricultural changes, achieved industrialization and economic modernization against the determined opposition of small business and agriculture, installed new mechanisms for government direction of the economy, and pressed (unsuccessfully) for fundamental changes in the free-enterprise system to provide for "association" and "participation" of workers in profits and business decisions.

In the last decade, the RPR demonstrated that its loyalty to de Gaulle's legacy does not prevent it from making significant adjustments in its doctrine. The RPR's economic policy is now more nuanced, with formal pledges for more free-market direction to the economy counterbalanced by continuing acceptance of the state as an important economic actor. The Gaullist party has worked for privatizing the public enterprises, not only those brought into the public sector by the Socialists in 1981, but also those firms de Gaulle nationalized in 1945. But privatization did not end state involvement in these enterprises.

Among the most important deviations from the Gaullist heritage has been the RPR's adjustment of its nationalist traditions to the needs of increasing globalization. In the aftermath of the cold war, the RPR now accepts the role of an intermediate power. Under Chirac's presidency, France has abandoned many of the traditional Gaullist foreign and defense policies that once set France apart from its western neighbors. For example, France now participates more fully in the North Atlantic Treat Organization. Above all, Gaullist governments have become increasingly supportive of European economic and political integration.

The Gaullist party is remarkably cohesive and well-disciplined compared with other French conservative movements, past or present. It has sought mass membership, although its dues-paying membership rarely went above 150,000.[18] The party has demonstrated strong voting discipline in the National Assembly,[19] an unusual trait for center-right parties in France. While local units are often inactive and sometimes paralyzed by internal divisions, they are readily mobilized at election times. The RPR national organization generally has been strong and effective in presenting a common front on policy and leadership selections.

More than anything, the Gaullist party has been a political machine to support the presidential ambitions of its leaders. After de Gaulle's relatively weak performance in the 1965 presidential election, Prime Minister Georges Pompidou devoted great attention to party building and turned the Gaullist party into a well-organized, mass-membership, and centralized party. It was such a personalized organization that after Pompidou's death in 1974 the party was not able to shift its loyalty to his presumptive successor. As a result, the Gaullist candidate in the 1974 presidential election, Jacques Chaban-Delmas, was defeated on the first ballot. Without a presidential contender at its head, the Gaullist party floundered for the next two years. Then, Jacques Chirac took over the party and made major organizational and leadership shifts that turned the RPR into a highly personalized political machine to support his candidacies in the next three presidential elections.[20]

With a party designed especially for presidential politics, the Gaullists have been less successful in local organizations and municipal elections. Over time, they have built strong local support, but the party remains a national one focused above all on presidential politics. This is not bad politics in France, where the presidential election has become the key political event.

Party unity and central control are key themes in the RPR's informal norms of conduct. But the party has had its share of divisive conflicts. In its early years, the Gaullist party had small but important factions of de Gaulle purists—the *Gaullistes de gauche* and the "keepers of the flame"— that contended with more pragmatic groups arrayed behind leaders such as Georges Pompidou or Jacques Chaban-Delmas. There were also important clashes between "currents" arrayed behind rival leaders. In general, however, the overarching loyalty to the party and its leader has limited such factionalism.

This has not prevented serious internal conflicts over the past decade. The three years after the defeats in the 1988 presidential and parliamentary elections represented a time of conflict that was "unprecedented in the history of the RPR."[21] Chirac's second defeat in as many tries in presidential elections motivated some to search for a more viable and electable presidential candidate. Some Gaullist leaders, notably Charles Pasqua and Philippe Séguin, criticized Chirac's lack of sufficient militance on immigration and law-and-order issues. Others were reformers with their own political ambitions who saw Chirac's defeats as evidence that the RPR needed fundamental reform and a new leader. Alain Carignon and Michel Noir were among those who aspired to change the RPR's leadership and to link RPR reformers with like-minded younger UDF leaders to give a new image and leadership to the center-right. A combination of factors enabled Chirac to retain control of the RPR: his leadership skills, the implantation of his supporters in key party positions throughout the country, some blunders on the part of his opponents, and a lot of good luck.

In 1992, the RPR faced another trial in the referendum on the Maastricht Treaty. Many Gaullists still share de Gaulle's mistrust of European integration. Formally, the party took no position on the 1992 referendum and declared a "free vote" for its members. Pasqua and Séguin led the "no" vote campaign and Chirac on a personal basis campaigned for a "yes" vote. In the confusion, slightly more than two-thirds of RPR voters supported the "no" position and a little under one-third came out for the treaty. This division reflects ambivalent feelings about European integration among many Gaullists. The party's division on the issue was again evident in the 1994 European Parliament elections when a dissident Gaullist list opposed to European integration ran against the official RPR-UDF list. After the bitter 1992 and 1994 European campaigns, Chirac was again successful in bringing the two sides together for the key national tests: the 1993 and 1997 National Assembly elections and the 1995 presidential election. Chirac bridged differences on the European issue, more through ambiguity than genuine compromise. The resulting delicate balance means that the RPR avoids raising Europe as an issue in national elections.

RPR cohesion was again tested by the 1995 presidential election. After the 1993 legislative victory, Chirac supported Edouard Balladur, a member of the RPR, to be prime minister. Mitterrand duly appointed him. At first, Balladur disclaimed any presidential intentions. His popularity, however, grew, and he eventually decided to challenge Chirac for the nation's presidency. Chirac's dominance in the party minimized the effects of this contention. The party's leadership and rank-and-file aligned themselves with Chirac. Balladur was forced to look to the UDF for support with only a few RPR leaders willing to join his campaign.

Beyond such personal rivalries, there is often discontent based on specific policy differences or general dissatisfaction, especially when the party is in government. For example, in 1996–1997 Prime Minister Alain Juppé faced harsh criticism from within the RPR over his failed economic policies and capitulation to public-sector strikers. In this case, and this is not unusual, the criticism of policies was accompanied by maneuvering by RPR parliamentarians to align with rival leaders in anticipation of a change in the office of prime minister.

Another era of internal strife broke out after the stunning defeat in the 1997 National Assembly elections. While Chirac remains president until 2002, his political judgment is discredited by his decision to hold early elections, and by the poorly managed campaign. Chirac's hold on the party is shaken by these events and by his need to remain aloof from openly partisan matters as he seeks to preserve what presidential prerogatives he can during cohabitation with the Socialists.

Meanwhile, other RPR leaders are contending with each other for party leadership, offering sharply different visions of the party's future directions and strategies. The initial victory went to Philippe Séguin, nationalistic on Europe, a supporter of harder lines on immigration and public order, and a *dirigiste* and statist in economic matters. It is not clear, however, that Séguin will be able to impose his leadership on the party. Nor is it clear that Chirac is prepared to surrender leadership of the party he remade.

With leadership squabbles, doctrinal disputes, confounded by how to respond to challenges from the far right and the declining morale of its rank-and-file membership, the RPR is once again in crisis. The severity of the challenge confronting the RPR at the end of the 1990s resembles the party's crisis after Pompidou's death. But this time, the emergence of a "new Chirac" to revive the party is hindered by Chirac's continued political presence. At this time of deep crisis, it is important to remember that pundits have announced the death of the Gaullist party on numerous occasions since 1958. Each time the party has revived and resumed its place as the leading party of the Fifth Republic. It may well do so again.

The Union for French Democracy

The Gaullist movement's success in the first 15 years of the Fifth Republic pushed other conservative and centrist parties to the political sidelines. The developing rivalry between Gaullists and the left destined the small anti-Gaullist centrist and conservative parties to political oblivion. The one exception was the Independent Republican party formed by Valéry Giscard d'Estaing in the mid-1960s. This party, now known as the Republican Party (PR), was founded by conservatives who rallied to de Gaulle but who refused to affiliate with the Gaullist party. The new party was based on those conservatives from the old Centre National des Indépendants who remained loyal to de Gaulle in the battle over Algerian independence and the 1962 referendum on popular election of the president. While some of these Independents joined the Gaullist party in 1962, others joined Giscard d'Estaing in a new, pro-Gaullist Independent Republican party (RI).

Giscard, de Gaulle's young minister of finance, soon dominated the Independent Republican party and made it a vehicle for his own political ambitions. The Independent Republicans, while remaining apart from the Gaullist party, became a part of the president's majority—often dubbed "the majority's minority." Independent Republicans filled prominent posts in successive Gaullist-led governments from 1959 to 1974. The RI party never succeeded in developing its own structures or membership. For the most part, it remained a party of notables dominated by long-time conservative leaders who aligned with Giscard while retaining their own autonomy at the local level.

In 1974, Giscard defeated the Gaullist candidate in the first ballot and went on to win the presidency. He and his party leaders felt that with Giscard as president, his followers should dominate the majority coalition. They directed efforts designed to make his own party the dominant force in the Gaullist coalition. However, the Republican party failed to attract new members or to undermine the Gaullist party.

As a result, in the preparations for the 1978 National Assembly elections, the Giscardians formed a broader Union for French Democracy (UDF). Giscard brought together his own followers with other conservatives and centrists who remained apart from the majority coalition. In the

1978 election campaign, UDF candidates were present in nearly all districts and challenged established Gaullist leaders. While the UDF drew close to the RPR in votes and elected deputies, it failed to achieve its goal of dominating the majority coalition. Furthermore, the competition within the majority left bitter memories that came back to haunt the Giscardians in 1981.

The UDF has remained a fragile coalition of weak parties. It is composed of the Republicans, several small centrist parties, remnants of French Christian democracy, the Radical party—a relic from previous French republics that refuses to disappear—and other center-right notables. None of these parties has a significant organization or membership base of its own. Each is based on a handful of personalities who use their small parties to pursue personal political ambitions. While the groups forming the UDF are too small to act independently, they refuse to surrender their separate identities in the UDF. They are more concerned with preserving their own distinctiveness than in building a strong alliance. With scarce resources of their own, the member parties of the UDF are reluctant to give much support to building the UDF itself. As a result, 20 years after its formation, the UDF still lacks its own organization, a clear identity, or cohesive leadership.

Under the Fifth Republic, parties must have credible presidential contenders within their ranks to hope for political success. The UDF has always had several contenders, but their very multiplicity reduces the party's political effectiveness. In recent years, these have included Giscard, Jean Lecanuet, Simone Weil, Raymond Barre, Alain Madelin, François Bayrou, and François Léotard. Rivalries among them have limited the UDF's ability to present credible presidential candidates. The UDF's leadership dilemma was well demonstrated by the 1995 presidential elections: there was no UDF candidate. Instead, several other center-right candidates contested the first ballot, with various UDF leaders and parties aligning themselves individually with either the RPR's Chirac or Balladur, with a slight edge in UDF leaders' endorsements to Balladur.

Giscardians faced the challenge of presenting a distinctive identity while serving as junior partners in a coalition dominated by Gaullists. When de Gaulle was president, the Giscardians defined their position as "*oui-mais*"— "yes, but." Yes, they supported de Gaulle as president, but they had reservations about many of his programs and about his aloof and often autocratic political style. The "buts" identified by the Giscardians as issues where they had differed with the Gaullists included more cooperation with the Atlantic alliance in foreign and defense policies, greater support for European integration, a more traditional liberal economic policy, greater respect for parliament, more openness to compromise and dialogue, and greater concern for civil liberties. In most cases, these differences were very subtle and reflected nuances rather than substantive policy divergences. They are well summarized by Jean Charlot:

> There was incompatibility of political temperament between Giscardians and Gaullists. Giscardians sought dialogue and compromise, whereas Gaullism was always ready to mobilize and wage war. Gaullism was strong-willed and intransigent with regard to the independence and greatness of France; Giscardianism was ready to accept the constraints that weigh heavily on a medium power.[22]

During Giscard's presidency (1974–1981) many of these purported differences disappeared. Giscard kept most of the independent foreign and defense policies that he earlier had criticized; his economic policies were basically the same as those he had managed as de Gaulle's minister of finance; he proved to be as aloof in his presidential style as were his Gaullist predecessors. During the 1980s, Giscardians accepted neoliberalism with somewhat more enthusiasm than did the Gaullists. They joined in the growing calls for reduced government economic regulation about the same time that the Socialist government of the time made similar commitments. Like the Gaullists, Giscardians remained more moderate in their positions on social welfare programs than conservatives in Britain or the United States.

The clearest difference between Giscardians and Gaullists was the Giscardians' more positive attitude toward European integration. Since the mid-1980s, even this difference has disappeared. Under Chirac, the Gaullists have overcome much of their earlier suspicion of a united Europe. Gaullist-led governments from 1986 to 1988 and 1993 to 1997 sought to keep France in the forefront of unification efforts. Indeed, the austerity economic policies that led to the center-right's defeat in the 1997 elections were motivated by Chirac's commitment to lead France into the single European currency. In effect, the RPR, the UDF, and most other French parties have accepted the reality of the European Union. They differ now only slightly in their interpretations of the best ways to defend French interests in European and global economies.[23]

The UDF still faces basic challenges to its own unity and identity. Member parties struggle more to assert their own positions than to achieve a unified front for the party. It lacks the means of identifying and developing likely presidential candidates. Their differences from the RPR are no longer distinctive policy-based differences but personal rivalries and histories of often bad relations. After the 1997 defeat, the UDF faces the same challenges confronting its Gaullist partner: demoralization, absence of a leader of presidential timber, and internal dissent confronted by its Gaullist partner.

Relations between the Gaullists and
the Union for French Democracy

The center-right coalition of the RPR and UDF (and their predecessors) is durable. Formed first in 1958, the coalition has contracted and expanded as smaller groups left the coalition and then returned. But the alliance between Gaullists and Giscardians has remained very much the same for 40 years. Smaller parties of the center and right have been unable to compete or to defend a separate identity outside the UDF or RPR. By 1974, virtually all of these smaller parties were incorporated in the coalition, usually through the UDF.

Within this coalition, the Gaullists have continued to be the largest force despite the effort of their allies to combine against them. The RPR begins with a broader and more reliable electoral base. The RPR has the additional advantage of a stronger party organization, greater cohesion, and a larger membership. The Gaullists have also been better at developing presidential candidates. In a system where presidential elections have become the central political event, that has given the Gaullists more leadership of the coalition than their political might merits. The two groups are nearly the same size in parliament (see table 2.3), but the Gaullists have been seen as the leader of the center-right coalition since 1986, when Chirac emerged as the center-right's preeminent presidential candidate.

Despite regular internal clashes and personal rivalries, the Gaullist-Giscardian coalition has maintained remarkable cohesion. Even at times of coalition stress, they vote together in the National Assembly, thus preserving their hold on politics and dominance of the policy process.[24] Their unity made the center-right coalition the hegemonic political force in France. Such long-term coalitions are unusual in French democratic history; in Europe only the unique German CDU-CSU coalition has lasted longer than the RPR-UDF partnership.

The two-ballot electoral system encourages competition within "political families" because separate parties can test their strength on the first ballot and then unite on the second. In fact, the center-right parties have more often than not avoided such first-ballot tests. In general, sitting deputies from one coalition party are not challenged by partners. Often, party leaders from the members of the coalition meet ahead of time to divide up open districts. For example, in the 1988, 1993, and 1997 National Assembly elections, the center-right parties agreed to endorse the same candidate in nearly all districts.[25] Head-to-head competition on the first ballot between Gaullists and their partners are thus the exception rather than the rule. The exceptions, however, often lead to mean-spirited campaigns where the center-right rivals direct their campaigns against each

Table 2.3   RPR and UDF Representation in the National Assembly, 1962–1997

Election Year	Number of RPR Deputies	Number of UDF Deputies
1962*	229	35
1968*	294	64
1973*	184	77
1978	150	139
1981	85	67
1986	151	126
1988	126	129
1993	247	213
1997	134	108

Source: Quid 1995 (Robert Laffront, 1995), pp. 793–795.
Note: *For the elections in 1962 and 1968, the figures are for the UNR/UDR and RI. The 1973 figure for the UDF includes the RI and the CDP (center-right politicians who had rallied to the majority).

other more than they address the left-wing candidates. Center-right voters generally overlook the bitterness of these campaigns and rally to support the center-right candidate who remains on the second ballot.[26]

The most serious attack on the coalition's unity came between 1974 and 1981.[27] This was the era when Giscard as newly elected president of the republic tried to assert leadership over the coalition. The UDF had the explicit aim of replacing the Gaullists as the strongest grouping in the majority. The Giscardians' open attack on the Gaullists stirred passions in the center-right coalition. Gaullists responded with efforts to renew their own organization and to challenge Giscard and his supporters in many contexts. The 1978 elections were the first (and only) legislative elections where the RPR and UDF directly confronted each other in nearly all districts. Giscardians came close to matching the Gaullist parliamentary delegation. But the intense competition soured relations within the coalition and resulted in a fierce contest between Giscard and the RPR's Chirac on the first-ballot 1981 presidential election.

When Giscard outpolled Chirac on the first ballot, some Gaullist voters and leaders refused to rally to him on the second ballot. A few weeks later, the RPR and UDF suffered even greater losses in the National Assembly elections called by Mitterrand to take advantage of the momentum from his solid victory in the presidential election. The RPR and UDF experienced their lowest voting results in the history of the Fifth Republic and found themselves a small minority in a National Assembly dominated by the first ever Socialist parliamentary majority.

Once in opposition, the Gaullists and Giscardians worked to rebuild their unity. It proved easier to cooperate in opposition to an increasingly unpopular left-wing government than it had been to stay unified while fighting each other for ascendancy within the governing coalition. The Left's pursuit of ideological goals brought unity back to the center-right. A more moderate course of action between 1981 and 1984 by the Socialist government might have accentuated divisions within the center-right. The left, however, moved ahead with ambitious plans for nationalizations and reopened the volatile clerical issue with attacks on private, Catholic schools. These programs enabled the center-right to put aside its internal conflicts in order to unite in opposition to Mitterrand.

The next National Assembly elections were conducted under proportional representation, which might have renewed their competition using even more strident terms since there would be no need for second ballot cooperation. Unity, however, was needed to demonstrate their ability to govern again and to face the new threat from the extreme right posed by Jean-Marie Le Pen's National Front. In the event, the RPR and UDF ran joint lists in 61 of 96 departments. In the 35 districts where they presented separate lists, they still campaigned with the theme of "governing together." Their election success confirmed the electoral and practical advantages of coalition unity rather than conflict.

It was a narrow victory, and that contributed to greater coalition solidarity. There remained tensions and rivalries but they were fought out discreetly. It was difficult to heal a decade's hostility, especially with the presidential elections less than two years away. There were two prominent center-right candidates in the 1988 presidential election: Raymond Barre (a former UDF prime minister under Giscard) and the Gaullist leader, Jacques Chirac. Their competition for the first ballot was intense but not divisive. The center-right was able to rally support for Chirac on the second ballot (but not enough to defeat Mitterrand) and to run a strong campaign for the ensuing National Assembly elections.

Tensions between Gaullists and the UDF continue, heightened now by recriminations over the 1997 losses. However, they are less intense than they were between 1974 and 1984 and do not compromise overall unity. The landslide parliamentary majority won by the RPR and UDF in 1993 did not produce the internal competition that many had feared. The coalition remained united in the 1995 presidential elections despite the presence of several candidates from the center-right (all of them Gaullists!). The partners went united into the 1997 elections and shared equally in the defeat. Following these elections, UDF leaders voiced strong challenges to the RPR's conduct of the election and sought to take advantage of the Gaullists' disarray. Without a presidential-type leader, however, the UDF is

Table 2.4 The Right in Power in France, 1958–1997

Years	Party of President	Party of Prime Minister
1958–1969	Gaullist	Gaullist
1969–1974	Gaullist	Gaullist
1974–1976	Giscardian	Gaullist
1976–1981	Giscardian	Giscardian
1986–1988	Socialist	Gaullist
1993–1995	Socialist	Gaullist
1995–1997	Gaullist	Gaullist
1997–	Gaullist	Socialist

not in a position to win control of the coalition. Some UDF and RPR leaders speak of a possible merger of the two movements. Such an action would be welcomed by their voters.[28]

The Right in Government

Above all, the RPR-UDF coalition is an alliance for government. That is the goal and the reality. The RPR-UDF alliance has dominated government since the establishment of the Fifth Republic in 1958 (see table 2.4). The Gaullist-Giscardian coalition has provided the prime minister and held a majority in the National Assembly for 29 of the 39 years since the Fifth Republic began. It has controlled the presidency for 25 years. This coalition lasted so long that the Gaullists and Giscardians were known simply as "the majority" and even the "ex-majority" until well into the 1980s.

During its long hold on power, the Gaullist-Giscardian coalition thoroughly dominated French government. Over the years, the majority successfully "colonized" much of the once-resistant bureaucracy.[29] There was extensive movement of individuals back and forth between the senior civil service and Gaullist or Giscardian party or government offices. Unconcerned that the opposition might win and use the same tactics against it, the center-right majority turned ministries into fiefdoms and civil servants into operatives. Partisan bias was often evident in the bureaucracy's conduct, notably in sensitive ministries such as interior, communications, defense, and public works. When the Socialists took office in 1981, they replaced many top-level civil servants, but there was no general purge of Gaullist influence in the bureaucracy. Personnel changes after the electoral shifts in 1995 and 1997 were even more modest, suggesting that senior civil servants may have become more discreet in their political activities.

Over the past dozen years, the center-right has faced a different governing challenge: sharing power or cohabitation. On two occasions, from 1986 to 1988 and then from 1993 to 1995, center-right parliamentary majorities had to govern under a Socialist president. Currently, a center-right president shares power with a left-wing government and parliament. The first cohabitation was complicated by the fact that the Gaullist prime minister, Jacques Chirac, was preparing for a presidential contest only two years away with the incumbent president as his likely opponent. There were frequent clashes between Chirac and Mitterrand as they tried to work out cohabitation and to maneuver for position in the presidential race. The RPR-UDF union maintained its solidarity in spite of occasional Socialist efforts to divide them, thereby allowing the center-right to regain its image of a cohesive and viable governmental alliance. Excluded again from government after the 1988 presidential and National Assembly elections, the center-right coalition retained its unity and furthered its public acceptance as a potential government coalition.

The next cohabitation episode, 1993–1995, went more smoothly. Once again, the center-right dominated parliament and government under a Socialist president. In part, the success of this second experiment with cohabitation was due to the fact that precedents on how to operate under cohabitation were in place, and the relationship between president and prime minister was better defined than it had been between 1986 and 1988. There were also personality differences: Prime Minister Edouard Balladur was less combative in dealing with the president, and Mitterrand was increasingly preoccupied by his declining health. Mitterrand did not need to assert himself since he did not intend to run again and there was no obvious Socialist candidate to replace him. Political considerations also played a part: the RPR-UDF majority was overwhelming with 80 percent of the seats in the National Assembly. This gave the RPR-UDF government a clear popular mandate that the Chirac government lacked in the earlier cohabitation.

The third era of cohabitation is different in that the president is from the center-right and the National Assembly majority is on the left. Early signs indicate that Chirac and Socialist Prime Minister Lionel Jospin will avoid open clashes. Jospin has already acknowledged the president's role in foreign and defense policies. Chirac gave a polite but reserved welcome to the newly appointed ministers. The real challenge for the center-right will come from Chirac's need to be "presidential" and above politics in order to maximize his governing role in cohabitation and his credibility among the citizenry. That nonpartisan stance will limit his ability to help revive his own party and to maintain RPR-UDF unity in the aftermath of their electoral disaster.

Despite the current left-wing government, it is still appropriate to picture the center-right as the "natural" governing parties in France. Just as the British Conservatives and the German CDU/CSU have dominated politics in their countries for most of the last 50 years, the center-right is the "normal" government in France. The current challenge is not due to a reduction in the popularity of the right: even in the 1997 elections, the parties of the right had a solid majority on the first ballot and the vote for the left actually shrank compared to its victories in 1981 and 1988.[30] The problem now is that the conservative vote in France is split between a pariah radical right and the traditional center-right parties.

The Center-Right and the National Front

The silencing of the far right was among the most important achievements of the early Gaullist era. The success of the Gaullist party and its allies overwhelmed the smaller far-right parties and gave their voters little choice other than to vote Gaullist. In the 1965 presidential election, with memories of de Gaulle's "betrayal" of Algeria still close in the hearts of France's nationalists, a well-financed and popular candidate of the far right, Jean-Louis Tixier-Vignancour, could only attract 5 percent of the voters. After that, the combined vote for the many parties of the radical right rarely attracted more than 1 percent in national elections.

The revival of the far right began in the early 1980s when extremist groups benefited from voter hostility to the expanding immigrant population. Voters also saw a vote for the far right as a way of demonstrating their total disenchantment with the Socialist government of the time. Under the dynamic leadership of Jean-Marie Le Pen, the National Front (FN) became a mighty political force and demonstrated its appeal in the 1984 European elections and the 1986 National Assembly elections. Initially, the FN was written off as a "flash party" produced by the Socialist experiment with proportional representation in 1986. However, the FN has now developed a substantial and durable electoral base and replaced the Communist party as the fourth-largest party[31] (see table 2.5). With over 15 percent of the vote in the 1997 National Assembly elections, the FN is the most successful party in the current resurgence of the far right in Europe, with the exception of the Austrian Freedom party.[32]

Much of FN support has come from voters who previously supported mainline center-right parties.[33] To their credit, the parties of the center-right have disdained cooperation with the FN even on those occasions when such cooperation might have helped their candidates. While their candidates have often benefited from FN voters in run-off elections, the RPR and UDF have refused any formal electoral negotiations with the

Table 2.5 Electoral Strength of Parties of the Right

| | Percentage of Total Votes Cast: | |
Election	RPR + UDF	FN
1983 Municipal Councils	50.8	0.1*
1984 European Parliament	42.3	11.0
1986 National Assembly	46.5	9.9
1986 Regional Assemblies	44.6	9.56
1988 Presidential	36.3	14.6
1988 National Assembly	40.5	9.7
1989 European Parliament	37.9	10.5
1989 Municipal Councils	45.0	9.6
1992 Regional Assemblies	37.1	13.6
1993 National Assembly	44.2	12.7
1994 European Parliament	37.9	10.5
1995 Presidential	39.4	15.0
1997 National Assembly	36.2	15.1

Source: *Quid 1995* (Paris: Robert Laffont, 1995), pp. 789, 794–797, 921; *Financial Times,* April 25, 1995; and *Le Monde,* May 27, 1997.
Note: *This figure is for all far-right candidates.

FN in both national and local elections, even in difficult situations. When outvoted by an FN candidate on the first ballot, the mainstream parties have urged abstention or even voting for the leftist candidate. The RPR backed up its policy with threats to expel any party member who collaborated with the FN. For its part, the FN has maintained its candidates for second ballot run-offs to defeat center-right candidates and where eliminated on the first ballot the FN urges its voters to support the opposition left rather than the center-right candidates. There have been a few exceptions to this policy where RPR or UDF candidates have made local deals, but those cases have brought angry criticism from within the center-right parties.

For the RPR and UDF, the FN remains a political pariah lacking commitment to democracy and advocating extremist positions reminiscent of fascist parties of the 1930s and 1940s. But the ability of the FN to hold the main parties electoral hostage in regional and National Assembly elections has led some in the RPR and UDF to reconsider their hostility to the FN. For them, the extreme right is "not an extension of the right" but an entirely different and alien political tradition. This stance is not entirely altruistic. The RPR and UDF know very well that the overwhelming majority of French voters regard the FN as a threat to democracy. Center-right collaboration with LePen would run the risk of at once alienating many of their own voters and enhancing the FN vote by giving it the stamp of democratic approval. Indeed a poll showed that 66 percent of RPR voters and 77 percent of UDF voters opposed any alliance with the National Front.[34]

For its part in National Assembly elections, the FN has maintained its candidates for second ballot run-offs to defeat center-right candidates, and where eliminated on the first ballot the FN urges its voters to support the opposition left rather than the center-right candidates. Indeed, as it has grown in electoral strength, it has targeted the voters of the center-right. The FN's success in the 1997 National Assembly elections was not in the number of deputies elected—only one. But the far right met the 12.5 percent threshold for participating in second-ballot contests in nearly one-fourth of all districts. That put the FN in the position of spoiler or power broker. Unable to get concessions from the mainstream center-right, the FN maintained its candidates putting RPR/UDF candidates into three-way contests against the left on the second ballot. The splitting of right-wing voters provided the margin of victory for the left.[35]

Obviously, center-right politicians are troubled by this strategy. Debate on the proper response continues. The mainstream parties still reject collaboration with the National Front, but this position will be tested frequently. Such was the case in the 1998 regional elections. A number of regional presidencies were lost when the RPR or UDF regional leaders refused to accept National Front support. In a few other cases, the center-right regional coalitions accepted FN support and faced expulsion from their parties. In a recent FN congress, Le Pen declared that "There will soon be nothing left between the socialo-communists and us."[36]

While the RPR and UDF have eschewed electoral cooperation with the FN, they have picked up on some of the themes championed by Le Pen and his followers. They have steered far clear of the anti-Semitism and extreme antiforeign rhetoric of the FN, but the RPR and UDF have taken harder positions on immigration, naturalization, and asylum issues since the mid-1980s. The center-right parties have also picked up on the FN's "law and order" issues by taking firm stands against urban crime and drug use. These hardline positions on immigration and law enforcement by mainstream parties led one observer to note that "it was reasonable to ask whether the National Front had not in fact won an [im]moral victory" for its issues.[37]

Relations between the National Front and the mainstream center-right parties will remain key points of contention in French politics. As long as the RPR and UDF can win national elections without the FN, they are likely to continue to regard the far right as beyond respectability. The two-ballot electoral system in use for the presidential and legislative elections facilitates the isolation of the National Front. The FN rarely is able to out-poll the mainstream candidates, and can keep its voters from rallying to center-right candidates in second-ballot run-offs only when the center-right is in power. The FN has been slow in translating its influence in national elections into local politics. Should this situation change due to electoral-system reform or further gains for the National Front, the matter of the relationship between the Front and the mainstream parties might well be re-opened.

The French Center-Right at the Turn of the Century

In its early years, the Gaullist coalition could justify its hold on government by pointing to the divided left, which had a strong Communist party at its heart and would implicitly—and sometimes explicitly—tell voters "it's us or the deluge." The left has now proven its capability to govern effectively and moderately. Further, the communist threat is gone not only because of the moribund state of the French Communist party but also because communism is no longer the great danger to Western civilization that it seemed to be during the cold war.

The Gaullists, with an assertive and combative political style, thrived during the long years that the French party system was polarized between an ideologically committed left and a more moderate and pragmatic center-right. That polarization is now also gone. After failing in their attempt to create a new socialist society, the Socialists have moderated their once dogma-based stances on economic policies, social issues, cultural values, and foreign policy. There remain important differences between the left and right in emphasis and priority of certain issues. But the choice between the Socialists and the RPR/UDF is no longer a choice between entirely different societies. As a result, French politics is likely to be more competitive than in the past.

It may seem surprising that the Socialists have accepted so much of the neoliberal economic agenda. But both Socialists and the center-right find themselves constrained to accept these policies, not because of a perceived new neoliberal consensus, but rather because the international economic competition discourages—and the European Union in some cases forbids—the state *dirigisme* of both Gaullists and Socialists. There is no public consensus in France for neoliberal notions of economists and politicians, who favor the state retreating from economic and social management. It is not surprising, then, that both the center-right and the left have definite limits to their acceptance of neoliberalism. The French center-right parties have not embraced free-market policies as the British Conservatives have done nor have the French Socialists gone as far as the British Labour party.

The limits of neoliberalism in France are well illustrated by the denationalization efforts launched by the RPR/UDF government in 1986. It was one of the most ambitious privatization programs in Western Europe. Under Gaullist direction, however, the state retained substantial influence over not only the privatization process but also over the resulting private firms.[38] When the Socialists regained power in 1988, they accepted the denationalizations that had already been accomplished, but moved ahead very slowly in further sales of state firms. This same cautious course was adopted by the RPR/UDF when they regained control of the government in 1993. The convergence of the left and right on denationalization illustrates the broad political consensus that has replaced the political party divisions that were so strong from 1962 to 1984. The limits of that convergence are evident, however, in Jospin's announcement of an end to denationalization of public enterprises that are part of the national heritage.

The political strength of the center-right in France is therefore not based on a new political consensus but rather on the skill of the RPR and UDF in adjusting their policies to expectations of French voters. A good example can be seen in Chirac's 1995 presidential victory. Observers contend that his victory was to his ability to convince French voters that he better than other center-right or even leftist candidates would forge a strong state to respond to the challenges of growing European and international competition.[39] The center-right's defeat in 1997 was linked to its government's failure to use state resources to reduce unemployment.

There are a number of challenges facing the French center-right at the end of the century. Some are socioeconomic, such as shifting importance of traditional cleavages. Others are more explicitly political. The center-right has lost its former political advantage of standing in opposition to extremism on the left and to the dangers of domestic and international communism. It also faces stiff competition from the extreme right FN that is unlikely to go away. The left has established its ability to govern and to stand as an alternative government party. The present political conjuncture allows voters to feel free to shift their support back and forth from the center-right to the left. Voter volatility is high[40] with voters more willing to vote against governments that displease them than vote for particular platforms.[41] This makes the political future in France more uncertain than at any time in the last 50 years. And the choice between the center-right and the Socialists will be meaningful. The differences between the left and center-right have diminished but remain important cues to voters interested in the issues of the day or in the personalities who aspire to be their leaders.

The strength of the center-right's position is nonetheless impressive. While it is likely that there will be more frequent rotation in power between the RPR/UDF and the Socialists, the center-right is also likely to remain as *the* party of government in France.

Notes

1. See Malcolm Anderson, *Conservative Politics in France* (London: George Allen & Unwin, 1974).
2. Eric Dupin, "RPR: Le Nouveau parti attrape-tout," *Libération,* February 9,1993.
3. Guy Michelat and Michel Simon, *Classe, religion et comportement politique* (Paris: Presses Universitaires de France, 1977).
4. Michael Lewis-Beck and Andrew Skalaban, "France," in Mark Franklin, Thomas T. Mackie, and Henry Valen, eds., *Electoral Change: Responses to Evolving Social and Attitudinal Structures in Fifteen Countries* (Cambridge, England: Cambridge University Press, 1992), p. 177.
5. Noona Mayer, "Elections and the Left-Right Division in France," *French Politics and Society* 13 (Winter 1995): 36–44. See also Daniel Boy and Noona Mayer, *The French Voter Decides* (Ann Arbor: University of Michigan Press, 1993).
6. Roy Pierce, *Choosing the Chief: Presidential Elections in France and the United States* (Ann Arbor: University of Michigan Press, 1995), pp. 148–161.
7. Guy Michelat, "In Search of Left and Right," in Boy and Mayer, eds., *The French Voter Decides,* pp. 65–90.
8. See Philippe Habert, Pascal Perrineau, and Colette Ysmal, eds., *Le Vote éclaté* (Paris: Presses de la FNSP, 1992) and Pascal Perrineau, "Election Cycles and Changing Patterns of Political Behavior in France," *French Politics and Society* 13 (Winter 1995): 45–53.
9. See the excellent analysis of the Gaullist electorate in Andrew Knapp, *Gaullism Since de Gaulle* (Aldershoot, England: Dartmouth, 1994), pp. 138–185.
10. Harvey G. Simmons, *The French National Front: The Extremist Challenge to Democracy* (Boulder, CO: Westview Press, 1996).
11. See Tony Judt, "The Social Question Redivivus," *Foreign Affairs* 76 (September–October 1997): 95–118.
12. *The Economist,* January 18,1997.
13. See D. B. Goldey, "The French Presidential Election of 23 April–7 May 1995," *Electoral Studies* 15 (February 1996): 97–109.
14. On the founding of the Gaullist party, see Jean Charlot, *L'UNR: Etude du pouvoir au sein d'un parti politique* (Paris: Armand Colin, 1967).
15. Frank L. Wilson, "Gaullism Without de Gaulle," *Western Political Quarterly* 36 (September 1973): 485–506; William R. Schonfeld, Vincent McHale and Sandra Shaber, "From Aggressive to Defensive Gaullism: The Electoral Transformation of a 'Catch-all' Party," *Comparative Politics* 8 (January 1976): 291–306; and Jean Charlot, *Le Phénomène gaulliste* (Paris: Fayard, 1970).
16. Knapp, *Gaullism Since de Gaulle,* pp. 40–137.

17. Ibid., p. 368.

18. Ibid., pp. 206–210.

19. Frank L. Wilson and Richard Wiste, "Party Cohesion in the French National Assembly," *Legislative Studies Quarterly* 1 (November 1976): 467–490.

20. On this process, see Kay Lawson, "The Impact of Party Reform on Party Systems: The Case of the RPR in France," *Comparative Politics* 13 (July 1981): 401–419.

21. Knapp, *Gaullism Since de Gaulle,* p. 114. See Knapp's excellent summary of this tumultuous era, pp. 113–133.

22. Jean Charlot, "The Fall of Giscard," in Howard Penniman, ed., *France at the Polls, 1981 and 1986: Three National Elections* (Durham, NC: Duke University Press, 1988), p. 28.

23. Patrick McCarthy, "Between Europe and Exclusion: The French Presidential Elections of 1995," *Occasional Paper: European Studies Seminar Series* (Bolonga: Johns Hopkins University Bologna Center, 1996).

24. Wilson and Wiste, "Party Cohesion in the French National Assembly."

25. For a description of how such joint candidates are agreed upon, see François Bachman and Guy Birnbaum, "Heurs et malheurs de la sélection des candidats RPR et UDF," in Philippe Habert, et al., *Le Vote sanction: les élections législatives des 21 et 28 mars 1993* (Paris: Département d'Etudes Politiques du Figaro and Presses de la Fondation Nationale des Sciences Politiques, 1993).

26. Pierce's study shows that between 85 and 88 percent of voters whose preferred candidate was eliminated on the first ballot voted for candidates of the same tendency (left or right) on the second ballot in the 1974, 1981, and 1988 presidential elections. Pierce, *Choosing the Chief,* pp. 175–176.

27. Jean-Luc Parodi and John Frears, *War Will Not Take Place,* London: C. Hurst, 1979).

28. A fall 1997 poll found 72 percent of RPR voters and 64 percent of UDF voters supporting the merger of their parties. *The Economist,* October 25, 1997.

29. Wilson, *French Political Parties Under the Fifth Republic.* pp. 79–83.

30. In 1981, the parties of the left took 55.1 percent of the vote; in 1988, they received 50.4 percent; in 1997, they were down to 47.7 percent. *Le Monde* June 5, 1997.

31. Harvey G. Simmons, *The French National Front: The Extremist Challenge to Democracy* (Boulder, CO: Westview Press, 1996).

32. The Austrian Freedom party took 21.9 percent of the vote in the 1995 elections.

33. Noona Mayer and Pascal Perrineau, "Why Do They Vote For Le Pen?" *European Journal of Political Research* 37: 891–906, and Jacqueline Blondel and Bernard Lacroix, "Pourquoi votent-ils Front national?" in Noona Mayer and Pascal Perrineau, eds., *Le Front National à decouvert* (Paris: Presses de la Fondation Nationale des Sciences Politiques, 1989).

34. *Le Nouvel Observateur,* July 10–16, 1997.

35. See James G. Shields, "La Politique du pire: The Front National and the 1997 Legislative Elections," *French Politics and Society* 15 (Summer 1997): 21–36.
36. *Libération,* October 20, 1997.
37. Simmons, *The French National Front,* p. 106.
38. Mairi Maclean, "Privatisation in France 1993–94: New Departures, or a Case of *plus ça change?*" *West European Politics* 18 (April 1995): 273–90. Michael Bauer, "The Politics of State-Directed Privatisation: The Case of France," *West European Politics* 11 (October 1988): 49–60.
39. McCarthy, "Between Europe and Exclusion."
40. Andrew Appleton, "Parties Under Pressure: Challenges to 'Established' French Parties," *West European Politics* 18 (January 1995): 52–77.
41. See the study of the 1993 elections, Philippe Habert, et al., *Le Vote sanction.*

CHAPTER THREE

The Christian Democratic Center-Right in German Politics

William Chandler

The terminology of left and right, although fundamentally spatial in origin, has come to connote divergence in belief systems and partisanship. Thus, we must first recognize that left or right may refer to a position in party competition and/or to a core ideology, but whether meant as position or value, the prevailing assumption has been that such distinctions can be meaningfully arranged along a single continuum. In comparative party research, both coalition-building and ideological/ programmatic traits have been set within this framework. However, as traditional class and social milieu-based party loyalties have eroded, it has become a matter of dispute whether voter preferences are so easily interpreted in this parsimonious way.

By combining ideological/partisan strands, the notion of center-right is unavoidably imprecise and open to differing national expressions. Equally problematic is the question of its scope and composition. Components may range from a single (typically catch-all) party, to a coalition of forces, or simply to an array of competing parties. Such variation depends in part on the constitutional order, the electoral system, and the underlying structure of societal cleavages. In a Westminster-type system, where single-member-plurality electoral rules apply, single-party majorities are normal. The British Conservative party has neither challengers nor partners making claim to the center-right label. By contrast, within continental parliamentary traditions, where more complex party systems, usually operating under some form of proportional representation, are the norm, we find the center-right comprising two or three parties—sometimes, but not always, in coalition.

Throughout the first five decades of the Federal Republic, the Christian Democrats of the Christian Democratic Union (CDU) and the Bavarian Christian Social Union (CSU) have dominated the center-right space in German politics by their electoral success and governing longevity. The character of the CDU/CSU is best analyzed from several vantage points: (1) its unique postwar formation, (2) its structural features, (3) its electoral support, (4) its programmatic character and (5) its role in the exercise of power. In addition, in the German case, the politics of unification has superimposed an unprecedented layer of complexity upon the consideration of most of these factors.

Foundations

Bismarck's unification of the German Reich in 1871 established free Reichstag elections under universal manhood suffrage and led directly to the development of modern party politics. However, governments remained accountable to the Kaiser rather than to parliament. Parties excluded from power developed into ideological defenders of subcultures rather than architects of governing coalitions and policy compromise. The result was a system composed of *Weltanschauungsparteien,* that is, class and milieu parties based on segmented, polarized patterns of representation.[1] This fragmentation and polarization contributed to the collapse of Weimar democracy and ended with the Nazi *Machtergreifung* (seizure of power) in 1933.

In the aftermath of World War II, parties were licensed by occupation forces on the basis of their noncontamination with the Nazis and therefore were regarded as instruments of democratization. Unlike British parties, which emerged from parliamentary factions as by-products of the gradual extension of suffrage within an existing constitutional order, post-1945 German parties themselves became the builders of the new constitutional order. It was in this context that the primacy of parties translated into the legitimacy of the party state.[2]

The 1949 Basic Law "constitutionalized" parties, with the aim of ensuring the legitimacy of the democratic rules of the game.[3] Article 21 sets conditions for party organization and function to avoid the earlier institutional flaws that had permitted the rise of antidemocratic extremism and led to the downfall of the Weimar Republic. This article prescribes that parties maintain internal democratic procedures; it further provides for the prohibition of antidemocratic parties, which led to the outlawing of both the neo-Nazi Socialist Reich party (SRP) and the German Communist party (KPD) in the 1950s. Even more important are the positive functions that Article 21 assigns to parties, especially the participatory role in forming the political will of the people.[4]

Both CDU and CSU emerged after the war as new entities. First licensed at local and regional levels, the CDU was little more than a collection of local/regional notables campaigning under a common umbrella, which then coalesced into a loose confederation. After 1949, federalism solidified these patterns.[5] With the birth of the Federal Republic, Konrad Adenauer quickly adapted the CDU into an electoral machine (Kanzlerwahlverein) dedicated to supporting him and his government. By the critical 1953 election, the chancellor's popularity and catch-all strategy were reinforced by the CDU/CSU's advocacy of recovery, prosperity, and anti-communism to effectively unite much of the non-socialist electorate. This inclusive Christian union soon became the prototype for catch-all parties across western Europe. With the exception of the 1972 election, Christian Democracy's electoral edge over the SPD of about 5 to 10 percent meant a standing asymmetry of the German party system and a governing advantage for the CDU/CSU.

In the Soviet zone, the CDU was established in June 1945 alongside the KPD, the Social Democratic party (SPD) and Liberal Democratic Party of Germany (LDPD). Members came from the pre-1933 Zentrum, DDP, and Christian, non-socialist trade unions.[6] In the beginning phase of building state socialism, autonomous "bourgeois" parties participated, allowing leaders like Jakob Kaiser, Andreas Hermes, and Ernst Lemmer to establish an interconfessional party of "socialism based on Christian values."[7] The CDU quickly expanded its membership to an estimated 211,000 in 1948.[8] When in the 1946 Landtag elections, the CDU won a surprising one quarter of the vote, it exposed itself as a potential threat to communist leadership.

Party pluralism was soon undermined by the Zwangsvereinigung (forced fusion) of social democrats with communists. Under Soviet tutelage, the newly created Socialist Unity Party (SED) increasingly concentrated political control. The formation of the Antifascist-Block directly compromised the autonomy of the CDU and LPD, by integrating them into the SED-led party system via the formation of unitary fronts. In 1947, the inclusion of mass organizations further diluted the role of non-SED parties. The incorporation of the CDU and other bloc parties into the National Front electoral alliance meant that from the first Volkskammer elections in 1950 all elections were conducted under the unity-list system, thus confirming the subordination of bloc-parties to SED hegemony.

Purification followed in an atmosphere of increasing repression. The 1945 expulsion from leadership positions of Hermes and in 1947 of Kaiser and Lemmer, as well as other purges under SED and Soviet pressure, favored the installation of more malleable "progressive" elites.[9] Between 1948 and 1953 some 572 CDU members were arrested on political grounds. Purging of dissidents was highlighted by the arrest of Foreign Minister Georg Dertinger followed by show-trials of members accused of espionage for the west-CDU.

Through a process of enforced uniformity *(Gleichschaltung)* in which ideological adjustments were designed to justify the "leading role of the SED," the CDU also completed its shift to subservient appendage. By 1952, the CDU formally recognized its own satellite status within the SED dictatorship. Under the leadership of Gerald Götting (from 1966 until 1989), the CDU as a loyal junior partner of the SED served to integrate the Christian sector into the system of SED rule, a function that gave no opportunity for autonomous influence. Consequently, membership declined to a low point in 1961 of 70,000, recovering thereafter, peaking at 140,000 in 1987. Motivations for belonging included career advancement and family connections, but not political opposition.[10]

Organizational Structure

As long as the Christian Democrats maintained their state-party preeminence, there was no need to revamp the cadre party style based on decentralized networks that combined the power of regional "barons" in the Länder with that of the chancellorship in Bonn.[11] However, the trauma of opposition, beginning in 1969, provoked serious consideration of organizational reform for the CDU. (The CSU had previously undergone its own shock of opposition from 1954 to 1957, when a four-party coalition in Bavaria forced an early organizational adaptation.)

Substantial renewal started in earnest for the CDU only after another defeat in 1972 and a change in the top leadership. Modernization involved a shift in the strengthening of the federal center, which increasingly set priorities and designed strategies. The 1970s marked a phenomenal explosion in CDU membership, from about 300,000 in 1969 to almost 700,000 in 1980. The CSU experienced a comparable expansion. This also meant an increase in women, youth, and Protestants, making the 1980s membership slightly more representative of the population as a whole. As seen in table 3.1, this period of development closed the membership gap between CDU/ CSU and the SPD. However, since the 1980s, the CDU has had trouble attracting new members, especially among youth and women. It has a low proportion of young members—only 5.2 percent under 30 years old—but 33.6 percent over 60, while women constitute only 24.9 percent of all members. Indeed, the age/gender gap has become a growing concern for the CDU/CSU. Within the electorate, the party suffers a severe weakness among younger women but draws strength among older women. As of 1994, 26.2 percent of Bundestag members were women, but

Table 3.1 Party Membership Development (in thousands)

	CDU	CSU	Ost-CDU	SPD	CDU/CSU as % of SPD
1947–1948	400	82	211	875	55.1
1960–1961	255	53	70	650	47.4
1970	329	77		820	49.5
1980	693	172		986	87.7
1983	734	185		925	99.3
1989	662	185	140	921	92.0
1990	777*	186	134	949*	101.5
1994	671*	176	78	849*	99.7

Source: Data adapted from Rudzio, pp. 175–176.
Note: * = East + West combined totals.

with only 14 percent women members of the Bundestag, the CDU/CSU had the lowest share among all parties represented.

The place of women within the CDU has provoked heated debate at recent party congresses. At the Bonn party congress in 1994, General Secretary Hintze and the women's caucus pressured Helmut Kohl to institute a women's quota for candidates to the executive bodies of the CDU (*Vorstand* and *Presidium*). This rule would have meant that one-third of party offices would be filled by women. Despite strong opposition, this proposal passed by 416 to 361 votes, with the measure to be incorporated into the party statutes the following year. However, the extent of resistance was underestimated, and it was narrowly defeated at the October 1995 Karlsruhe congress. Peter Hintze then cobbled together a diluted, face-saving compromise that proposed that any round of voting for the *Vorstand* or *Presidium* that produced less than one-third women winners would be invalidated, thus requiring a second ballot. The purpose was to assure that slates of candidates would include a minimum of one-third women. This modified quota system was adopted at the Hannover party congress.

As a party incorporating diverse tendencies,[12] an important part of the CDU's organizational depth has always depended upon its social and economic affiliates (*Vereinigungen*), which by party statute have official status and overlapping memberships. In particular, a youth organization, a women's association, employees' groups, the union-affiliated social committees, a small business association, a local government association, and an organization representing refugees and expellees are all integrated into party life by *Proporz,* that is, the proportional allocation of offices and candidate positions on the all-important party lists. The resultant balance of client groupings internally gives the CDU a consensus-building style that reinforces its pragmatism and catch-all strategy.[13]

Although the 1970s witnessed two important organizational changes, the development of the central headquarters and a rapid expansion of membership, neither fundamentally altered the traditional structure of the party. Despite significant professionalization, party organization in the CDU has remained essentially election oriented.[14]

The CDU-CSU Partnership

The structural character of the center-right has been shaped in part by the special relationship between CDU and CSU. In 1949 they formed a single Bundestag caucus (*Fraktion*) but did not create a unified federal party organization. This unique partnership between two sister parties is based on electoral noncompetition and parliamentary fusion. This allowed the CSU to function as an autonomous regional party in alliance with the CDU.[15] Ever since, the CSU has protected its dualistic status.

In the 1970s in reaction to the social-liberal era, the CSU increasingly defined itself as a conservative anchor and defender of Christian, western values,[16] thus exposing an inherent tension with the more centrist CDU, whose preference was for a Christian-liberal majority. In opposition, tensions over chancellor-candidate selection came to dominate CDU-CSU relations. In 1972 Rainer Barzel was reluctantly accepted by the CSU, while in 1976 Helmut Kohl was initially opposed by Franz-Josef Strauss. The low point in CDU-CSU relations was manifested in post-election November 1976 when Strauss, at the famous Bad Kreuth meeting, led his CSU *Landesgruppe* to vote to establish an independent *Fraktion* and expand nationally. Only the threat of a CDU *extension* into Bavaria forced the CSU to rescind its proposal.[17] In 1980 a cohesive CSU *Landesgruppe* found allies within the CDU to thwart Kohl and permit Strauss to be chosen as chancellor-candidate. Ultimately this enduring personal rivalry was decisively rebalanced in Kohl's favor when he assumed the chancellorship in 1982, but the rivalry still lingered on until Strauss' death in 1988.

In the early phase of the GDR's democratic transition, the newly formed German Social Union (DSU) was sponsored by the CSU and appeared to offer an indirect way for the CSU to expand its national influence. However, the quick demise of the DSU cut short any prospects for CSU expansion.[18] Party chairman Theo Waigel successfully argued against repeating the Kreuth separation, preferring to work cooperatively with Kohl and the CDU federally. After the 1990 elections in which the CSU lost its status as second party in the coalition to the FDP, the prospects were uncertain for the CSU as a partner in Bonn. However, as FDP support eroded and as the CSU reconfirmed its regional dominance in the 1994 Bavarian elections, relations between CDU and CSU have been characterized by moderation and harmonization in the post-unity era.[19]

Fusion and Integration

Institutionally, the accession of the German Democratic Republic (GDR) to the Federal Republic of Germany (FRG) involved an unprecedented transfer of laws and regulations to the territory of former East Germany. Political parties, too, had to extend themselves (prior to and following formal unification) into the territory and society of the former GDR. For the CDU this challenge took on special meaning, because as the dominant governing force in Bonn, it had the most direct voice in the unfolding process of unification. As well, the Christian Democratic Union (like the FDP but unlike the SPD) inherited a former bloc-party, the Ost-CDU, burdened by a record of support for the discredited SED-State. Despite complicity in the East German system of power, the Ost-CDU survived into the postcommunist era. From September 1989 on, it began to distance itself from the SED's democratic centralism. Götting was forced to step down, replaced by the unknown Lothar de Maizière on November 10, 1989. One month later, the East German CDU rejected its bloc-party role and asserted its commitment to a market economy, although it remained within the Modrow transitional government until January 1990 when it rejected any future alliance with the SED/PDS. The CDU in Bonn had long avoided contact with the Ost-CDU. However, reservations about dealing with the former bloc-party dissipated as the party began to reform itself through internal democratization. From early 1990, with the CDU lagging behind the SPD in early opinion polls, the urgency for a stronger organizational basis in the east necessitated closer contacts between the two CDUs.

The eastern party, by virtue of its heritage, possessed an organizational infrastructure, including property holdings and an established membership (although many quit during the collapse of GDR). Other potential partners for the federal CDU were the newly founded opposition groups, the DA (*Demokratischer Aufbruch*) and DSU, but both remained organizationally feeble and were naturally apprehensive about dealing with the Ost-CDU. As the *Volkskammer* elections drew near, all three were joined under the electoral umbrella, Alliance for Germany. Under Kohl's leadership, the western CDU took over the campaign, advocating rapid unification, currency union based on parity of exchange, and defense of the market economy. The result was an astounding Alliance victory of 48.1 percent, with 40 percent for the CDU. The de Maizière government was formed with a mandate to negotiate the Treaty on Monetary, Economic, and Social Union, and the unification of the two Germanys.

The reconstruction of the former bloc-party involved an input of western money, resources, and personnel, paving the way to ultimate fusion, which was formalized on the eve of unification at the October 1990 Hamburg party congress. However, serious obstacles to party-building in the new *Länder* have persisted. The dependence culture in which competition was denigrated provided no training for pluralist participation. Forty years of dictatorship left a nonparticipatory residue that the new parties in the east have yet to overcome. The eastern wing of the CDU continues with a large party staff but only skeletal local memberships.[20]

With the important exception of the PDS, which has retained a grass-roots basis among former SED activists, other parties appear to many easterners to be largely exogenous imports. Serious difficulties in attracting new members, and low organizational density remain characteristic of both CDU and SPD in the east and reflect the limited legitimacy of western imports. It also has meant that the eastern party organizations remain dependent on massive financial transfers from their federal party organizations. These problems have been most acute for the SPD, which lacked any bloc-party foundation.[21]

Persistence or Renewal?

Unlike most revolutions, the collapse of the GDR involved no systematic purge of political activists (apart from the top elites) from the old regime. Although the initial takeover of the Ost-CDU by old cadres was challenged in 1991 in a wave of pressure for renewal, coming from members without ties to the past, the failure to attract new members has also left the majority of rank and file still consisting of pre-1990 members (with almost three-fourths of CDU members having joined under the old regime). Disillusionment with failed promises, higher taxes, and job losses also contributed to a drop-off in membership—from about 130,000 in 1990, to less than 110,000 by 1992, and down to 78,000 by 1994 (see table 3.1). The loss of members from the bloc-party era has not been matched by any equivalent replacement of new members. Former GDR activists have as well remained strongly represented among eastern parliamentarians.[22] Organizational integration has meant an awkward partnership within a party still largely made up of veteran cadres, many with possible Stasi (secret police) connections. The unresolved tensions between older "Blockis" and the newer "Renewalists" has cast a shadow over the CDU's ability to mobilize new support and recruit candidates after unification. As Clay Clemens has noted, "Merger did not just expand the CDU but exacerbated its challenge of integrating heterogeneous components."[23]

Popular Support

Studies of the history of German partisanship document the importance of both sectarian and social class divisions for shaping party loyalties. Despite the fact that postwar Christian Democracy, unlike its Zentrum predecessor, was explicitly interdenominational in character, practicing Catholics have continued to provide a bedrock of support. Yet, the forces of modernization and secularization, over the long term, have also meant that this confessional core has shrunk as a proportion of the population and as a share of the Union parties' electorates. In addition, the eastern *Länder* are both more secular (with 73 percent having no church ties) and more Protestant than in the west. Although the CDU found crucial support among those identifying with religion, the total share of confessional voters remains limited and the Catholic proportion only a small minority.[24] As a consequence the confessional bases of CDU (but not CSU) support have shifted. In terms of age and gender, the Union parties enjoy their greatest strength among older female voters but suffer a deficit among younger women. Such age differentials are less evident among men or within other party electorates.[25]

Despite the fact that the SPD's traditional social bastion is found among skilled blue-collar workers, the CDU/CSU has also effectively mobilized support among Catholic and/or nonunion industrial workers (see tables 3.2 and 3.3). Even so, its occupational strong points have always been farmers, the self-employed, public servants, and the small-business *Mittelstand*. Perhaps more important, the largest and still expanding occupational group, the salaried white-collar sector, which is characterized by weaker partisan attachments, has become the primary battleground for electoral competition.

The CDU and CSU are not identical in bases and strength of support. Religiosity has remained a stronger factor in Bavarian party loyalties, but the CSU's regional hegemony has its foundation in the fact that it also claims a majority in all other social and occupational categories, with Catholic workers being key to sustaining its broad interclass character. By the mid-1960s, the position of the CSU as the party of power was assured, with the mid-1970s being the high-water mark of its electoral strength.[26] As the *Land* party of government, the CSU has pursued economic modernization without endangering its traditionalist core support. CSU preeminence is primarily attributable to its success in attracting the expanding new middle classes and a substantial portion of

Table 3.2 Occupation and Major Party Support

	1990		1994	
	CDU/CSU	*SPD*	*CDU/CSU*	*SPD*
West				
Blue Collar	39.0	46.7	35.0	49.5
White Collar	43.0	35.9	39.9	37.7
Civil Servants	43.8	33.1	43.8	33.1
Farmers	65.4	11.9	65.4	11.9
Self-Employed	56.9	16.3	53.0	17.1
	CDU	*SPD*	*CDU*	*SPD*
East				
Blue Collar	48.5	24.7	40.6	35.1
White Collar	35.9	25.0	32.0	30.7
Civil Servants	29.9	24.4	29.9	24.4
Farmers	59.0	22.2	59.0	22.2
Self-Employed	48.8	16.1	48.3	19.7

Source: Data adapted from Wolfgang Gibowski, "Election Trends in Germany: An Analysis of the Second General Election in Reunited Germany," *German Politics* 4 (no. 2, 1995): 44–45.

Table 3.3 Religion and Major Party Support

	1990		1994	
	CDU/CSU	*SPD*	*CDU/CSU*	*SPD*
West				
Catholics	56.3	34.6	51.6	30.6
Protestants	39.6	39.7	36.5	43.7
Non-affiliated	30.3	35.2	28.0	40.1
	CDU	*SPD*	*CDU*	*SPD*
East				
Catholics	65.8	11.5	68.5	19.5
Protestants	53.4	20.1	53.4	28.9
Non-affiliated	33.3	28.7	27.1	34.1

Source: Data adapted from Wolfgang Gibowski, "Election Trends in Germany: An Analysis of the Second General Election in Reunited Germany," *German Politics* 4 (no. 2, 1995): 46–47.

blue-collar voters. By contrast, the Bavarian SPD has been able to capture a plurality of support only among protestant workers.[27]

Electoral Trends

Prior to unification, the CDU/CSU, already in power for about eight years, was manifesting signs of fatigue. After the 1987 election—and especially after the damaging Barschel affair in 1988—but prior to the pressures of unification, CDU/CSU vulnerability had become evident in slumping polls and in *Landtag* election setbacks. Political fortunes suddenly reversed when the GDR collapsed, yet victories in the unity elections of 1990 did not erase electoral anxieties for the CDU/CSU.

Traditionally the north-south divide has constituted the primary line of regional differentiation in party politics. Christian Democratic bastions have tended to be located in southern Germany and the Rhineland, both of which are predominantly Catholic. Of course, the merger of east and west shifted the primary regional cleavage from north-south to east-west. This applies within the CDU as it does to the entire political system.

Unification has, at least for the present, also drastically altered traditional bases of support. As it extended eastward, the CDU found no natural electoral clientele (few Catholics, small middle class) so that its own internal diversity was unavoidably accentuated. Nor could the trade-union basis for the SPD be carried over into the new *Länder*. The 1990 elections produced a surprising inversion of support patterns, with the CDU emerging as strongest among working-class voters. Persisting into 1994, despite significant losses, the CDU's continued attraction to working-class votes indicates a stabilization of a new class cleavage.[28] More generally, eastern parties have been characterized by relatively unstructured social bases of support and therefore potentially high volatility in patterns of party competition. The lack of solid social bases of party support in the new *Länder* has meant that eastern voters are highly sensitive to immediate issue factors.[29]

Unification exposed the hidden reality of a corroded East German economy. The collapse of industrial production with massive layoffs confronted Bonn with policy overload in an atmosphere of economic and social stress. As the major governing party, the CDU/CSU suffered from unpopular restructuring, which inevitably fuelled mass disenchantment. The necessity of tax increases was effectively used by the opposition to label Kohl and his majority as "tax-liars." Coincidentally, the opening of eastern borders led to an influx of refugees and prompted popular anxiety over the asylum question. In Baden-Württemberg, the 1992 *Landtag* election resulted in significant CDU losses to the far-right *Republikaner* (who won 10.9 percent) and led to a grand coalition between CDU and SPD.[30]

In Germany, there has always been a close link in voters' minds between economic performance and the popularity of governments. Although the CDU/CSU has generally held an advantage over the SPD on perceived competence in economic management, the dislocations and costs of unification compounded by recession undercut the government parties. CDU popularity plummeted sharply in the east, from 43 percent in 1990 to about 20 percent by 1992, and led many to erroneously predict that the CDU would be devastated in the next round of elections in 1994.[31] As signs of economic recovery turned pessimism into optimism, Kohl once again engineered a remarkable political reversal, initially seen in a strong showing in the 1994 European elections. Also important was the defusing of the asylum issue, which during 1991–93, had become a preoccupation among western Germans. This was accomplished through an interparty compromise revision of the asylum rights provisions in the Basic Law. Even with this sharp turnaround, CDU support in the 1994 Bundestag election remained considerably weaker in the east than in the west. Only among western voters was the CDU/CSU fully effective in mobilizing its core electorate.[32]

The CDU/CSU and the Far Right

Since 1949, right-wing extremism has rarely shown enough strength to become a factor in German party politics. However, on two occasions, in the late 1960s with the rise of the National Democratic party (NPD), and in the late 1980s and early 1990s with the *Republikaner* and German People's Union (DVU), such movements threatened but ultimately failed to establish themselves as viable forces. As a result, the CDU/CSU has been spared the difficulty of contending with an extremist force to its right. On both occasions the key question was whether the extremist impulse signified an ephemeral outburst of frustration or some more fundamental structural transformation.[33]

The *Republikaner* (or REP), with an estimated membership of about 23,000, had the greatest potential for breakthrough. Their initial foray in the 1986 Bavarian elections produced only modest results of 3 percent. However, in the 1989 Berlin elections, the REP unexpectedly surged to a 7.5 percent vote share and repeated this in the June 1989 European elections (7.2 percent) with notable gains in southern bastions of both CDU and CSU (an astounding 14.6 percent in Bavaria and 8.7 percent in Baden-Württemberg), reflecting a creeping rural discontent over EC farm policy as well as growing public concern over the influx of asylum-seekers. In the first three years of unification, disillusionment with the established parties widened and deepened, and the potential for protest and extremism correspondingly increased. Although the far right remained insignificant in the unity elections of 1990, it resurfaced in several Land elections in conjunction with the economic slow-down, the influx of asylum-seekers, and anxiety over European integration prompted by the debate over Maastricht. By mid-1993, national support for the *Republikaner* lingered just above the 5 percent minimum, suggesting a possible 1994 entry into the Bundestag. Such an outcome would have plunged the party system into crisis and could have altered dramatically coalition alternatives, perhaps forcing a CDU/CSU-SPD grand coalition. As in the 1966–69 period, the lack of major-party opposition could have then intensified rejection of the "cartel of elites" in Bonn. Extremism certainly served as a vehicle for diverse discontents, with some two-thirds expressing frustration and anxiety through populist protest.[34] This made for an unstable electorate, without firm social anchoring.

The electoral law means that a fringe party normally only becomes a minor party by surpassing the 5-percent hurdle for Bundestag representation. This requires either a reliable core or "loaned votes" on the second ballot, as has become usual for the FDP. With regard to the first condition, the new rightist phenomenon failed to establish a solid clientele. For the second, as long as the far right was rejected as a viable coalition partner by the CDU/CSU, major-party voters had no motivation to split their ballots in order to help the extremist alternative.

The Center-Right in Power

Program and Policy

The ideological roots of Christian Democratic thinking can be traced to Catholic social thought stressing solidarity and subsidiarity. The former gave impetus to social intervention, while the latter implied that conflicts should be resolved first within the lowest possible community. Such broad values, falling short of any rigorous ideology, have allowed a pragmatism to prevail. Moreover, Adenauer's early catch-all strategy meant that the CDU/CSU would develop by accommodating disparate economic and social interests, even though a basic division has always remained between social progressives and national conservatives. In general, its self-definition as an "office-oriented" party has constrained inclinations toward dogmatic conservatism.[35]

In the founding years, some regionally autonomous CDUs formulated strongly progressive goals, as in the 1947 Ahlen Program in the British zone and Jakob Kaiser's illusory hope for a achieving a Christian socialism in the Soviet zone. However, following the success of Erhard's June

1948 currency reform and victory in the first Bundestag elections in 1949, the paradigm of the social-market economy became the foundation for subsequent CDU/CSU economic thinking. Complementing this was the success of Adenauer's *Westpolitik,* based on integration and reconciliation.[36] These anchors of Christian Democratic policy thinking have reinforced a conservative yet centrist strategy based on a consensus dynamic that has facilitated interparty compromise and, occasionally, even grand coalition politics. Thus program followed from, rather than produced, policy. Indeed, in the 1950s there was no clear distinction between government policy and party program, the latter tending to be as much campaign material as policy guidelines.[37] In the CDU/CSU it is accurate to say that strong leaders and governing experience have heavily influenced programmatic content.

After 1969, when the CDU/CSU was forced into opposition, programmatic debate intensified. The commission on basic principles (*Grundsatzkommission*), chaired by Richard von Weizsäcker, sought to develop a new programmatic profile. The ensuing discussion about the proper relationship between state and society culminated in the *Grundsatzprogramm* of 1978. In essence a new statement of party identity, it was in large part a reaction to the social reform agenda of the social-liberal (SPD-FDP) majority.[38] The 1982–83 return to power (*die Wende*) did not mark a neoconservative renunciation of the socioeconomic policy consensus of the past several decades. However, subtle changes in internal party debate surfaced in the 1980s. In particular, there was growing concern for technological adaptation in a rapidly changing social and economic order, the importance of science and technology, and the need to adapt economic policy to maintain competitiveness. As well, in response to growing public awareness of ecological dangers (and the coincident rise of the Greens), a new Christian Democratic sensitivity to environmentalist concerns became evident.

Party extension due to unification has accentuated ideological diversity. New east-west disparities within the CDU correspond to fundamental differences in social and economic interests. In terms of occupational structure, the eastern wing underrepresents the self-employed and professionals and overrepresents workers (comprising four times the number of manual workers as does the SPD). As Stephen Padgett notes, this mixed social composition translates into "ideological eclecticism" reflected in stronger eastern preferences for statist intervention, while on social issues like abortion, the more secular easterners tend to be liberal.[39] The eastern delegation in the Bundestag (65 members) has become an informal regional lobby, pressing eastern policy priorities. While the CDU has sought to integrate eastern leaders into the federal party hierarchy, by the mid-

1990s, with some exceptions (e.g., Angela Merkel and Claudia Nolte), few easterners as yet occupied prominent posts in the federal government.

Generally, the 1990s have witnessed a programmatic adaptation to economic and social stress points, notably to persisting high unemployment, slow economic growth, high labor costs, and threats to economic competitiveness in the global economy. After the narrow victory in the 1994 Bundestag elections, the CDU's party congresses in Bonn (December 1994) and Karlsruhe (October 1995) gave new urgency to these economic challenges, particularly the need to fight unemployment. The general message was one of rethinking the role and costs of the social state, of restructuring the economy, and of the need for new flexibility in the labor market, the latter implying new compromises between business and labor. These concerns were consistent with Kohl's subsequent encouragement of tripartite discussions on the basis of the "Alliance for Jobs" advocated by the head of the metalworkers' union, Klaus Zwickel. These discussions failed to produce any new settlement, but the programmatic thrust of economic renewal within the CDU/CSU paved the way for the government's controversial 50-point action program and its 1996 drastic cost-saving measures (*Sparpaket*) involving cutbacks for most ministries and benefits of the generous welfare state.

On the external side, although the commitment to NATO remains unchanged, the end of the cold war, the collapse of the Soviet Union, and the revolutionary transformations across central Europe have given urgency to rethinking European security priorities, including Germany's military role in future international crises. Recent party congresses also confirmed both the CDU/CSU's and the chancellor's deep commitment to the widening and deepening of European integration, including the unpopular goal of European monetary union.

Chancellor and Party

Crucial to the development of the center-right was the fact that the CDU/CSU immediately became the party of government. Of course, it is impossible to know what might have evolved had Konrad Adenauer not been elected chancellor by just one vote (his own) in 1949. What is clear, however, is that control of state power allowed him to pursue an integrative strategy, coopting voters and activists from smaller conservatives forces. This gave the CDU/CSU a tremendous advantage over the SPD in achieving dominance. With the significant exception of the 13 years (1969–82) during which the Social-Liberal majority prevailed, the center-right has constituted the normal coalitional majority, with the CDU/CSU being the primary party of government.

Leaders normally reflect the values of their party, yet they may also themselves reshape the character of parties. This phenomenon is more likely within parties of the center-right, whose typically flexible/pragmatic ideologies allow leaders to redefine basic objectives. The real impact of the leader, as in the case of Margaret Thatcher (see Jorgen Rasmussen's chapter in this volume) is unmistakable. In rather different ways, comparable effects can be found within German Christian Democracy, with particular reference to the two most dominant chancellors, Adenauer and Kohl. Christian Democracy has been shaped by its leaders, and CDU/CSU strategy and programs have always reflected a link to governing.

The constitutional advantages accorded to the chancellor are no guarantee of effective influence. Chancellor authority has depended on a strong relationship between chancellor and party. Dominant leaders like Adenauer and Kohl have enjoyed both control over and support from their own parties. Weaker chancellors like Ludwig Erhard and Kurt-Georg Kiesinger have lacked this. Adenauer of course also benefited from his standing in public opinion, which he translated into a chancellor-bonus at election time. Kohl, certainly prior to becoming the unity chancellor, enjoyed no such bonus—leading many to underestimate his power and durability. But Kohl, even more than Adenauer, has retained and cultivated his roles as party manager and coalition balancer. Clay Clemens' landmark analysis concludes that "durable party backing is essential to the German chancellor's authority, and that broad voter appeal has not been vital to securing such support."[40]

As head of government, Kohl's style has been to seek consensus positions through a slow maturation based on deliberation.[41] This informal consultative process often gives the impression of indecision and even weakness. The media developed an image of Kohl as an *Aussitzer*, one who would rather wait for problems to go away. This no doubt hurt his public standing and caused dismay among supporters. Yet Kohl's longevity and authority have rested consistently on his managerial control over his own party and his extensive network of loyalties developed over many years of careful cultivation. Unification assured for Helmut Kohl a place in history. It also made his leadership image such a political asset that Kohl himself became the exclusive focus of the Union parties' campaign in 1994.[42]

Coalition Politics: The Christian-Liberal Model

Governments in Bonn have always been coalitional, with the FDP normally serving as the minor partner either for the Christian Democrats or for the Social Democrats. Its pivotal ability to shift alliances has given the small FDP extraordinary governing presence and influence. In practice, federal center-right coalitions have been carefully constructed balances among three partners: CDU, CSU, and FDP. The grand coalition alternative of CDU/CSU sharing power with its usual opponent, the SPD, also occurs, either as a formal coalition, as in the 1966–69 period, or as a de facto mode of interparty policy bargaining, which becomes a necessity when the federal opposition enjoys majority control in the Bundesrat. Within the *Länder*, various governing coalitions may exist simultaneously. In Bavaria, the CSU governs alone, while elsewhere, CDU-FDP, CDU-SPD or SPD-FDP-Green coalitions may be found.

Christian Democrats and Free Democrats have for most of the postwar era found themselves in alliance, but not always in policy agreement. The FDP's economic conservatism provides an ideological common ground with the CDU/CSU, while its civil libertarian views have often been a source of dispute, especially with the CSU. Coalitional politics involving the FDP have often generated tension between CDU and CSU. For the former, the FDP has been seen as a natural partner, fully compatible with the need for moderate appeals to undecided and unattached voters. The latter has looked forward to building a solid conservative majority without the FDP, which it regards as too left-liberal on many issues.

Because the Free Democrats have lacked a sizable electoral core, they have perpetually found themselves relying on ticket-splitting from other parties' supporters. Although unification appeared to strengthen the liberal electorate after 1990, the FDP proved unable to transform immediate gains into a solid base and organization, leading to defeats in a string of Landtag elections prior to the October 1994 Bundestag elections. A feeble 4.1 percent in the 1994 Euro-elections signaled a looming crisis. In these Bundestag elections, the FDP absorbed massive losses compared to 1990, but did survive with 6.9 percent. Had the FDP fallen below the 5 percent minimum, the coalition consequences for the CDU/CSU would have been drastic. Its electoral weakness has accentuated the importance of Christian Democratic strategic voting designed to keep the FDP in the Bundestag. In the 1994 election, it is estimated that over 60 percent of the second ballots cast for the FDP came from CDU\CSU ticket-splitters.[43] Without firm roots or a stable core, the FDP reliance on "itinerant" voters remains its Achilles' heel. In the public mind, the party no longer has a distinctive role, and to a considerable extent, the FDP has been overtaken by the Greens as the third party in the *Länder* and in public opinion.

Do German Parties Make a Difference?

Proponents of the null-hypothesis that parties do not matter claim that because elections are won at the center, convergent dynamics tend to blur ideology and minimize policy differences between major competing parties or coalitions. Chancellor Kohl's expressed view that Germany should be governed from the center matches not only his leadership style but fits well within a tradition set by prior chancellors. While centrism as a governing mode surfaces most fully under "grand coalition" power sharing between the two major *Volksparteien*, interparty bargaining and consensus-based outcomes have come to characterize the German policy process regardless of which coalition forms the majority.

The development of party competition has also fostered convergence. In the 1950s the CDU/CSU built a broad interconfessional and interclass base that stabilized its governing dominance with a centrist vocation. The SPD as the major opposition force was driven, out of necessity, to imitate this catch-all strategy. With its 1959 Bad Godesberg rejection of its class-party heritage, the SPD moderated its programmatic stances on economic and foreign-policy questions in order to capture a portion of the growing middle-class electorate. The classic thesis of the end of ideology implied that convergence would become an embedded trait of modern German democratic politics. This made credible the view that fundamental policy difference between the two major parties would eventually evaporate, yet this prediction has never been fully achieved.

Of course, alternations in power provide the best tests of partisan impact, but because no such power shift has occurred since 1982, we must rely on evidence of partisan policy conflict to infer probable impacts. It is certainly true that on significant issues CDU/CSU and SPD have often found common ground. However, even with interparty compromises with regard to the social-market economy, European security/NATO, and European integration, German parties continue to differ. Indeed, based on tensions emerging in the 1990s, we can identify zones of conflict between the center-right majority and the SPD-Green opposition from which it is reasonable to expect significant policy differences depending on which party/coalition is in government.

The most intense battleground involves government control and management of the economy. Redistributive issue conflict has increasingly dominated political debate as the performance capacity of the German social-market economy has been called into question by slow growth, plant closings, and the loss of production to locations outside Germany. As unemployment in the 1990s has reached unprecedented levels, the tension has surfaced between two visions: *Modell Deutschland,* long held up as the basis for Germany's economic success and social peace, and *Standort Deutschland,* resting on a neoliberal imperative of adjustment to a changing global economy. The CDU/CSU-FDP government increasingly has argued that the loss of competitiveness, resultant from Germany's high labor and production costs, has led to loss of investment and jobs.

The Kohl government's post-1994 agenda for economic restructuring proposed budgetary rigor, cuts in welfare-state spending, and deregulation. Parties of the center-right have increasingly perceived a looming economic crisis associated with the negative effects of the postwar economic compromise based on the mixed economy, corporatist labor-management relations, and an inclusive welfare state. The center-left, by contrast, remains committed to these arrangements, to which they credit German economic prosperity and success. There is corresponding pressure on German corporatist bargaining among the "social partners" that in the past has brought benefits to employees at the expense of the taxpayer. Employers claim that high labor costs are due not just to wages but, crucially, to the non-wage costs necessary to finance the many benefits that have accrued over decades, while trade unions naturally defend their hard-fought gains.

Foreign/security policy and European integration constitute areas in which the balance of partisan division remains far less clear. Both CDU/CSU and SPD have long supported Germany's place within the western alliance and remain committed to the goal of building a supranational Europe, yet policy divergence has been manifested on many specific issues. After 1969, the SPD-FDP government under Willy Brandt took Germany in the direction of détente and *Ostpolitik* at a time when the CDU/CSU certainly would not have done so. Similarly, with the end of the cold war, Kohl's government moved toward a "normalization" of German participation in international peace-keeping that has involved troop deployments out of the NATO area; again a policy shift that the SPD resisted and would not have initiated. In this case, policy resolution was accomplished only via rulings of the Federal Constitutional Court.

European integration has remained an area characterized by stable interparty elite consensus, despite the fact that the German public is profoundly disenchanted with the idea of European Monetary Union. By 1997 the strains of meeting the Maastricht convergence criteria exposed tensions both within and across party lines. Voices in both major camps are expressing doubts about EMU while hinting at its possible delay. The SPD's Gerhard Schröder (minister-president in Lower Saxony and 1998 chancellor-candidate) has questioned the wisdom of meeting the convergence criteria and the social costs involved. There are also potential fissures within Christian Democratic ranks where the Bavarian minister-president, Edmund Stoiber, has occasionally allowed himself to utter Euro-sceptic thoughts.

In these important policy domains, the varying degrees of partisan divergence that give reason to expect different policy outcomes, depending on which party or coalition forms the majority, challenge the null-hypothesis that parties do not matter. Generally, such policy examples point to the limits of centrist consensus. The new polarization based on redistributive issues furthermore implies a hardening of economic class divisions and increased strain on the consensual mode of conflict resolution.

Erosion or Endurance?

A partially new party system prompts the question of the future for the center-right. Unification has created two distinctive patterns of party competition and coalitional options. In the west, a four-party struggle among CDU, SPD, FDP, and Greens persists, but in the east, both the FDP and the Alliance 90/Greens have faded almost out of existence, while the PDS has stabilized as a third force. Even in the old *Länder*, the FDP has been marginalized electorally, often surpassed by the Greens, although retaining its coalition role federally in the 1994–1998 governing period. Only the two catch-all parties retain their viability in both regions.[44] Although the parties of the old Federal Republic have survived the shock of unification, several unknowns remain and may be briefly summarized in the debate over erosion or endurance.

The erosion thesis proposes that the CDU/CSU's *Volkspartei* status is in danger. After more than 15 years in power, some observers contend that the CDU/CSU suffers from a crisis syndrome, and doubts persist about the CDU's ability to remain a party of wide integration. This concern is far less relevent to the CSU, which has retained its dominance in Bavaria. There is certainly evidence of shrinking electoral cores. Only 18 percent of CDU support now comes from its Catholic base.[45] Both *Volksparteien* find themselves increasingly dependent on floating voters or potential nonvoters. These trends have reduced the capacity of both to maintain their majority vocations.[46]

Erosion may also imply organizational reversion to a *Kanzlerpartei* model or to a party of notables.[47] If the extent of membership decline measures such erosion, the status of the CDU is unclear. There certainly has been stagnation and a failure to recruit younger voters, but there has been no mass exodus. As noted above, membership problems are, however, a serious source of concern in the new *Länder.*

The case for erosion also rests on signs of internal discord. Unification has made the CDU more diverse and has expanded the potential for disunity. Of course, some of the pressures of internal diversity were already evident prior to unification but now are greater. As Clemens says, the CDU has been more a victim of events than an agent for change, yet the stabilization evident in the 1994–1998 majority suggests that this impact remains unclear.[48] While the CDU is now more fragmented, a loose collection of interests, with east–west fissures on many issues, it is yet to become "two parties or one."[49]

The endurance thesis counters that the extent and potential for erosion is overstated. Proponents of endurance argue instead that the center-right can retain its dominant place in German politics. While it is true that over four successive Bundestag elections between 1983 and 1994, Christian Democratic support has stagnated, the CDU/CSU has not suffered alone. Both *Volksparteien* lost ground due to dealignment effects, but the weakening of the SPD has been even more severe, so that by 1990 the popular support gap between the two expanded to about 10 percent. If the CDU/CSU has lost some of its integrative capacity, it is crucial to recall that the SPD, too, remains burdened by its unresolved divisions between moderate materialist and more radical postmaterialist wings. Even more serious is the vitality of opposition to its left. Since the 1980s, the Greens have repeatedly drained the electoral pool of the SPD. In the 1990s, the stabilization of the PDS has created a similar problem in the east. For the CDU/CSU, the relative absence of a challenge on the far right has spared it the problem of dealing with a more radical opposition. To the contrary, the far and new left, by undercutting the SPD, have aided the CDU/CSU to maintain its advantage.

With regard to the question of internal disunity, there is some evidence of convergent trends with eastern voting patterns beginning to look more similar to those in the west. Wolfgang Gibowski, in arguing that the 1994 results attest to the relative durability of the CDU/CSU electorate, notes that the multiple negatives during the first five years of unification did not result in massive losses. Moreover, the extensive tactical voting designed to save the FDP and the coalition artificially cut into Christian Democratic support.[50] However, by 1998 the capacity of the CDU/CSU to dominate from the center-right, based on its tradition of the "politics of the middleway" was seriously in question. The 1998 watershed elections would reduce the uncertainty about whether this tradition would continue to shape German politics into the new millennium.

Notes

1. Gordon Smith, *Democracy in Germany*, 3rd ed. (New York: Holmes and Meier, 1986), pp. 9–16.
2. Kenneth Dyson, "Party Government and Party State," in Herbert Döring and G. Smith, eds., *Party Government and Political Culture in Western Germany* (London: Macmillan, 1981), p. 84.
3. Nevil Johnson, *State and Government in the Federal Republic of Germany* (Oxford: Pergamon, 1982), p. 155.
4. Smith, *Democracy in Germany*, pp. 67–8; Russell J. Dalton, *Politics in Germany*, 2nd ed. (New York: Harper-Collins, 1993), p. 278.

5. William Chandler, "The Christian Democrats," in Peter Merkl, ed., *The Federal Republic at Forty* (New York: NYU Press, 1990), pp. 294–95.

6. Thomas Ammer, "Parteien in der DDR und in den neuen Bundesländern," in Alf Mintzel and Heinrich Oberreuter, eds., *Parteien in der Bundesrepublik* (Bonn: Bundeszentrale für politische Bildung, 1992), p. 460.

7. Stephan Zeidler, "Entstehung und Entwicklung der Ost-CDU, 1945–89," *Aus Politik und Zeitgeschichte* 16 (no.17, 1996): 23.

8. Dieter Segert, "The East German CDU," *Political Parties* no. 4 (1995): 590.

9. Zeidler, "Entstehung und Entwicklung der Ost-CDU, 1945–8," pp. 24–8; Segert, "The East German CDU," pp. 590–92.

10. Segert, "The East German CDU," p. 591.

11. Wulf Schönbohm, *Die CDU wird moderne Volkspartei. Selbstverständnis, Mitglieder, Organisation und Apparat 1950–1980* (Stuttgart: Klett-Cotta, 1985), pp. 31–48.

12. Wolfgang Rudzio, *Das politische System der Bundesrepublik Deutschland,* 4th ed. (Opladen: Leske and Budrich, 1996), p. 146.

13. Peter Haungs, "Die Christlich Demokratische Union Deutschlands (CDU) und die Christlich Soziale Union in Bayern (CSU)," in Hans-Joachim Veen, ed., *Christlich- deomkratische und konservative parteien in Westeuropa,* vol. 1 (Paderborn: Schoningh, 1983), pp. 130–42, 51–64; Chandler, "The Christian Democrats," pp. 302–6; Schönbohm, "*Die CDU wird moderne Volkspartei. Selbstverstaendnis, Organisation und Apparat, 1950–1980,"* pp. 219–29.

14. Peter Haungs, "Die CDU: Prototyp einer Volkspartei," in A. Mintzel and H. Oberreuter, eds., *Parteien in der Bundesrepublik* (Bonn: Bundeszentrale für politische Bildung, 1992) p. 198.

15. Alf Mintzel, "Die CSU als Forschungsobjekt—Entwicklung, Stand, Defizite und Perspektiven der CSU-Forschung," in Oskar Niedermeyer and Richard Stöss eds., *Parteien und Wähler im Umbruch* (Opladen: Westdeutscher Verlag, 1994) p. 104.

16. Alf Mintzel, "Die Christlich Soziale Union in Bayern" in Mintzel and Oberreuter, eds., *Parteien in der Bundesrepublik,* pp. 231–33.

17. Mintzel, "Die Christlich Soziale Union in Bayern," p. 256; Haungs, "Die CDU: Prototyp einer Volkspartei," pp. 210–13; Merkl, *The Federal Republic at Forty,* pp. 59–60.

18. Juergen Falter and Siegfried Schumann, "Konsequenzen einer bundesweiten Kandidatur der CSU bei Wahlen," *Aus Politik und Zeitgeschichte* 11:12 (1991): 33–45.

19. Eckhard Jesse, "Die CSU im vereinigten Deutschland," *Aus Politik und Zeitgeschichte* 6 (1996): 29–35.

20. Barbara Donovan, "Transfer or Transformation? Volksparteien in the Five Eastern States," Chicago, paper presented at the 19th Annual Conference of the German Studies Association, 1995, pp. 6–9.

21. Stephen Padgett, "*Superwahljahr* in the New Länder: Polarisation in an Open Political Market," *German Politics,* 4:2 (1995): 77–8.

22. Rudzio, *Das politische System der Bundesrepublik Deutschland,* pp. 174–77; Segert, "The East German CDU," p. 597.

23. Clay Clemens, "Disquiet on the Eastern Front: The Christian Democratic Union in Germany's New Länder" *German Politics* 2:2 (1993): 208.

24. Padget, "*Superwahljahr* in the New Laender: Polarisation in an Open Political Market," p. 82.

25. Matthias Jung, "Die Union nach der Bundestagswahl 1994," in Gerhard Hirscher, ed., *Parteiendemocratie zwischen Kontinuität und Wandel* (Munich: Hanns-Seidel-Stiftung eV, 1995), pp. 185–87; Wolfgang Gibowski, "Election Trends in Germany: An Analysis of the Second General Election in Reunited Germany," *German Politics* 4:2 (1995): 39.

26. Mintzel, "Die Christlich Soziale Union in Bayern," pp. 225–56.

27. Rainer-Olaf Schultze, "Die bayerische Landtagswahl vom 14. Oktober 1990: Bayerische Besonderheiten und bundesrepublikanische Normalität" *Zeitschrift für Parlamentsfragen* 22:1 (1991): 54; Mintzel, "Die CSU als Forschungsobjekt—Entwicklung, Stand, Defizite und Perspektiven der CSU-Forschung," p. 90; Haungs "Die CDU: Prototyp einer Volkspartei," pp. 242–45, 256.

28. Russel Dalton, "A Divided Electorate?," in Gordon Smith, William E. Paterson, and Stephen Padgett, eds., *Developments in German Politics* (Durham: Duke Univ. Press, 1996), pp. 39–40; Rainer-Olaf Schultze, "Widersprüchliches, Ungleichzeitiges und kein Ende in Sicht: Die Bundestagswahl vom 16. Oktober 1994," *Zeitschrift für Parlamentsfragen* 26:2 (1995): 340.

29. Padgett, "*Superwahljahr* in the New Laender: Polirasation in an Open Political Market," pp. 81–2; Gibowski, "Election Trend in Germany: An Analysis of the Second Election in Reunited Germany," p. 43; Hans-Joachim Veen and P. Gluchowski, "Die Anhängerschaften der Parteien vor und nach der Einheit" *Zeitschrift für Parlamentsfragen* 25:2 (1994): 165–85.

30. Dieter Roth, "The Volksparteien in Crisis? The Electoral Successes of the Extreme Right in Context" *German Politics* II:1 (1993): 1–20.

31. Oskar Niedermeyer, "Party System Change in East Germany," *German Politics* 4:3 (1995): 75–91.

32. Gibowski "Election Trends in Germany: An Analysis of the Second General Election in Reunited Germany"; Roth, "The Volksparteinen in Crisis?"

33. Hans-Joachim Veen, Norbert Lepszy, and Peter Mnich, *The Republikaner Party in Germany* (Westport, CT: Praeger, 1993); H. G. Betz, "The New Politics of Resentment: Radical Right-Wing Populist Parties in Western Europe" *Comparative Politics* 25 (July 4, 1993): 413–28.

34. Veen et al., *The Republikaner Party in Germany,* pp. 41–54; Lepszy.

35. David Conradt, *The German Polity,* 6th ed. (White Plains: Longman, 1996), pp. 119- 20.

36. Chandler, "The Christian Democrats," p. 291.

37. Rudzio, *Das politische System der Bundesrepublik Deutschland,* pp. 146–48; Haungs, "Die CSU: Prototyp einer Volkspartei," p. 183.

38. Haungs, "Die CSU: Prototyp einer Volkspartei," pp. 184–85.

39. Padgett, "*Superwahljahr* in the New Laender: Polarisation in an Open Political Market," pp. 79–81.

40. Clay Clemens, "'The Chancellor as Manager:' Helmut Kohl, the CDU and Governance in Germany," *West European Politics* 17:4 (1994): p. 47.

41. Clay Clemens, "The Chancellor as Manager," p. 34; Gordon Smith, "The Resources of a German Chancellor " *West European Politics* 14:2 (1991): 48–61.

42. Conradt 1996, p. 8.

43. Gibowski, "Election Trends in Germany," p. 37; Conradt, 1996, pp. 5, 19; Jung, "Die Union nach der Bundestagswahl 1994," p. 181.

44. Oskar Niedermeyer, "Party System Change in East Germany," *German Politics* 4:3 (1995): 80–86.

45. Jung, "Die Union nach der Bundestagswahl 1994," p. 190.

46. Oskar Gabriel and Angelika Vetter, "Die Chancen der CDU/CSU in den neunziger Jahren," *Aus Politik und Zeitgeschichte* 6 (January 1996): 9–19.

47. Dettling, Warnfried, "Ende oder Wende. Was wird aus der CDU?" *Aus Politik und Zeitgeschichte* 1 (January 1994): 3–7.

48. Clemens, "Disquiet on the Eastern Front," pp. 217–18.

49. Peter Lösche, "Zur Metamorphose der politischen Parteien in Deutschland," *Gewerkscahftliche Monateshefte* 43 (1992): 9.

50. Gibowski, "Election Trends in Germany," p. 48.

CHAPTER FOUR

The Greek Right:
Between Transition and Reform

Stathis N. Kalyvas

New Democracy (*Nea Dimokratia*—ND) emerged as the dominant Greek right-wing party immediately after the transition of the country to democracy in 1974. Although challenged by extreme right-wing parties, as well as by splinter parties, ND has managed to uphold its hegemony of the center-right political space in a way unmatched by most European conservative parties. However, it has failed to translate this hegemony into broader political domination. In fact, the ambiguity of its achievements is impressive: its success in reinventing itself while building and dominating the new democratic regime after 1974, stands in striking contrast to its dismal performance after 1981. ND was continually in power from 1974 to 1981 but has remained in opposition for 12 out of the last 15 years. After its defeat in the 1996 elections, ND is entering a period of 4 more years out of power. Its predicament exemplifies a problem faced by a number of conservative parties across the world, which have had their economic and political agenda taken over by center-left parties.

The evolution of ND raises some interesting theoretical issues. In just 22 years, ND experienced an unusually diverse organizational trajectory, in many respects a condensed equivalent of the organizational development of Western European parties during the entire century. ND underwent several major organizational mutations, evolving from an elite (or cadre) party to one with successively pronounced mass, catch-all, and now cartel characteristics. Surveying this organizational trajectory is essential in explaining the way in which changing patterns of party competition affect the form of party organization. Finally, the overlap of democratic transition and consolidation processes with the emergence and evolution of ND allows the examination of the interaction between democratization and party development.

Historical Background

The Greek party system is defined by the presence of cleavages with deep historical roots in two civil conflicts. The first one, known as National Schism, began during World War I over the issue of Greece's participation in the war. It evolved during the interwar period into a conflict between republicans and royalists. The republican camp, also known as *venizelist* (from the name of its leader Eleftherios Venizelos), was dominated by the Liberal party, while the royalist camp (the *antivenizelists*) was dominated by the People's party. The second conflict is the Civil War (1946–1949) between the pro-western bourgeois parties and the communist-dominated left. Although the venizelist political establishment sided with the royalists, significant venizelist popular segments fought with the communists. During the 1960s, the attempt by the king to obstruct the exercise of power by the venizelist Center Union provoked a major political crisis that reactivated the old royalist-republican cleavage and paved the way for the 1967 military coup.

The succession and superimposition of these two historical cleavages have produced a lasting division in three political families: The right, the center, and the left as they were called in the postwar period.[1] The communist and postcommunist left is presently represented by the Communist party and the leftist coalition. The center-left is dominated by the Panhellenic Socialist Movement (PASOK), founded in 1974 by Andreas Papandreou and led since 1996 by the present prime minister, Kostas Simitis. Although created as a totally new party seeking to fill the until-then empty socialist slot, PASOK successfully appropriated the venizelist tradition. It has been continually in power since 1981, with the exception of a brief spell in 1989–93 (see table 4.1).

New Democracy has a long and clear partisan lineage. It follows on the steps of the interwar People's party, and the postwar Greek Rally (founded in 1952) and National Radical Union (ERE—founded in 1956). This continuity is expressed in terms of both electoral support and political personnel—most strikingly in the person of Konstantinos Karamanlis. Having founded and led ERE, Karamanlis went on to found ND in the wake of the collapse of the military dictatorship in 1974. ND is presently headed by Karamanlis' nephew, Kostas Karamanlis, the party's sixth leader.

Table 4.1 Election Results, 1974–1994 (in percentage of votes cast)

	1974	1977	1981	1981*	1984*	1985	June 1989	1989*	Nov. 1989	1990	1993	1994*	1996
ND	54.4	41.8	35.9	31.3	38.0	40.8	44.3	40.4	46.2	46.9	39.3	32.7	38.1
Other Right	1.3	7.9	1.7	2.8	2.6	0.6	1.3	3.1		0.8	5.0	10.0	2.9
Center	20.8	12.0	1.6	7.6	2.0	0.3	0.5	1.2	0.1				
Greens							0.1	2.6	0.9	1.1	0.2		
PASOK	13.6	25.3	48.1	40.1	41.6	45.8	39.1	36.0	40.8	39.4	46.9	37.7	41.5
Communists/ Left Coalition	9.5	12.1	12.3	12.2	15.1	11.7	13.1	14.3	11.0	10.5	7.4	12.6	10.7
Other Left	0.4	0.5	0.2		0.7	0.4	1.0	2.4	0.4	0.4	0.2		4.4
Other		0.4	0.2		0.4	0.6		0.6	0.9	1.0		5.6	2.28

Note: *Elections to the European parliament

Despite the party system's tripolar structure, competition has been bipolar between the ND and PASOK. The two parties have overwhelmingly dominated both the party system at large and their own respective political space, as shown in table 4.2.

Electoral Support and Social Basis

Greece ranks last in the structural determination of the vote according to a 16-country study. It is also the only Western European country where ideological party cleavages are more powerful predictors of voting than structural ones.[2] A recent electoral study confirms these findings and shows that contrary to the other Southern European countries, the main predictor of Greek voting behavior is not class or religiosity but ideology in the sense of the voters' positioning on the left-right axis.[3] The ideological cleavage in Greek politics reflects partisan identities largely shaped by the legacy of past civil conflicts. Still, a number of variables, such as socioeconomic status, urban vs. rural lifestyle, and age have a limited impact and allow us to track the evolution of some general trends. Most significant is the modernization of the social basis of ND toward a younger, better educated, more urban profile from 1981 to 1989 and the gradual reversal of this trend after 1993.

Historically, the Greek right has tended to rely on rural support.[4] In 1963, ERE won 12.8 percent more votes in rural areas than in urban ones, a feature inherited by ND. However, the rural component of the right-wing vote declined steadily between 1981 and 1993: In 1981 ND was stronger in rural areas (+8.6 percent), but in 1985 this difference had shrunk to 3.7 and in 1989 to 2.5. Interestingly, PASOK followed the

Table 4.2   ND and PASOK Domination: 1981–1993 National Elections

Election	Votes Polled by ND and PASOK	ND Share of the Right Vote (%)	PASOK Share of Center-Left Vote (%)
1974	2068.0	98.3	39.5
1977	2067.1	84.1	67.8
1981	2083.9	95.4	96.7
1985	2086.6	98.5	99.3
June 1989	2083.4	97.1	96.5
November 1989	2086.8	100.0	97.6
April 1990	2085.5	98.3	97.2
1993	2086.2	88.7	99.5
1996	2079.8	92.9	90.4

opposite path: Whereas in 1981 it won more votes in urban areas (+4.3 percent), in 1985 its support was almost uniform (+0.9 in urban areas), and in 1989 the balance was reversed (+5.2% in rural areas). Class became a somewhat sharper determinant of the vote in 1985 with significant segments of the middle and upper socioeconomic groups deserting PASOK for ND.[5] Parallel to this trend was the rising attractiveness of ND among the more educated and younger segments of Greek society. This development is even more striking if contrasted with the notorious difficulty of ND in attracting support from younger voters. In 1977, for instance, age differentiated more than any other demographic factor the voters of the two major parties.[6] In sum, ND largely succeeded during the 1980s to "modernize" its social basis.

However, this trend is currently being reversed. PASOK's right shift after 1993, and especially the 1996 election of the modernizer Kostas Simitis at its head had a significant impact on the social basis of both parties. Significant middle and upper income groups (such as professionals and educated private-sector workers) shifted their support away from ND and toward PASOK.[7] In the process, ND became markedly less "modern": the rural component of its vote climbed back to +3.6 in 1993 and +5.3 in 1996 (as opposed to PASOK's +2.5 and +3.4 respectively). Likewise, whereas older voters (60 years and up) were in 1996 6.8 percent more likely to vote for ND than for PASOK, younger ones (18–29 years), were 4.1 percent more likely to vote for PASOK. The social segments in which ND fared well in 1996 included the older and better educated homemakers, the better educated retirees, and the farmers (respectively 19.5, 11.4, and 7.8 percent more likely to vote for ND than PASOK). ND did poorly among public-sector workers (irrespective of education level) and the less educated workers and retirees of the private-sector.[8] In fact, whereas 40 percent of party representatives in the 1996 PASOK congress were public-sector employees, only 13 percent of party representatives in the 1997 ND congress were employed in the public-sector.

Party Organization

Throughout its existence, New Democracy has been a hybrid party in terms of organization: the clientelistic features of an elite party coexist with key elements of a mass party—membership size, use of mass mobilization, and the role of organization in creating and representing a collective identity. Likewise, catch-all party features such as membership heterogeneity, focus on policy and social amelioration rather than societal change, low emphasis on members' obligations, and power differential between leadership and party cadres, coexist with cartel party features such as state connections, growing professionalization, and a view of political competition as a matter of efficient and skilled management.[9]

The organizational hybridity of ND points to the inadequacy of the classification tools. True, party types are ideal types, "heuristically convenient polar types, to which individual parties may approximate more or less closely."[10] Still, the very exercise of classification is ultimately futile because it is based on a perception of parties as snapshots rather than dynamically evolving organizations. What is needed instead is a more dynamic (hence contextual and historical) understanding of a party's trajectory. Below, I survey the origin and development of ND using an analytical framework that relies on simple rational choice assumptions combined with a historical/contextual analysis.

ND is distinguished by two surprising organizational features. First, it is the European conservative party with the second most encapsulating organization. In 1996, ND claimed 383,428 members distributed across 3,500 local branches. This is the official number of participants in the 1996 party elections—most probably an inflated number. Table 4.3 provides data on the evolution of the party's membership over the last 20 years. This membership corresponds to a ratio of party members to party voters (M/V) of 14.53, and a ratio of party members to the electorate (M/E) of 4.46. These numbers place ND in a higher position than the Belgian, German, Italian (before their demise) and Dutch Christian Democrats, and the Danish, Norwegian, Swedish and British Conservatives. Only the Austrian Conservatives have a higher M/E ratio (see table 4.4).

The second feature worth noticing is the representativeness of ND's organization. According to a recent comparative study, ND is the European party (across all party families) most representative of its electorate. Based on Eurobarometer data, ND ranks first in terms of gender, age, and class representativeness of its electorate.[11]

Both features are surprising, cross-nationally as well as longitudinally. Center-right parties (particularly non–Christian Democratic ones) tend to be weak in terms of mass organization and representativeness. In fact, ND is the only representative conservative party.[12] Moreover, Greek parties, while relying on powerful collective identities, have traditionally been personalistic and clientelistic, shunning formal, and even more, mass organization. Indeed, Karamanlis established ND singlehandedly in 1974 without prior consultations with the legitimate ERE leadership.[13] Most telling is the fact that the official symbol of the party up to 1979 was Karamanlis' picture.

The military dictatorship had a profoundly modernizing impact on Greek parties—albeit a gradual one. Charismatic leadership was a feature of both ND and PASOK: Karamanlis and Papandreou were both charismatic

Table 4.3   ND Membership Figures

Year	Membership	Local Organizations
1976[a]	20,000	40
1977[c]	20,000	233
1978[b]	100,000	missing data
1979[a]	150,000	missing data
1981[a]	missing data	580
1983[a]	220,000	2,000
1987[a]	400,000	3,500
1991[a]	400,000	3,500
1996[d]	383,428	3,500

Sources: [a]official party figures (cited in Pappas 1995; Clogg 1985)
[b]Katsoudas 1987
[c]official party figures (cited in Loulis 1981)
[d]official party figures (cited in *Tò Vima,* March 24, 1996)

Table 4.4   Ratio of Party Members to the Electorate (M/E)—Selected Countries

CDA (Netherlands)	1.10 (1989)
CDU (Germany)	1.56 (1987)
Conservatives (UK)	2.32 (1987)
CSU (Germany)	0.41 (1987)
DC (Italy)	3.97 (1987)
M (Sweden)	1.27 (1988)
ND (Greece)	4.46 (1993)
ÖVP (Austria)	9.40 (1990)
PSC/CVP (Belgium)	2.59 (1987)

Source: Katz et al. (1992), except Greece.

personalities who founded and dominated their parties. But these parties survived and eventually transcended the advent of their charismatic founders. They introduced formal rules regulating their activities, built a mass structure, and democratized to a considerable extent their organizations. PASOK was the first noncommunist Greek party to introduce large-scale mass organization, but was able to reform its internal organization and escape from the autocratic embrace of its founder only after Papandreou's death in 1996. ND's initial attempts to build a modern party organization were only moderately successful, but the party survived successfully five leadership changes after Karamanlis moved to the presidency in 1980.[14] The party organized a first congress in 1979 and built an impressive mass organization after 1981.

New Democracy's organizational development followed four distinct phases. In a first phase (1974–1979), the party leadership set out to create a national organization with regional and local branches. However, the party emphasized the articulation of a modern ideological message rather than the recruitment of members and the development of a grassroots organization. Indeed, membership remained very low and the party was run by its leader with traditional notables in control of the regional level. As the party's general director acknowledged in 1977: "During this first organizational period, the leader . . . instructed and supervised the party organs, determined their membership, their activities, their sector of responsibility, their ways and methods of action."[15]

In a second phase (1977–1981), the party leadership made vigorous efforts to institutionalize its organization and develop a mass structure. A preliminary congress took place in 1977, the first opportunity for members of a Greek conservative party to participate in party proceedings, and in 1979 the party convened its first congress. At the same time, a well advertised membership drive was launched under the slogan "you are a friend; become a member." As a result membership climbed from 20,000 in 1977 to 150,000 in 1979.[16] Still, the development of party organization was slow: "The party was far less significant as a mass organization than as a group of leaders and professional politicians."[17] Party "members" were often indistinguishable from the personal clienteles of party potentates.

In a third phase (1981–1989), the party carried out a process of "structural modernization"[18] by building an impressive mass organization and succeeded in beating PASOK at its own game. Membership swelled, reaching a stunning 400,000 members; the party created powerful youth, student, and professional organizations. Strikingly for a non–Christian Democratic party, it set up party branches in trade unions. It mobilized tens of thousands of supporters, both during elections and in between for a variety of activities, ranging from canvassing and poster-plastering to participation in demonstrations and mass rallies. In short, during this period the party adopted many of the mass party's features—a development consistent with Maurice Duverger's hypothesis of "a contagion from the left" according to which all parties are forced to become mass parties in order to compete with the left.[19] However, ND never became an ideal-typical mass party. While "active participation of members grew sharply," the party was still dominated by its leadership.[20] Still, the emphasis ND placed on mass mobilization and the central role afforded by a historically grounded collective identity differentiated it from catch-all parties and gave it a definite mass profile.

Finally, since 1989 the party has been experiencing organizational decline coupled with a limited democratization of its organization. On the one hand, ND is quickly shedding mass mobilization, replacing it with professional teams running media-oriented electoral campaigns. On the other hand, the declining party membership is offered new opportunities for participation: Members' representatives were included for the first time in 1993 in the electoral college which elected the party president, while the present leader was elected by the party congress.[21]

In short, ND's 22-year organizational trajectory represents in a much condensed form the trajectory of many West European parties, a process which took place in the span of over a century. Interestingly, this accelerated organizational trajectory mirrors the process of Greece's transition from an agrarian to a service economy in just 30 years. Such processes are bound to produce outcomes that parallel the models they emulate, but diverge from them in significant ways.

Below, I explain party development by focusing on the way political competition shapes the incentives and strategies of party elites and party sympathizers. I rely on simple rational choice assumptions: On the one hand, party elites seek reelection. In a parliamentary system with strongly disciplined parties, an electoral system favoring the winner, and pronounced clientelistic features, this is equivalent to seeking the party's victory. On the other hand, party sympathizers seek to maximize the benefits derived from their participation in politics. These benefits take the form of selective incentives (both material and symbolic) which, if exceeding the cost of active participation, solve the collective action problem by making party membership an attractive option. This framework also stresses agency. Party organization is the outcome of choices made by party elites and sympathizers in response to changes in the structure of political competition rather than the result of impersonal structural forces. In turn, these choices are constrained by various political and institutional factors but in ways that leave room for choice. As indicated by table 4.5, predictions diverge slightly from actual outcomes. As a result, I supplement this framework with a contextual analysis. Two factors, in particular, turn out to be significant: The transition to democracy and the legacy of past choices.

Explaining the Organizational Trajectory

In July 1974, New Democracy's founder and leader, Konstantinas Karamanlis steered the country to democracy. The elections that followed reflected this particular circumstance: ND won an unprecedented 54 percent of the votes against divided opponents (the Center Union and PASOK)

Table 4.5 Political Competition and Party Organization

Features of Political Competition	Incentives of Party Elites	Incentives of Sympathizers	Predicted Outcome	Actual Outcome
ND domination (1974–1977)	Restriction of party resources/elite politics	Personal clientelistic ties	Personalistic party; no formal rules	Introduction of formal rules
Erosion of ND domination; rise of a mass-organized challenger (1977–1981)	Limited opening to outside groups	Limited participation	Institutionalization of party organization; limited member recruitment	Institutionalization of party organization; limited member recruitment
Defeat; loss of state resources (1981–1989)	Decisive opening to outside groups	Active participation	Active member recruitment; mass organization	Active member recruitment; mass organization
Alternation in power/new media landscape (1989–now)	Liquidation of mass organization	Gradual Atomization	Decline of party organization; professionalization	Slight decline of party organization; professionalization; democratization

and assumed full control of the state. Party elites had no incentive to create a formal or mass party structure. Such organizations are costly and time-consuming to build, while they restrict the freedom of action of party elites by creating a competing political class of party cadres.[22] Even if a formal party structure was in place, party sympathizers would have lacked the incentive to join, since they prefer instead to maintain individual clientelistic links with party notables. The prediction that follows is that neither formal nor mass organization would emerge. However, while no mass organization was built during this time, the party leadership began a concerted and sustained effort to create a formal party structure that amounted to a "voluntary, yet carefully controlled, transfer of intra-party power from the top to the base."[23] This development is even more puzzling because it was the charismatic leader himself who pushed for formal party organization.

The paradox of a charismatic party leader creating a formal party structure can be unraveled once a contextual factor, the transition to democracy, is integrated into the analysis. The transition to democracy affected the preferences of the party leadership and provided an incentive for the modernization of the right. Karamanlis' ambition to create a "modern" party of the right, distinguishable from the pre-1967 ERE in terms of organizational and ideological outlook, proved a powerful motor of reform. In pushing for the creation of party organization, Karamanlis was motivated primarily by his objective to consolidate Greek democracy.[24] As he pointed out in his 1974 founding declaration of ND, "it will be necessary . . . to rally people into powerful political formations able to protect democracy not only from communism and fascism, but also from the causes that occasioned its downfall."[25] Likewise, Karamanlis was convinced that powerful and enduring parties had to be democratically organized so as to be independent of their leader's fate.[26] It is important to emphasize here that the impact of democratic consolidation on party development is contingent of political competition: Karamanlis could indulge in his endeavor only because his party dominated Greek politics. A higher level of competition might have prohibited him from concentrating on the development of formal party institutions. The case of ND is, thus, significant from a theoretical point of view. While we begin to understand the role of political parties in processes of consolidation, the question of how consolidation processes affect party development remains largely unexplored.[27]

Since party institutionalization was geared toward democratic consolidation rather than party competition, the new formal institutions remained inactive. Predictably, parliamentarians opposed the expansion of local party organization "in the hope of retaining personal control over contacts with prospective voters."[28] Likewise, the party's administrative committee, which was composed exclusively of nonparliamentarians, was ignored by Karamanlis, who ran the party with his own staff.[29] Finally, while the party introduced new personnel in Greek politics (out of 220 deputies elected in 1974, 127 ran for the first time), it was immediately dominated by unreformed notables of the old ERE.[30]

In 1977 the political landscape began to change. Democracy appeared stable, hence consolidation was exhausted as an incentive for party institutionalization. Moreover, the pattern of political competition changed. Even before the November 1977 elections, it became clear that the dominant position enjoyed by ND could no longer be taken for granted. ND won these elections but suffered extensive losses (a drop of 12.5 percentage points), both to its right (the extreme-right made substantial inroads into ND's electorate) and to its left. PASOK, supported by its mass organization, emerged as the main opposition party and a powerful challenger, a development that "panicked" the leadership of ND.[31] Finally, the anticipation of Karamanlis' retirement in the context of the mounting PASOK challenge raised the pressure for the institutionalization of party organization.

The renewal of the party's efforts to develop a formal organization during this period can be explained by this shift in political competition.[32] The expansion of regional and local party branches, the initiation of a drive toward mass organization-building, the organization of the first party congress and, ultimately, the successful replacement of Karamanlis through formal procedures rather than obscure backroom deals, as was often the case in the past, were all expressions of this effort. Membership benefits for party sympathizers remained quite low compared to the costs they faced, but were higher than in the previous period. A party apparatus was now in place, providing the most committed sympathizers with incentives for participation—even professional opportunities as party cadres. The party leadership encouraged member participation.[33] As a result, party cadres began to demand openly that the party "get rid of the hitherto absolute dominance of its elites, that is, of what has been characteristically called deputocracy.'"[34] Still, these inroads were limited. The 1979 party congress reinforced the role of the parliamentary group within the party, while local and regional organizations were, as a party memorandum noted, "not representative, lack[ing] quality, and hence competence to carry out the party organization, as well as to mobilize the voters for the forthcoming election campaign."[35]

Many observers expected that ND would not survive Karamanlis' 1980 departure from the party he founded to the presidency of the republic. They also speculated that the party might not be able to withstand the shock of its 1981 electoral defeat and the ensuing internal fighting.[36] These observers were extrapolating from past history: Events such as the departure of charismatic leaders, crucial electoral defeats, and open internal infighting (not to mention the electoral victory of a leftist party), constituted extraordinary circumstances in the context of Greek politics that, in the past, had affected the political system in profound and disruptive ways. That ND overcame these obstacles and survived as a party, is testimony to its successful institutionalization—a result of the organizational strategy followed after 1974.

The 1981 crushing defeat of ND came as a shock to party leaders and sympathizers alike. Accustomed to long and uninterrupted periods in power, they were now deprived of their main resource, the state. Karamanlis' successor, the moderate George Rallis, was blamed for the defeat and replaced (through formal procedures of the parliamentary group) by the hard-liner Evangelos Averoff. The new party leadership set out to fight PASOK with its own weapons. Despite an initially old-fashioned discourse suggesting that the party was retrogressing "in both ideological and organizational terms,"[37] this period marked the beginning of a remarkable overhaul: The party succeeded in building a formidable mass organization. The prior empty party shell was filled by the expansion of party branches, the creation of ancillary organizations, and the active recruitment of members. Party membership swelled, eventually reaching twice the size of PASOK's. The party gave special emphasis to its youth organization (ONNED) and its professional branches.[38] Elections in professional associations and unions (from high school students to legal and medical doctors associations) became bitterly contested along partisan lines and their outcome commanded broad attention and carried substantial political relevance. The result was a rise in political polarization and the wholesale politicization of Greek society.[39]

The decision to build a mass organization can be explained as an effect of the 1981 defeat on the incentives of both party elite and sympathizers. The party lost its state-related resources while having to face mass mobilization, a mode of political competition promoted and mastered by PASOK. Hence, it made sense to undergo the substantial costs and risks of mass organization-building. The evolution of the party is indeed compatible with Duverger's "contagion of the left" hypothesis, but only in the limited sense that it represented the outcome of a particular configuration of political competition, rather than some universalistic wave of the future. Personal connections to party notables lost a great part of their significance for party sympathizers because these notables could no longer provide benefits. However, this development alone would have only produced a growing disaffection from politics on the part of sympathizers rather than an incentive to join the party as members, an act of more intense participation. In any case, the expectation of clientelistic benefits did not disappear since the party was expected to return to power, sooner or later. Moreover, the idea of political activism was foreign, even suspect, to the conservative ND electorate, since it was perceived as behavior only fit for leftists. Why, then, did sympathizers join the party? To a great extent, it was PASOK's behavior in power that raised the participation incentives of ND sympathizers. Not only did these sympathizers lose their privileged access to the state, they also discovered that the state itself turned against them. Indeed, PASOK's actions in power appeared vindictive to many. Together with inflamed rhetorical attacks against the right, constantly pounded by the government-controlled electronic media, the new government sent negative signals about its impartiality. For instance, public-sector employees who were known ND sympathizers felt threatened by the imposition of politically motivated professional sanctions. Furthermore, party membership offered an important symbolic benefit for a substantial segment of ND sympathizers—a sense of belonging and a confirmation of their identity at a time when their traditional references were lost and their identity challenged. The party complemented symbolic incentives with material ones. Party branches began to organize a variety of popular nonpolitical activities (such as community events, excursions, dances, festivals), and offer a wide range of services, going as far as helping members find employment in the private sector. The outcome of the 1984 European elections intensified the transformation of sympathizers into members by demonstrating beyond any doubt that the PASOK government was not a fleeting phenomenon but a lasting reality.

It took eight years for ND to return to power. After three successive elections in 1989 and 1990, ND beat an electoral system designed by the PASOK government to penalize it, and achieved a tiny parliamentary majority despite a landslide victory. The expansion of the public sector during the previous years had led to the deterioration of the country's economic situation, and EC pressure for structural reforms were growing. Patronage sources shrank, while the liberalization of the electronic media led to the creation of private radio and TV stations. The combination of these trends entailed a move away from mass mobilization and toward fundraising, greater professionalization, and "mediatization" of politics.

As a result, both parties are now engaged in a process of "cartelization," evolving into parties "whose campaigns are now almost exclusively capital-intensive, professional and centralized, and who rely increasingly for their resources on the subventions and other benefits and privileges afforded by the state."[40] In the 1993 elections both parties downgraded mass mobilization and concentrated instead on media campaigning. The 1994 European elections confirmed this trend: Television was flooded by party commercials, and for the first time the three major parties did not hold their ceremonial mass rallies in the center of Athens during the closing of the campaign. ND even decided against holding a mass rally in the 1996 elections. The shift of campaigning away from mass mobilization and toward the intensive use of the media is further confirmed by a look at campaign expenditures. The 1993 elections cost ND $36.4 million, as opposed to just $5.8 million in 1990; out of this sum $12 million were spent on advertising alone.[41] The 1996 elections cost ND close to $7 million in TV commercials alone.[42] In addition, mass organization became a cost rather than a fundraiser for the party. Although no data are available about the economic contribution of party members, it is clear that it was not substantial.[43] In fact, party organizations received a $560,000 subsidy from the central party during the 1993 campaign.[44] Since the main benefit that party organization could deliver, mass mobilization, was downgraded, the overall tab was now largely negative.

Still, contrary to what this analysis would predict, this latest shift in political competition has not yet led to as sharp of a decline of membership as one would expect.[45] This is the second instance where the actual outcome diverges from the prediction offered by the framework of analysis. Apparently, the creation of a mass organization is likely to have lasting consequences, transcending the effects of political competition alone. What is more, party members appear to have wrested additional power within the party, most important the right to participate in the election of the party president. The present party leader, Kostas Karamanlis, was elected for the first time by an enlarged party congress, composed of 3,604 representatives (up from 1,983.)[46] While it is too early to say if the relative persistence of mass organization is not just due to a time lag, it does underline the weight of past choices. Likewise, it remains to be seen whether the empowering of party members will counteract the decline of the party's mass organization.

Internal Politics and Splinter Parties

New Democracy has not been immune to internal disputes. In some instances these disputes were driven by ideological concerns. For instance, when ND lost the 1981 elections, the hard-line deputy Evangelos Averoff orchestrated the ousting of the moderate George Rallis and steered the party to the right. Often, these conflicts had a more personal dimension, like the conflict between Miltiadis Evert and his predecessor, Konstantinos Mitsotakis. Some times disputes were centered around demands by party cadres for more power within the party and/or critique of party strategy. Most disputes had mixed origins, blending ideological, strategic, and personal concerns. The party has generally failed to develop democratic procedures for the airing and discussion of grievances, reflecting a political culture often suspicious of open expression of disagreement.

While disputes were frequent, only twice did they develop into full-blown party splits, threatening the party's domination of the center-right political space. The first split took place in 1985 when the defeated contender in the party leadership contest, Kostis Stephanopoulos, resigned from the party, followed by nine deputies, to form a new party called Democratic Renewal. As its name indicated, the party's objective was to renovate the center-right. However, it never managed to articulate a clear identity and remained torn between its message of political renewal and the conservative and old-fashioned character of its leadership. The second split took place in 1993 and initially appeared more threatening. It was caused by a personal clash between Konstantinos Mitsotakis and his young foreign affairs minister, Antonis Samaras. The latter resigned over a dispute about the Macedonian issue and left ND to form a new party, Political Spring. When two ND deputies defected to join his party they deprived ND government of its slim parliamentary majority and caused its downfall.

Samaras strove to convey the image of the leader of a young and dynamic political force battling against the "dinosaurs" of the "old parties" (ND and PASOK), while simultaneously promoting an uncompromising nationalistic stance. Otherwise, its program did not differ from that of New Democracy. Initially, the new party capitalized on the prevailing disenchantment from the lackluster performance of the two major parties; just after it was formed surveys estimated its support at between 15 and 20 percent.[47] However, the party did not make the expected breakthrough and obtained a meager 4.9 percent and ten seats. The results of the 1994 European elections, when the party won 8.6 percent of the votes and emerged as the third strongest party, reinforced its presence. However, the party failed to reach the 3 percent threshold in the 1996 elections (it got 2.94 percent) and lost its parliamentary representation. The advent of new younger leaders in the two major parties, the decline of nationalist feelings in the country, and the formation of a new protest party (the PASOK splinter DIKKI), contributed to the party's defeat, whose future is bleak. On the other hand, although the extreme right is politically represented by various small parties, it has not succeeded in securing any significant representation since 1977. The threat it has posed to ND remains, hence, insignificant.

Ideology and Policy

New Democracy emerged in 1974 as an essentially pragmatic party lacking a well-defined ideological profile. This attitude was reflected in its early attempt to deny the relevance of political cleavages. The categories right, center, and left were rejected as being misleading, arbitrary, artificial, and insignificant.[48] The party defined itself in its statutes with vague and all-encompassing terms: "Democratic, modern, popular, social, radical, liberal, European, and national." This vagueness is explained by the Greek right's past self-definition, which was based to a considerable extent on opposition: *anti*venizelist during the interwar years, it became *anti*communist afterwards. On the "affirmative" side, one could find nationalism and royalism. These ideological features were appropriated, and subsequently discredited by the colonels' dictatorship (whose main justification for the coup was precisely the presence of a communist threat).[49]

The bankruptcy of the traditional ideology of the right forced Karamanlis to liquidate the past. He swiftly did away with anticommunism and royalism by legalizing the Communist party (outlawed in 1947) and abandoned the monarchy to its final defeat in the 1974 referendum.[50] ND engaged in a vigorous effort to deemphasize its association with "obsolete parties of the past" and to stress that it was neither a "mere continuation of ERE" nor a "personal party."[51] While Karamanlis was successful in freeing the right from its traditional ideological anchors, he had trouble replacing them with new ones. His bet was that a European liberal profile, coupled with his project to get the country into the European Community, would provide the new party with a compelling and attractive ideology. He attempted to develop a new ideological profile under the ambiguous label of "radical liberalism," which was said to be lying between traditional liberalism and democratic socialism. This ideological project eventually failed: Joining the European Community was an abstract undertaking and radical liberalism was predictably too bland to inspire. The party's "confusing and contradictory image" contributed to its difficulties in the face of the rise of the ideologically aggressive PASOK.

Typical of the ambiguity of the party's profile was its position on the issue of state intervention in the economy. ND governments promoted vigorous state intervention and Karamanlis proudly underlined the implementation of wide-ranging nationalizations in the wake of the transition to democracy. The stress on state intervention was not surprising in a time of Keynesian hegemony and rising expectations following the collapse of the dictatorship. Again, Karamanlis justified his emphasis on social justice by stressing the goal of democratic consolidation: "When a people cannot attain social justice in the framework of democracy their trust in the ideal of democracy is shaken."[52]

The 1981 defeat disassociated New Democracy from the state and forced a general rethinking of its ideas. Promoting a sharper ideological profile was also seen as central in attracting members to the party's emerging mass organization. The attacks against PASOK proved useful in the short run but could not sustain the party's effort after 1984. The emerging neoliberal project came in handy. Its attractiveness lay in its coherent and clear set of principles (as opposed to wishy-washy pragmatism) and its opposition to the traditional, paternalistic, and state-oriented tradition of the right, which appeared obsolete. Moreover, neoliberalism provided the right with the opportunity to recast itself into a party that was modern rather than old-fashioned; ideologically assertive rather than defensive; and liberal rather than conservative. However, the attractiveness of the neoliberal project in a society extremely dependent on the state was bound to be limited. For the masses of public-sector employees and the self-employed linked to the state, the neoliberal agenda was a threatening prospect. There was considerable resistance within the party as well. The debate around this issue was temporarily settled by the adoption of a neoliberal party manifesto (issued in February 1985 and entitled "New Proposal of Freedom"), which turned freedom into "the basic overriding principle of all political and governmental activity." The expansionist public-sector policies and the "exceedingly powerful state" were castigated; "the limitation of the extent of the state, particularly in the economy" became the party's overriding priority.[53] The party ran the 1985 electoral campaign around the theme of "Liberal New Democracy." However, even assuming that neoliberalism could be attractive in Greece at the time, this ideological shift came too late to convince the electorate. Surveys indicate that close to 50 percent of respondents thought that the new theme was a mere "electoral trick."[54]

The defeat of the party in 1985 was blamed by many within the party on "excessive liberalism," leading the leadership to reassess its ideological message and tone down its neoliberal agenda. The party's 1989–90 manifesto (entitled "Greece will not turn back") while still inspired by the neoliberal project was now promoted together with the slogan "Freedom-Creation-Social Protection." This program advocated an extensive program of privatizations, a drastic reduction in the number of appointments in the public sector, and a liberalization of the labor market. However, the debate during these elections revolved, initially at least, less on the economy and more on issues of corruption and scandals. The deterioration of the economy during 1990 and the collapse of the communist regimes of Eastern Europe provided a handy shortcut that allowed ND to promote its program while avoiding an extensive and potentially dangerous debate on its content.

After obtaining a parliamentary majority in April 1990, ND appeared poised to innovate with respect not only to PASOK's policies but also to its own past practice. Its symbolic reconciliation with the left, in the context of the coalition government of June-November 1989, indicated a spirit of renewal and innovation. Its willingness to introduce economic reform was reinforced by the dismal economic situation of the country. On the basis of virtually any macroeconomic indicator Greece's performance was negative, diverging significantly from the other EU countries. Problems included high inflation rates, large public deficits, and uncertainty with respect to the basic rules of the economic game and the line separating the private from the public sector, leading to low rates of investment, decreasing international competitiveness, and low growth.[55] The EU pressured Greece to introduce radical economic measures by making major loan packages contingent on the achievement of certain performance targets. The convergence criteria for participation in the EMU put additional pressure on Greece. Structural adjustment reforms were no longer a choice predicated on ideological considerations, but a necessity imposed by international and domestic constraints.

However, results hardly measured up to expectations. On the political front, the ND government got entangled in the protracted and eventually damaging corruption trial of ex-prime minister Andreas Papandreou and several high-ranking PASOK officials. On the economic front, the far overdue program of privatizations was implemented with great delay and proved to be far more limited than promised. Some loss-making state-controlled enterprises were either sold or liquidated. But the two biggest privatizations were botched. While the government's deflationary policies (such as the freezing of public-sector wages and pensions) were predictably unpopular, they failed to bring under control the public deficit and public debt, bring down inflation substantially, and reduce the number of public-sector employees.[56] Widespread social agitation generated by union action contributed to the program's failure. Overall, the ND government proved "quite incapable of overcoming an image of generalized inefficiency, inertia, and sheer incompetence."[57] Predictably, ND came under sustained attack in the 1993 elections, both for the substance of its policies and the way it handled them. PASOK denounced the "sellout of public property" and pointed to the social costs of economic reforms. Besides its dismal record, ND was also hurt by allegations of corruption related to its handling of privatizations. Unable to assume the political cost of economic reforms, the perceived ineffectiveness of its policies, and the fallout from corruption allegations, ND was soundly defeated. After this defeat, Mitsotakis resigned and was replaced by Miltiadis Evert.

Following its 1993 victory, and under pressure from both the EU and the pressing problems of the Greek economy, PASOK gradually revised its statist agenda and undertook a program of economic reforms.[58] Indeed, the 1996 OECD report on the Greek economy, though calling for tougher measures, took note of the progress Greece made in implementing structural reforms.[59] After his election as the head of the party in 1996, Kostas Simitis turned the modernization of the economy and the participation of Greece in the European monetary union into his central projects.

PASOK's bet was that it could implement these reforms more efficiently and less harshly than ND, while using its ties to unions to preserve social peace. During the electoral campaign, Evert attempted to stave off this challenge by adopting a populist discourse with nationalist overtones so as to attract the discontented. His strategy failed: PASOK suffered significant losses only on its left (to the Communist party, the Leftist coalition, and particularly the PASOK splinter DIKKI). It preserved its core centrist constituency and managed to expand its influence on its right, eroding the traditional social basis of New Democracy. This victory pinpoints PASOK's ability to transform itself despite political and economic constraints hostile to its (initial) ideology and the welfare of large segments of its supporters. In the long run, however, it is doubtful whether the PASOK government will be able to go forward with the implementation of these reforms without alienating increasingly wider segments of its social basis. Either it will carry out the tough reforms required by the present state of the Greek economy, thus provoking an acute internal party crisis and the prospect of desertion of a large part of its traditional electorate—especially the salaried public-sector workers; or, in an effort to preserve its social outlook it will settle on halfhearted reforms that will ultimately fail to address the country's economic problems and will undermine its credibility. How PASOK addresses this dilemma will have a decisive impact on Greek politics.[60]

The 1996 defeat led New Democracy into a deep and protracted crisis. The inability of the party to benefit from the political shift to the right and win the elections was, predictably, a big disappointment. Evert was heavily criticized; he initially accepted responsibility for the defeat and resigned on election night, but recanted a couple of days later. He submitted his candidacy anew, won reelection in an atmosphere of internecine fighting, and contributed to the deepening of the party crisis.[61] The March 1997 party congress elected a new party leader, the 41-year-old Kostas Karamanlis, a Thessaloniki deputy and nephew of former prime minister, president, and party founder Konstantinos Karamanlis. In the first round of the three-way contest, Karamanlis won 40 percent of the votes as opposed to 30 percent for Giorgos Souflias and 25 percent for Evert. In the second round, the congress rallied behind Karamanlis, who won 69.16 percent of the vote. Karamanlis, a young and relatively obscure politician with little experience, came from nowhere to win the party leadership. He was put forward by the party's conservative old guard who sensed Evert's imminent defeat and wanted to prevent Souflias' election. In the first round, Karamanlis won the support of the massive party contingent from Macedonia. He was practically endorsed by Evert before the second round. Karamanlis' candidacy combined two contradictory features: novelty and tradition. The desire of party members for a young leader untainted by internecine fights was matched by the memories of past glory conveyed by his name (a popular chant at the congress was "here comes the new Karamanlis"). Obviously, youth and novelty are no guarantees for sound leadership, while an illustrious name is no substitute for experience. It remains to be seen whether Karamanlis will rise up to the tremendous challenge of redefining the party's strategy (even its character) and inspiring supporters.

Conclusion: Prospects for the Right at the Turn of the Century

New Democracy is confronted by two sets of challenges. The first one is related to the social and political impact of structural reforms; the second one concerns the particular strategy to adopt in order to face PASOK's successful right shift.

Both ND and PASOK will face serious challenges as a consequence of the widespread social disruption caused by the implementation of economic reforms. Large segments of Greek society will be directly affected and, as a result, the political landscape is likely to change radically. For example, the reduction of tax evasion will devastate the underground economy, a sector that accounts for 31 percent of the GNP and provides secondary jobs to one out of two public-sector employees. At the same time the existing welfare infrastructure is totally inadequate for dealing with such massive disruptions.[62] Related to the consequences of economic reforms is the process of erosion of traditional collective political identities, expressed in the growing popular disaffection with the two parties— and politics in general. This trend was particularly visible in the 1996 elections (see table 4.2). Moreover, the abstention rate rose, while blank and invalid ballots reached record levels—up 100 percent from the previous elections.[63] Public-opinion surveys confirm the growing dissatisfaction with existing political parties: In April 1995, for instance, the number of respondents who felt underrepresented by the existing parties reached a record 64.6 percent.[64]

Such developments open the door to political entrepreneurs willing to try their hand at populism. The fact that the European Union is seen as the primary force behind these economic reforms might generate an anti-European backlash. In such a context, issues like immigration and crime are increasingly likely to become politicized. For instance, immigration is a new social phenomenon which began in the early 1990s. Like Spain and Italy, Greece was a country of emigration which suddenly finds itself on the opposite side: There are currently 100,000 legal, and between 400,000 and 500,000 illegal immigrants in Greece, the latter making up about 13 percent of the labor force. Illegal immigrants, mostly from Eastern Europe and the Middle East, are chiefly employed in agriculture, where they make up 31 percent of the labor force. Even though most immigrants live in rural areas, do not strain welfare services, and constitute a cheap and plentiful source of labor, their presence is viewed negatively by the public.[65] The perception that the surge in crime is related to immigration is likely to reinforce xenophobic attitudes. Likewise, relations between Greece and Europe might also generate populist mobilization. European attitudes toward Greece and the interpretation of such attitudes in Greece, constitute an issue of identity, relatively easy to politicize. Greece's economic performance and policies vis-à-vis its neighbors have attracted considerable criticism from its European partners and their media, and Greece is often portrayed as an "insufficiently European" country.[66] Greek reaction to such criticism has often been defensive, stressing precisely the distinct cultural dimension of Greek identity. While culturalist and isolationist arguments have so far failed to make any significant inroads in public opinion (particularly if compared to other European countries), the social consequences of economic reforms combined with the decline of the traditional political identities are likely to reinforce electoral volatility and centrifugal tendencies within parties, and provide an opening for populist and nationalistic mobilization outside the two dominant Greek parties.

On top of these broad challenges, New Democracy needs to respond to PASOK's move to the right. Its predicament is in many ways similar to that of the Spanish right during the 1980s—and many Eastern European and Latin American center-right parties today. Apparently, socially costly economic reforms enforced by international agencies in the absence of a socialist tradition and strong independent unions can lead to the wholesale adoption of neoliberal policies by left-wing parties—often under a "social" or even a populist discourse.[67] Indeed, PASOK has successfully taken over what was, only a few years ago, widely considered to be a neoliberal agenda. Faced with a choice between two parties that promote broadly similar policies, the median voter is likely, other things being equal, to opt for the party that appears more efficient and promises a more socially sensitive application of the reforms.[68] Programmatic similarity might also turn the electorate's attention to other factors, such as the personality of party leaders.[69] This situation is particularly ironic, since ND was at a marked disadvantage during the 1980s, when the societal consensus was in favor of state expansion, and remains in the same position even though public opinion has shifted to the right.

New Democracy's economic program remains unchanged in its promotion of radical economic reforms, especially privatizations.[70] Tight international and domestic constraints make structural reforms inescapable: growth is still sluggish (2.1 percent in 1996); public debt reached 114 percent of the GNP in 1995; although inflation is down 20 percent from five years earlier (8.3 percent in 1996) it is still higher than the EU average, while unemployment rates are rising. Yet, at the same time, the party kept relying on a populist discourse that denied the reality of these economic constraints. This contradiction reflects the strategic impasse in which New Democracy finds itself following its recent defeat. The party faces the following dilemma: It can either choose a right-wing populist strategy in order to attract the losers of the adjustment process, or opt for an uncompromising modernizing strategy built around the argument that ND can better implement the reform agenda than PASOK. The populist strategy might be profitable in the short run, but it can also prove unconvincing, as indicated by the 1996 elections. ND lost upper-middle-class support to PASOK but failed to erode PASOK's discontented lower-middle- and working-class voters who were tempted by left-wing parties. Furthermore, whatever the electoral benefits of this strategy, it carries tremendous political costs in case ND wins and is forced to implement the very reforms it condemned as an opposition. On the other hand, the modernizing strategy might fail to tap effectively into mass discontent and would place the party at an initial disadvantage vis-à-vis PASOK's strategy of combining the implementation of reforms with some modicum of a social agenda. In the longer run, however, ND might benefit from the difficulties likely to be experienced by the PASOK government on the economic front and the internal divisions that will follow. What strategy is eventually chosen will determine whether New Democracy will regain its dominant position in Greek politics.

Notes

1. George Th. Mavrogordatos, *Rise of the Green Sun: The Greek Election of 1981* (London: Centre of Contemporary Greek Studies, King's College, 1983), p. 5.
2. See S. Ersson, K. Janda, and J. E. Lane, "Ecology of Party Strength in Western Europe: A Regional Analysis," *Comparative Political Studies* 18:2 (1985): 170–205; Oddbjörn Knutsen, "The Impact of Structural and Ideological Party Cleavages in West European Democracies: A Comparative Empirical Analysis," *British Journal of Political Science* 18:3 (1988), 323–352; and Yannis Papadopoulos, "Parties, the State and Society in Greece: Continuity Within Change," *West European Politics* 12:2 (1989): 54–71.

3. Richard Gunther and Jose Ramon Montero, cited in Takis Spyros Pappas, "The Making of Party Democracy in Greece" (Ph.D. diss.,Yale University, 1995), p. 322.

4. The absence of national election studies and reliable longitudinal survey data makes it difficult to track long-term trends. Reliable data from public-opinion surveys conducted at regular intervals, panel studies, and exit polls, became available only recently.

5. See Elias Nikolakopoulos, "I Eklogikiepirroi ton politikon dynameon" [The electoral influence of political forces], in *Ekloges kai kommata sti dekaetia tou 80* [Elections and Parties during the 1980s], ed. by Christos Lyrintzis and Elias Nikolakopoulos (Athens:Themelio, 1990).

6. John C. Loulis, "New Democracy: The New Face of Conservatism," in *Greece at the Polls:The National Elections of 1974 and 1977,* ed. Howard R. Penniman (Washington: American Enterprise for Public Policy Research, 1981), p. 76–77.

7. This trend was particularly visible in upper-middle-class Athens districts, where electoral support for ND collapsed to levels never seen after 1981 (with a significant parallel increase of PASOK and smaller parties). See Yannis Mavris, "Nees tasis tou eklogikou somatos" [New trends in the electorate], *I Kathimerini,* Sept. 29, 1996.

8. See Elias Nikolakopoulos, "'Apofasismenoi' kai 'anapofasistoi': I simvoli ton dimoskopiseon exo apo ta eklogika tmimata stin analisi tis psifou" ["'Decided' and 'undecided' voters: The contribution of exit polls for the analysis of the vote"]. Paper presented at the Hellenic Political Science Association conference on the 1996 elections, Athens, December 3, 1996.

9. Richard S. Katz, and Peter Mair, "Changing Models of Party Organization and Party Democracy: The Emergence of the Cartel Party," *Party Politics* 1:1 (1995): 5–28.

10. Ibid., p. 19.

11. Anders Widfeldt, "Party Membership and Party Representativeness," in *Citizens and the State,* ed. by Hans-Dieter Klingemann and Dieter Fuchs (Oxford: Oxford University Press, 1995).

12. Richard S. Katz, et al., *Party Organization: A Data Handbook on Party Organizations in Western Democracies, 1960–1990* (London: Sage, 1992); Widfeldt, "Party Membership," p. 173.

13. Richard Clogg, *Parties and Elections in Greece: The Search for Legitimacy* (Durham, N.C.: Duke University Press, 1987), p. 154.

14. Karamanlis was replaced by George Rallis in 1980, followed by Evangelos Averoff in 1981, Konstantinos Mitsotakis in 1984, and Miltiadis Evert in 1993.

15. Quoted in Pappas, "The Making of Party Democracy," p. 162.

16. These numbers should be treated with caution. For instance, it is well known that at least in the early stages many deputies registered massively their local clients in order to control the party delegates to the congress. See Loulis, "New Democracy," pp. 79–80.

17. Ibid., p. 72.
18. Michalis Spourdalakis, "Securing Democracy in Post-authoritarian Greece: The Role of Political Parties," in *Stabilizing Fragile Democracies: Comparing New Party Systems in Southern and Eastern Europe,* ed. Geoffrey Pridham and Paul G. Lewis (London and New York: Routledge, 1996), p. 174.
19. Maurice Duverger, *Political Parties: Their Organization and Activities in the Modern State* (London: Methuen, 1954), p. xxviii.
20. Dimitrios K. Katsoudas, "The Conservative Movement and New Democracy: From Past to Present," in *Political Change in Greece: Before and After the Colonels,* ed. by Kevin Featherstone and Dimitrios K. Katsoudas (London: Croom Helm, 1987), p. 100.
21. In 1993, Evert won 141 ballots out of the 182 cast by an electoral college comprising the members of the parliamentary group and party representatives.
22. See Stathis N. Kalyvas, *The Rise of Christian Democracy in Europe* (Ithaca, NY and London: Cornell University Press, 1996).
23. Pappas, "The Making of Party Democracy," p. 151.
24. Ibid., p. 150. Concern about democratic consolidation is a more powerful explanatory variable than additional factors suggested by Pappas, such as the new political landscape which made old-style politics "simply not possible" and the desire of Karamanlis "to eliminate the autonomous power of his opponents" within the party. The first factor begs the question, while the second disregards the fact that formal (but no mass) party organization is no substitute for charismatic leadership when it comes to internal divisions.
25. Quoted in Clogg, *Parties and Elections in Greece,* p. 224.
26. For Karamanlis, "democratically constituted parties" stood in opposition to "short-lived ones." He argued that "a political party cannot exist for any reasonable length of time unless it is democratically organized so as not to identify its own fate with that of the leader." Even accession to the EC was justified in terms of democratic consolidation: As Karamanlis told the Athens ambassadors of the member-states the day the Greek petition was presented in Brussels (June 13, 1975), the Greek application was "first and foremost political, as it is concerned with the consolidation of democracy and the future of the nation." See Susannah Verney, "To Be or Not to Be Within the European Community: The Party Debate and the Democratic Consolidation in Greece," in *Securing Democracy: Political Parties and Democratic Consolidation in Southern Europe,* ed. by Geoffrey Pridham (London and New York: Routledge, 1990), p. 208; Clogg, *Parties and Elections in Greece,* p. 226; and Pappas, "The Making of Party Democracy," p. 145.
27. See Leonardo Morlino, "Political Parties and Democratic Consolidation in Southern Europe," in *The Politics of Democratic Consolidation: Southern Europe in Comparative Perspective,* ed. by Richard Gunther, P. Nikiforos Diamandouros, and Hans-Jürgen Puhle (Baltimore and London: Johns

Hopkins University Press, 1995); and Geoffrey Pridham, ed., *Securing Democracy: Political Parties and Democratic Consolidation in Southern Europe* (London and New York: Routledge, 1990.)

28. See Loulis, "New Democracy," p. 13.

29. Ibid., p. 69.

30. George Th. Mavrogordatos, "The Greek Party System: A Case of 'Limited but Polarized Pluralism?'" in *Party Politics in Contemporary Europe,* ed. by Stefano Bartolini and Peter Mair (London: Frank Cass, 1984), p.158; Christos Lyrintzis, "Political Parties in Post-Junta Greece: A Case of 'Bureaucratic Clientelism?'" *West European Politics* 7:2 (1984): p. 106.

31. Pappas, "The Making of Party Democracy," p. 195.

32. This mechanism might operate in an indirect fashion: The expectation of the charismatic leader's retirement at a crucial moment for the party's fate forced party elites to develop a formal organization guaranteeing party continuity, in order to ensure their political survival. The interesting question here is, why did the UCD party elites in Spain, seemingly facing a similar situation, fail to maintain the unity of their party?

33. It has been noted about the 1977 preliminary party congress, that "far from being a mere facade of party activism, [it] offered its participants an opportunity for considerable involvement in the party's internal affairs." See Pappas, "The Making of Party Democracy," p. 156. The second party congress took place only six years later, in February 1986. In contrast, PASOK held its first congress in 1984, its second one in 1991, and its most recent (which elected Papandreou's successor) in 1996.

34. Ibid., p. 167.

35. Ibid., p. 275.

36. See Lyrintzis, "Political Parties in Post-Junta Greece."

37. See Mavrogordatos, "The Greek Party System," p. 159.

38. ONNED expanded from 220 branches in 1979 to 470 in 1986, recruiting 50,000 members. The importance of this organization within the party was recognized in the 1986 congress, which doubled the number of ONNED representatives to party congresses. Likewise the workers' and farmers' party organizations (DAKE and SYDASE), were formed and became key players in their respective fields during the same period.

39. See Stathis N. Kalyvas, "Consolidation, Legitimacy, and Iteration: Party Politics and Democracy in Greece, 1980–1985." Paper presented at the 1995 Symposium of the Modern Greek Studies Association.

40. See Katz and Mair, "Changing Models of Party Organization," p. 20.

41. See *Oikonomikos Tachydromos,* June 2, 1994. The state subsidy reached $22 million in 1993.

42. See *Eleftheros Typos,* September 25, 1996.

43. The official 1995 ND budget lacks an entry for members' contributions; it only reports income from fundraising campaigns (generally undertaken on an ad hoc basis). PASOK reports an income of $281,800 from members' contributions, while the Communist party reports $860,000. This is

probably a good indicator of the "quality" of the parties' mass organizations. See *Oikonomikos Tachydromos,* June 20, 1996.

44. See *Oikonomikos Tachydromos,* June 2, 1994.

45. On this issue, see Susan E. Scarrow, *Parties and Their Members: Organizing for Victory in Britain and Germany* (Oxford: Oxford University Press, 1996).

46. Prior to the 1997 party congress there was strong disagreement about the method of appointing representatives to the congress. The party leadership argued for the appointment to the congress of the (elected) boards of local and professional party organizations, whereas the party opposition demanded the direct election of congress representatives by party members. At the end, the position of the leadership prevailed. There is no evidence that indirect election is necessarily less representative of members' opinions. For instance, in the electoral college vote following the 1996 party's defeat, most parliamentarians voted for the outgoing president, M. Evert, while most party cadres supported the challenger, G. Souflias, thus reflecting the preferences of party members as registered in surveys. As Michalis Spourdalakis points out, "the role of [ND] membership goes beyond the mere legitimizing junction shaping party strategy." See Spourdalakis, "Securing Democracy in Post-authoritarian Greece," p. 174. Party members have also obtained (on paper rather than in practice), some input in the drafting of the party's candidate list. Candidates to the parliament are selected by the president and the party's executive committee from a list of potential candidates drawn after elections have taken place in regional party organizations. See Giorgos Papadimitriou and M. Spourdalakis, *Ta katastatika ton politikon kommaton* [The statutes of political parties] (Athens: Sakkoulas, 1994).

47. Panayote Elias Dimitras, "The Greek Parliamentary Election of October 1993," *Electoral Studies,* 13:3 (1994): 235–239.

48. Karamanlis' speech at the First Congress of ND, May 1979. See Clogg, *Parties and Elections in Greece,* p. 227.

49. Royalism was discredited as well, because of the widespread perception that the king's interventions in politics during the 1960s paved the way for the dictatorship.

50. See Mavrogordatos, "The Greek Party System," p. 158.

51. ND party literature, quoted in Spourdalakis, "Securing Democracy in Post-authoritarian Greece," p. 174.

52. Quoted in Katsoudas, "The Conservative Movement and New Democracy," p. 98.

53. Quoted in Clogg, *Parties and Elections in Greece,* pp. 228–233.

54. Katsoudas, "The Conservative Movement and New Democracy," p. 101.

55. Loukas Tsoukalis, "Is Greece an Awkward Partner?" in *Greece in a Changing Europe: Between European Integration and Balkan Disintegration?,* ed. by Kevin Featherstone and Kostas Ifantis (Manchester and New York: Manchester University Press, 1996); George Tridimas, "Greek Fiscal Policy and the European Union," in *Greece in a Changing Europe: Between European*

Integration and Balkan Disintegration?, ed. by Kevin Featherstone and Kostas Ifantis (Manchester and New York: Manchester University Press, 1996).

56. According to one estimation, at least 60,000 new employees were hired in the public sector during the 1991–1994 period. See *To Vima*, December 18, 1994.

57. George Th. Mavrogordatos,"Political Data Yearbook: Greece," *European Journal of Political Research* 26 (1994): 315–316.

58. European Union subsidies are crucial in sustaining the Greek economy—but they are declining. Greece's net benefit from the EU reached $3.3 billion in 1995, as opposed to $3.9 billion in 1994 and $5.5 billion in 1992. See Tridimas, "Greek Fiscal Policy and the European Union," p. 55, and *To Vima*, January 21, 1996.

59. See OECD report quoted in *Eleftherotypia*, July 31, 1996.

60. The first indications conveyed by the 1997 budget are that the PASOK government has not yet managed to address this dilemma: On the one hand, the level of fiscal discipline is relatively low given the convergence targets, and no privatizations have been planned; on the other hand, the budget is not "social" enough to satisfy the party's populist wing and its lower-income constituency.

61. Evert won by 103 votes, while ballots were cast in favor of his competitor, G. Souflias.

62. For data on the underground economy, see a KEPE study, cited in *I Kathimerini*, December 13, 1992. Unemployment compensation stands at one-third of the European average despite the fact that the average Greek income is about two-thirds of the average European one; health spending per person (as percent of the GDP) is the lowest in the EU. See *Eleftherotypia*, July 26, 1996 and *The Economist*, August 3, 1996.

63. See *To Vima*, October 20, 1996.

64. See *Ta Nea*, April 19, 1995.

65. See Anna Triandafyllidou, "Greek Migration Policy: A Critical Note," *Synthesis: Review of Modern Greek Studies* 1:1 (1996): 15–22; G. Voulgaris, et al., "He proslepse kai he antimetopise tou allou ste semerine Ellada. Porismataempirikis erevnas" [The reception and confrontation of the other in contemporary Greece. Results of empirical research], *Greek Political Science Review* 5 (1995): 81–100, and *Eleftherotypia*, February 27, 1996. Still, the presence of foreigners in Greece only ranks as the tenth most important problem in Greece. See Voulgaris, et al., "He proslepse kai heantimetopise tou allou," p. 100.

66. See Featherstone and Ifantis, *Greece in a Changing Europe*. Bideleux echoes this attitude when he argues that the cold war "induced the West to treat Greece as part of Western Europe, in blatant defiance of cultural and geographical facts." See Robert Bideleux, "The Southern European Enlargement of EC: Greece, Portugal, and Spain," in *European Integration and Disintegration: East and West*, ed. by Robert Bideleux and Richard Taylor (London and New York: Routledge, 1996), p. 129.

67. See Kenneth M. Roberts, "Neoliberalism and the Transformation of Populism in Latin America: The Peruvian Case," *World Politics* 48:1 (1995): 82–116.

68. 1996 survey data indicate that 40.3 percent of respondents thought that a PASOK government headed by Kostas Simitis would be more efficient than a ND government headed by Miltiadis Evert (as opposed to 27.4 percent who thought the opposite). See *Ta Nea,* March 15, 1996. This perception can be attributed, to some extent, to the failure of the ND government in 1993–96.

69. Simitis was seen positively by 49.5 per cent of the respondents, as opposed to Evert's positive rating of 27.4 percent. See *Ta Nea,* March 15, 1996.

70. ND's recent "propositions for the economy" promote a radical privatization program, which includes a substantial part of the banking sector (close to 90 percent of which is still under state control), refineries and petrochemicals, shipyards, tourist enterprises, and basically all state enterprises operating in fields where the private sector can take over. The party is also proposing the partial privatization of the so-called natural monopolies (electricity, transportation).

CHAPTER FIVE

Looking for a Center of Gravity: The Reconstitution of the Italian Right

Dwayne Woods

The Christian Democratic party (DC) dominated the Italian center-right from the epochal 1948 elections until its collapse in 1994.[1] To its right were minor political parties, most notably the fascist *Movimento social Italiano* (MSI). To its left were the minor centrist Liberal and Republican parties. After the 1948 elections, the DC became the dominant party in the numerous governments that formed in Italy over the next four-and-a-half decades. In fact, it would dominate the prime minister's office and other key ministries, such as interior and public works, until 1982, when Giovanni Spadolini became the first non–Christian Democratic prime minister in over 30 years. The DC was an hegemonic force. The dominant political actor on the Italian political landscape, it was the party of government and of order; the party of the Catholics; the bulwark against the threat of communism, represented by Western Europe's largest communist party—the Italian Communist party (PCI).

Despite significant changes in Italian society and periodic declines in its electoral support, the Christian Democrats remained the dominant governing party until the fall of the Berlin Wall and the end of the communist threat from the East. Along with the changes in the East, Italy's Communist party moved away from its Leninist and Stalinist past. The Italian Communist party became the Democratic Party of the Left (PDS).[2] As a consequence, the DC was no longer expected to be the dominant anticommunist force in the country. Long before the collapse of communism, the other factors that had assured the DC its hegemonic position, the party of Catholics and of order, had already declined in importance. By the mid-1980s, the DC remained the dominant political party simply because Italians saw no alternative to them. The rise in nonvoters and negative opinion polls signified dissatisfaction with the party and the government.[3]

Years of political stalemate, corruption, and abuse of authority ended when the Christian Democratic party imploded in 1994. With the party's demise, an enormous political vacuum opened up in the Italian political system. There was no longer a dominant center-right party. As with the fall of Humpty Dumpty, the Italian right has been struggling to put the pieces back together. This chapter explores the manner in which the Italian center-right is reconstituting itself. Different political actors are jockeying to claim the mantle to represent the political space vacated by the Christian Democratic party. The reconstitution of the Italian center-right is grounded in the various, often contradictory social and political currents of the defunct Christian Democratic party. This includes the populist regional movement, the Northern League, *Forza Italia* (FI), the neo-fascist National Alliance (AN), as well as the small political formations which eventually emerged from the old Christian Democratic party—the *Centro Cristiano Democratico* (CCD), and the *Cristiano Democratico Union* (CDU).

To better appreciate how the new center-right parties are trying to fill the vacuum left by the DC, this chapter will present a brief history of the Christian Democrats. After a brief history, this chapter will focus on the different political and social forces that presently constitute the center-right in Italian politics. No single party has succeeded in recreating an electoral coalition similar to the one that had kept the Christian Democrats in power for so long.[4]

The Triumph of the Christian Democratic Party

After the 1948 elections, the Christian Democratic party (DC) emerged as the dominant political force in the country, with nearly 50 percent of the popular vote. Although the DC never regained an absolute majority in subsequent elections, the party managed to govern by forming coalitions with the small center-right parties (Liberals, Republicans, and Social Democrats) in parliament, and after 1963 with the Socialists.[5] In a politically and socially fragmented society, the DC integrated a diverse set of Italian social groups into a mass political party. The DC did so by occupying a shifting center position in Italian politics against extremes on both the left and the right.[6]

The party's ability to integrate these groups largely depended on its capacity to deliver political and ideological services. The DC provided these services by attracting anticommunist voters, by channeling state resources through clientelistic ties, by appealing to a growing middle-class strata of the population, and by relying on the mobilization of a core Catholic constituency. In this way, the party connected the periphery to the political center through local notables in the south, and the cultivation of a Catholic and middle-class constituency in the north. Over time, though, the Christian Democratic party maintained its diverse political base by colonizing government agencies and through its position as the party of order in the country. With its influence over nationalized corporations and public spending, the DC established a diffuse, yet effective, distributive system. Distributive resources cemented a broad constellation of social groups to the party.[7]

Through these resources, the DC stabilized interparty relationships between national and local elites. In gaining access to the top as well as intermediary and lower positions in the public sector, the DC used this privileged access to place "party leaders in jobs in the public sector, thereby decreasing the economic burden on the party." Moreover, in the south, as Mario Caciagli stated, "the DC occupies the key positions in the economic system. . . . It has been the party that controlled all channels through which flow grants and financial resources."[8] In return for public-sector employment, "party activists carry out two roles: part-time party worker and conduit for party policies and preferences in the administrative apparatus of the state."[9]

The Christian Democratic Party and its Many Faces

Because of its multiple and diverse ties, the Christian Democratic party developed many different faces. In various ways, it was a "catch-all party," that is, for as long as it continued to draw electoral support from different social classes and regions. The many faces of the DC reflected both its strengths and weaknesses. On the one hand, the party could mobilize a broad section of Italian society. On the other hand, the party had to accommodate the different social and economic groups that supported it. Endeavoring to accommodate these different segments of Italian society, the party assumed a variety of political traditions.[10]

One vocal segment of the party conveyed a conservative Catholic tradition. In the "white" (Catholic) areas of Bergamo, Brescia, and Veneto, the DC represented the party of family values, entrepreneurship, and order. It was rooted in a coherent Catholic subculture that provided a sense of identity to its voters.[11] Other elements in the party renewed a more populist strain with its origins in the Popular party of the early twentieth century. This element had ties with the country's labor movement. In the south, the DC eventually succeeded in overtaking the more traditional, reactionary, fascist, and monarchist forces through a combination of clientelistic politics and local elite cooptation. The party's political authority rested on the influence of prominent political families, such as the Gava clan in Naples.

These various segments had links to different factions within the party. In fact, much of the postwar history of the DC was the difficult and complicated act of balancing this diverse social base and the factions that, more or less, corresponded to them.[12] Despite the effects of economic modernization and the secularization of Italian society, the DC had succeeded in keeping the various components of the party in some balance. By the 1980s however, evidence of a growing gap between the DC and Italian society appeared in the overall decline in votes for the country's major governing parties as well as a sharply negative perception of government actions (see table 5.1).

The coup de grace for the party was the corruption scandals of the early 1990s and the change in the electoral system from proportional representation to majoritarian. The judiciary inquiries led by Milan prosecutors—known as *Mani Pulite* (clean hands) revealed a party system steeped in corruption and indifferent to public opinion. As the scandal spread and implicated an ever wider spectrum of the country's political class, the already fragile legitimacy of the DC eroded even further. What led to the party's demise, however, was the change in the country's electoral rules. Following a successful referendum led by a former Christian democrat, Mario Segni, Italians selected a predominantly majoritarian electoral system, although 20 percent of the seats remained under proportional representation rules.[13] This new electoral system precipitated the collapse of the DC.

The Fragmentation of the Italian Right

Anticipating the anti-center impact of a majoritarian system, the DC, already internally divided, split into two groups: the *Partito Popolare Italiano* (PPI) and the *Centro Cristiano Democratico* (CCD). Silvio Berlusconi, the television magnate, created the *Forza Italia* in February 1994 in an effort to capture the moderate voters of the old DC. The PPI and CCD joined forces with the *Forza Italia*. This alliance led to the break up of the PPI: the left-wing of the party broke with the right. Roco Buttiglione, the leader of the right faction, left the PPI and created the *Christiano Democratico Union* (CDU). The CDU entered into a loose federation with the

Table 5.1   Decline in Votes for Italy's Major Parties, 1972–1994*

	1972	1976	1979	1983	1987	1992	1994
DC	33.7	38.7	38.3	32.9	34.3	29.7	15.7
PCI	27.1	34.4	30.4	29.9	26.6	16.1	26.4
PSI	9.6	9.6	9.8	11.4	14.3	13.6	2.2
DC + PCI	65.8	73.1	68.7	62.8	60.9	45.8	42.1
DC + PCI + PSI	75.4	82.7	78.5	74.2	75.2	59.4	44.3

Sources: Instituto Centrale di Statistica (ISTAT), DC (Christian Democratic Party), and PDS (Democratic Party of the Left).
*By the 1994 elections, the Italian Communist Party (PCI) had split into two distinct political formations. The majority of the old PCI became members of the newly named Party of the Democratic Left (PDS), while a minority faction created the Refounded Communist Party (PRC). Also, the Christian Democratic party changed its name to the Popular party. Less than a year after the 1994 election, the Christian Democratic and Italian Socialist parties collapsed under the weight of corruption charges and public-sector mismanagement.

CCD. Although these two small political parties have not officially merged, they are basically the same. They share the same electorate and Christian ideology. Moreover, they contest elections together. Henceforth, these two small centrist parties will be referred to as the CCD-CDU. In addition to the former Christian Democratic forces, *Forza Italia* entered an electoral alliance with the neofascist National Alliance and the Northern League to contest the 1994 elections. For the first time in 42 years, the center-right electorate in Italy faced a competitive political market with new players.[14]

Many analysts assumed that the 1994 elections, based on majoritarian rules, would bring some clarity to a political situation in flux. Despite the regrouping of center-right forces into a political coalition (see table 5.2), the election produced an unstable alliance between the smaller Christian Democratic forces—the CCD-CDU, the volatile Northern League, *Forza Italia,* and the neo-fascist National Alliance (AN). While FI emerged as the largest right-wing formation throughout the country, it did not dominate the political landscape enough to dictate its agenda to the Northern League and the National Alliance.

The new electoral system polarized the country's political landscape between left and right blocs, but it did not generate a stable majority on either side (see table 5.3). More important, the 1994 election results showed that the diverse electoral base of the Christian Democratic party could not be easily reconstituted through a loose center-right coalition.

Table 5.2 Composition of Electoral Alliances in 1994 and 1996

1994

Polo (Pole):

    Lega Nord (Northern League), Forza Italia, Centro Cristiano Democratico (Center Christian Democrats), Unione de Centro (Union of the Center), Polo Liberal-democratico (Pole of Liberal Democrats), MSI-Alleanza Nationale (National Alliance)

Centro:

    Partito Popolare Italiano, Patto segni

Progressives (Progressiti):

    Partito della Rifondazione Communista (Refounded Communist Party), Partito Democratico della Sinistra (Party of the Democratic Left), Verdi (Greens), Partito Socialista (Socialist Party), Alleanza Democratica (Democratic Alliance), Cristiano Sociali (Social Christians), Renascita Socialista (Reborn Socialists)

1996

Polo delle Liberata (Pole for Liberty):

    Forza Italia (FI), Alleanza Nationale (AN), Centro Cristiano Democratico (CCD), Cristiano Democratic Uniti (CDU)

Progressisti:*

    Partito della Rifondazione Communista (PRC)

Ulivo (Olive):

    Partito Democratica della Sinistra (PDS), Verdi (Greens), Rete (Network Party), Cristiano Sociali (CS), Partito Popolare Italiano (PPI), Unione Democratica (UD), Repubblicano, Lista Dini

Others:

    Lega Nord, Movimento Sociale Tricolore (MST), Pannella-Sgarbi, Sudtiroler Volkspartei

Note: *The PRC and PDS shared an agreement not to compete in districts in which one of them had a higher plurality of votes.

Factors that the DC had successfully mediated in the past—such as subregional identification, economic divisions between the north and the south, secular/Catholic divisions, age, and income—divided the "pole for liberty," as the center-right coalition was called, more than it united it.[15]

It is, therefore, more appropriate to analyze the dynamics of the center-right in an unaggregated way. At this point, there is no coherent center-right. Each party is in the process of attempting to capture and dominate the center-right. In doing so, they are caught in a strategic game amongst themselves regarding which party will become the hegemonic force on the center-right and between themselves and the Italian electorate, which continues to identify itself along a left-right spectrum.

Table 5.3   Parliamentary Votes by Party Coalitions, 1992–1994

Party Coalition	1992	1994
Right		
MSI (National Alliance)	5.6	8.6
Lega Nord (Norhern League)	8.6	8.4
Forza Italia	0	21.0
Total	14.2	42.9
Center		
PSI (Italian Socialist Party)	13.6	2.2
PSDI (Italian Social Democrats)	2.7	0
PRI (Italian Republican Party)	4.4	0
DC (Christian Democrats)	29.7	15.7
PLI (Italian Liberal Party)	2.8	0
Total	53.3	17.9
Left		
PDS (Democratic Party of the Left)	16.1	20.4
PRC (Refounded Communist Party)	5.6	6.0
Verdi (Greens)	2.8	2.7
La Rete (Network	1.9	1.9
Total	26.4	31.0

Source: The Italian Ministry of Interior.

The Populist Right

The Northern League likes to present itself as a political formation transcending left-right divisions. In this respect, it would contest being placed on the right. In fact, because of its open hostility to the National Alliance, it helped to topple Berlusconi's government less than nine months after the "pole for liberty" won the 1994 elections. There are, however, a number of objective criteria that show its electoral base as mostly center-right (see table 5.4). The Northern League has thrived in the prosperous northeast and to a lesser extent in the northwest. In the 1994 and 1996 elections, it did particularly well among former Christian Democratic voters in small- and medium-sized cities throughout the north.

The League's key supporters are shopkeepers, small-industry businessmen and workers, and artisans. They are generally 18–45 year-old males with high school educations living in small towns of less than 20,000 inhabitants. The League has strong roots among workers in small- and medium-sized firms of the northeast. In the April 1996 elections, 30 percent of the League's voters were workers, giving the League the largest working-class base in Italy (see table 5.5).[16] It, however, is a well-off

124

Table 5.4 Party Identification of the Italian Electorate

	All Voters	AN-MSI	Forza Italia	Lega Nord	PPI	PDS	PRC
Left	9.8	1.2	1.6	4.5	0.8	46.2	66.9
Center-Left	16.2	2.0	5.1	6.0	8.0	47.2	31.8
Center	29.6	6.5	34.3	32.8	71.7	5.0	0.3
Center-Right	19.0	39.3	42.6	41.0	9.9	0.5	0.8
Right	8.6	49.7	11.9	11.5	8.4	0.1	0.2
Total	100	100	100	100	100	100	100

Source: Adapted from Gabriele Calvi and Andrea Vannucci, *L'elettore sconosciuto: Analisi socioculturale e segmentazione degli orientamenti politici nel 1994* (Bologna: il Mulino, 1995), p. 41.

Table 5.5 Composition of the Italian Electorate by Profession

	Total	AN-MSI	Forza Italia	Lega Nord	PPI	PDS	PRC
Employed							
Entrepeneur/Liberal Profession	2.2	4.1	3.3	3.3	0.9	1.3	0.8
Commerce/Shopkeepers	11.6	13.9	13.8	16.6	7.9	9.8	14.3
White Collar	16.7	20.7	11.8	13.2	21.3	22.3	23.9
Workers	18.4	18.9	18.4	30.1	12.0	25.8	18.4
Non-Employed							
Students	6.4	7.4	6.0	9.0	5.6	6.0	10.2
Housewives	19.7	14.6	21.8	13.0	19.4	12.0	13.0
Pensioners	19.6	11.1	17.2	13.8	29.6	18.1	12.9
Other	5.4	9.2	7.8	1.1	3.3	4.7	6.5
Total	100	100	100	100	100	100	100

Source: Adapted from Gabriele Calvi and Andrea Vannucci, *L'elettore sconosciuto: Analisi socioculturale e segmentazione degli orientamenti politici nel 1994* (Bologna: il Mulino, 1995), p. 24.

working class. Their incomes place them above the national average. Although part of a wage-earning category, they strongly identify with the economic success of the small firms they work for and the small towns in which they live. Thus, they empathize with the anger of local entrepreneurs and shopkeepers that the central government in Rome has ignored their interests and concerns.[17]

The Northern League has tapped into an electorate traditionally part of the Catholic subculture. This electorate has done well economically and claims that its economic success has resulted from its own individual initiatives at the local level. The Northern League has, however, captured a center-right electorate affected by the secularization and economic transformation of Italy.[18] Thus, it is far from a traditional right-wing constituency. As Renato Mannheimer notes, "various 'cores' exist within the Lega, differing in their socioeconomic components and in some of their attitudes and opinions, but to a large extent united in their negative attitude toward the traditional parties." Over time however, there is a "progressive increase in the percentage of *Lega* voters considering themselves center-right."[19]

The Northern League mobilized this electorate by appealing to some of the subcultural elements once exploited by the old Christian Democratic party. As Umberto Bossi noted, "the breakdown of the traditional relationship between the Christian Democratic party and the Catholic church explains, in part, the success of the League in Catholic strongholds of Lombardy and Veneto." He claims that the League "has assumed many of the values close to Catholic voters, such as defense of the family, education, and against the myth of money and material success."[20]

In his speeches, Bossi speaks of lost community values and identity, and in his autobiography he points out that this decline of community identity shaped his own political philosophy. While Bossi nostalgically regards traditional Italian village life, he emphasizes that Italians cannot return to the past. They must secure their present local and urban identities within a well-managed regional entity. Furthermore, this entity must respect local traditions and interests better than the centralized nation-state. The League's ideological appeal is not based only on lost community life. The movement's appeal is also tied to Bossi's ability to blame the crisis of northern community life on "outside elements." The us/them dichotomy so typical of populist movements contrasts Lombards with the corruption and parasitism of the south and Rome's politicians.

Bossi's movement successfully blends several distinct issues that concern northern Italians.[21] The first is the crisis of confidence in Italy's governing institutions. He has used the alienation many Italians feel for the dominant parties to cast the Lombardy movement as the antithesis of party politics.

In his speeches, Bossi likes to point out that the League is not a party but a popular movement that embodies Lombard's needs and demands. Second, the League blames all of Italy's problems on corrupt politicians in Rome. Moreover, the misallocation of resources and the poor quality of public services results from the domination of the Italian bureaucracy by southern Italians. This bureaucracy drains tax revenue from the north and redistributes it toward the south.[22]

Until the right addresses the source of appeal of the Northern League, it will remain divided. Bossi's movement brought down the Berlusconi government and played a central role in preventing the right from winning the 1996 elections. Clearly, some of the center-right's electorate still values a party that claims to reflect local identities and interests. Neither *Forza Italia,* the smaller Christian Democratic parties, nor the National Alliance succeeded in attracting this electorate during the last elections. Both *Forza Italia* and the National Alliance overestimated their ability to take these voters away from Bossi. They assumed that earlier evidence of the decline of the Northern League, based on regional elections, would ensure their success in the North. The League, however, proved to be a spoiler.

The Centrist Right: Berlusconi's Forza Italia

Forza Italia's unexpected victory in the 1994 elections demonstrated that the center-right electorate was literally up for grabs. Silvio Berlusconi successfully created an electoral movement in merely a few months before the elections; nevertheless, his movement came in first with 22 percent of the vote. Several factors explain *Forza Italia's* rapid success: First, the personality of the movement's leader; second, the vacuum created in the political center with the collapse of the DC; third, the media and marketing services at Berlusconi's disposal; and finally, the absence of a competitive rival on the right.[23]

While personalities have always played an important role in Italy's political system, Berlusconi's personalization of a political movement was unprecedented. Voters identify *Forza Italia* with Berlusconi. Without him, the movement has no independent status; it has no historical roots; and, it still lacks a stable organizational hierarchy that could survive without Berlusconi's presence. Between January and March 1994, the staff of Publitalia, the advertising affiliate of Berlusconi's television company, organized throughout Italy about 13,000–14,000 clubs (80 persons a club). These clubs served as the basis of the electoral campaign of Berlusconi.

In theory, the clubs are implanted locally and are connected to a national association of clubs. This association, in turn, has close links with FI. *Forza Italia* establishes the political line for the clubs and also selects the movement's candidates. The clubs are directly subordinate to a national committee dominated by Berlusconi. They enjoy very little autonomy and are not sufficiently structured to serve as a solid party institutional base.[24] Thus, three-year-old *Forza Italia* remains an effective electoral organization at the national level, but lacks roots at the local and regional levels. The repeated failures of *Forza Italia* in local and regional elections largely resulted from the party's weak infrastructures at these levels.[25] As Leonardo Morlino notes, "in this poorly institutionalized party the experience of being in office and the conflicts with its coalition partners have brought internal dissent and clearly distinguishable groups, though not factions. As an additional consequence, the MPs have become key figures in this organization, linking the centralized undisputed leadership with the local level of the clubs."[26] Berlusconi has had only limited success with his efforts to move beyond the personalization of *Forza Italia*.[27]

Forza Italia's electoral strength shows in national elections, with the media playing a central role. Berlusconi's electorate relies heavily on television, especially the television stations he owns, as their primary source of information. This is particularly true for the party's core supporters, housewives. They are not especially active in politics and rely heavily on television for their political information. Overall, *Forza Italia's* electorate derived from the conservative center (see table 5.4). They see themselves as moderates on most issues; however, they are more hostile to the left than to the extreme right. Berlusconi succeeded in attracting a moderately well-educated but economically well-off stratum of the population that had been alienated from the Christian Democratic party for some time. With the secularization of Italian society, this electorate no longer felt tied to the party because of any salient identification with Catholicism. As their alienation grew, this electorate increasingly divided its votes between the Republican, Liberal, and Socialist parties. Berlusconi attracted them to *Forza Italia* by making claims for an efficient and effective government, for the lowering of taxes, and for rewarding individual initiative. That Berlusconi accomplished none of this when he came to power influenced the perception of centrist voters in the 1996 elections that the center-left won.

While *Forza Italia's* success at the polls catapulted Berlusconi into power, his government lasted less than nine months. From its inception, the government was weakened by opposition from the center-right, led by the smaller Christian Democratic parties and the Northern League. The main tension in the coalition government existed between the Northern League and the neofascist National Alliance. The Northern League attacked the AN as a statist and centralizing party, out simply to take over the state long dominated by the Christian Democrats, rather than to reform it. Berlusconi's failure to establish an effective *modus vivendi* between the neofascists and the Northern League undermined a fragile reconstitution of the Italian right.[28] The refusal of the Northern League to govern with AN deprived the right a portion of its electorate. More important, in the 1994 elections the presence of several different right-wing candidates from the same district allowed the left to win.[29] Thus, the divisions on the right were more costly than those on the left (see table 5.6).

The Neofascist Right

The other major component of the Italian right is the National Alliance (AN). In some ways, the success of AN in the 1994 elections and the subsequent entry into the Berlusconi government is more surprising than *Forza Italia's* unexpected rise to power. Unlike *Forza Italia,* the core of AN, the Italian Social Movement (MSI), has deep roots in Italian history. Since its creation in 1946, the MSI has been on the extreme right of the Italian political map. While at different times it has flirted with legitimizing itself by establishing closer ties with the Christian Democrats, it remained strongly attached to its fascist tradition. In fact, MSI directly descended from the defeated fascist movement of the prewar era. It was founded by individuals formerly active in the Republic of Salÿ, a more radical and violent element of the Italian fascist tradition. At its inception, MSI embodied the

Table 5.6 Parliamentary Votes by Party Coalitions, 1996

Electoral Alliances	1996
Left	
PDS	21.1
PPI–Prodi–UD	6.8
PRC	8.6
Dini List	4.3
Total	40.7
Right	
Forza Italia	20.6
National Alliance	15.7
CCD–CDU	5.8
Total	42.1
Unaffiliated	
Lega Nord	10.1
Verdi (Greens)	2.5
M.S. Fiamma (Flames)	0.9

Source: The Italian Ministry of Interior.

anticapitalist, antibourgeois, and national-socialist principles of the radical/popular form of Italian fascism.[30] Apparently, the founders of MSI still considered Italian fascism a revolutionary movement.[31]

Over the next five decades, MSI would oscillate between being a radical anti-system movement on the extreme right to a right-wing party willing to make compromises with those in power. The dualism derived, in part, from the party's fascist ideological tradition and its potential electoral appeal. Contrary to extreme right-wing parties in other western European states, MSI remained attracted to a segment of the Italian electorate. Less than two years after the end of the second world war, MSI was an extremely competitive political force in the south.[32] It drew support from both the monarchists and Christian Democratic supporters. In the north, however, MSI had a much more difficult time inserting itself as a legitimate political actor into the postwar political landscape. As a consequence, the party would be more radical and violent in the north than in the south. In other words, "MSI reflected its environmental contexts: militant, semiclandestine and dedicated to extra-legal activity in the north, while it functioned as a pro-monarchist and pro-church force in the south."[33]

Throughout the 1950s, the right wing of the Christian Democratic party sought to integrate MSI into the political system by bringing it into the government as a coalition partner. These efforts failed because of left-wing opposition from within the DC and from radicals within MSI. Nevertheless, in the south, the two parties often worked closely together. With the ideological polarization of Italy in the 1960s, however, MSI intensified its anti-system position. It presented itself as the bulwark against the decadence of modern Italian society and against the communist threat. In this period, MSI retreated into its radical fascist identity. Also, it became implicated in the wave of right-wing violence that struck Italy in the 1970s. Many saw MSI as a dangerous fascist movement that rejected the legitimacy of Italian democracy.[34] The radicalization of MSI isolated the party. Its links with the DC in the south dissolved, and the party increasingly attacked both the Communist party and Christian Democrats. The ideological radicalization of the party contributed to its electoral decline. Throughout most of the 1970s, MSI found itself on the defensive and torn internally over its ideological identity. The leader of the party, Giorgio Almirante, attempted to mediate between the moderate and radical elements within the party, with only limited success.

In 1977, he backed Gianfranco Fini as the new leader of the fascist youth movement. In doing so, Almirante was grooming Fini as his successor.[35] He saw Fini as representing a moderate and less radical form of fascism. Over the next decade, Fini worked closely with Almirante to bring the party out of its isolation. As planned, Fini succeeded Almirante upon his death in

1988. Despite being Almirante's designated successor, Fini had a difficult time in containing the more radical elements within the party. At the party's 1990 congress in Rimini, Fini was replaced by Pino Rauti, a long-time advocate of a radical antibourgeois and antidemocratic ideology for the party. Initially, it appeared that MSI would remain an isolated party, despite the changes taking place on the left after the fall of the Berlin Wall.

Rauti's stewardship of the party, however, lasted only nine months. After a disastrous showing in regional elections, Fini was reelected as leader of the party. Fini retook the reins of MSI when the broader political context in Italy was changing. The growing crisis of the Christian Democratic party and its eventual collapse created new opportunities for the party. Almost overnight, the electorate on the right had lost the party it had voted for since the mid-1950s. While the MSI had become increasingly isolated since the 1960s, it still had roots and elected deputies in the south. Moreover, after the collapse of the DC, a number of former Christian Democrats joined the party. Therefore, the party logically sought the voters on the right, particularly in the south.

MSI profited more than any other party from the collapse of the old political system, without undergoing any major internal changes of its own. Unlike the transformation of the Italian Communist party into the Democratic Party of the Left (PDS) and a painful break with its past, the MSI moved out of its political ghetto without renouncing its fascist tradition. Indeed, the only significant change the party made leading up to the 1994 elections was its name. Fini transformed the party from the MSI to the National Alliance, claiming that the MSI was now part of a larger political formation of the center-right. As Piero Ignazi and others have shown, however, the AN made no break with its fascist past; it made no significant change in its militants; and, it did not consistently denounce fascism as an antidemocratic ideology.[36]

Nevertheless, in the 1994 elections AN received nearly 14 percent of the vote, and more significantly, its electoral support was not exclusively concentrated in the south. It had become a national neofascist party, although still drawing disproportionate support from the south. Ignazi outlines some of the reasons for this success:

> The reasons for the success of the National Alliance can be traced to a number of long-term and short-term developments. The long-term factors are the decline in the sharp ideological divisions within Italy between left and right and the historicism of Italian fascism. The short-term factors are the crisis of the partitocrazia system; the media image of Gianfranco Fini as a moderate; and, the acceptance by Berlusconi of MSI as a legitimate political actor.[37]

Beyond these elements, AN-MSI provided a home to an element of the Italian electorate that strongly identified with the right, while having lost the right-wing factions within the DC as their point of reference (see table 5.4). For many years, the AN had oscillated between becoming an acceptable party on the far right or remaining an anti-system political force mired in nostalgia regarding its fascist heritage. With the collapse of the Christian Democrats, a segment of the Italian electorate was now available to the party that shared many of its ideological positions without partaking in its nostalgia. Thus, the AN has been able to become a viable party on the right because a significant segment of the Italian electorate harbor few fears of its fascist past.

While AN-MSI success contributed to the rapid mainstreaming of a virtually unreformed neofascist party, the lack of reform later proved to be an albatross for the party. The relative failure of AN-MSI in the 1996 national elections is due, in part, to the party's inability to attract more centrist voters and the draining away of votes on the right by the dissident MSI party.[38]

The 1996 Elections and the Defeat of the Italian Right

The 1994 elections created the illusion of the Italian right reconstituting itself amid the ruins of the Christian Democratic party. The success of the smaller Christian Democratic parties, the Northern League, the neofascist National Alliance, and Berlusconi's *Forza Italia* appeared to lay the foundation for a gradual development of a coherent formation on the right. This was not to be. The divisions within the center-right electoral alliance ultimately kept the center-right electorate from coalescing into a coherent political bloc.

The divisions resulted from several different sources. First, the smaller Christian Democratic parties apparently viewed their electoral alliance with Berlusconi as a prelude to them absorbing *Forza Italia* and its electorate, rather than the other way around. Though the CDU and CCD garnered less than 8 percent of the vote between them, their leaders vainly believed that their political formations would be the basis of a reconstruction of a Christian Democratic center-right. This is somewhat surprising since they draw most of their support from an electorate that is over 60 and still strongly identifies with Catholicism. In other words, CCD-CDU have been moderately successful in reconstituting the core Catholic constituency of the former DC; however, they have to share this electorate with PPI and, to a lesser extent, with FI.[39] In any case, neither party has shown any capacity to replace FI as the main centrist party on the right. Their significance lies in the fact that neither *Forza Italia* nor the National Alliance can govern without them.

Second, *Forza Italia* underestimated how hostile the Northern League felt toward the National Alliance. Even more significantly, both the FI and AN underestimated the nature of the electoral support for the Northern League. They assumed that Bossi's electorate would switch to them. Berlusconi and Fini believed that Bossi would be penalized for causing the collapse of the center-right government in 1995. Soon after the League left the government and threw its support behind the "technical government" led by Lamberto Dini, survey data suggested that the Northern League was in decline. On closer analysis of the data, it seems that the Northern League lost ground in larger cities such as Milan to *Forza Italia,* but maintained its support in small urban centers throughout the northeast.[40]

Consequently, Bossi's political movement increased the level of competition on the right in the north. As Giacomo Sani states, "Whereas in 1994 almost three-fourth of the districts could have been classified as 'safe' (a margin of 15 percent or more), in 1996 almost half of the northern arenas would have deserved the label of 'marginal' (margins of less than 5 percent)."[41] Essentially, the *Lega* took votes away from center-right candidates by creating a three-way race, thus helping center-left candidates.

The tensions and contradictions prevented any one party on the right from gaining an hegemonic position in any way reminiscent of the old Christian Democratic party. Even more significant for the 1996 elections, the divisions on the right and their hostility to the government in power, essentially a centrist government, pushed them further to the right without leading to an organized political force on the right.

When the half-hearted attempt by FI and PDS to come to an agreement on a new constitution without first calling for new elections failed, the Italian right went into the April 1996 elections with some serious handicaps. First, the Northern League refused any coalition with the right this time. Thus, unlike the past, any votes that the League received would be at the expense of the right coalition. Second, the decisions by Berlusconi to seek a constitutional agreement with the PDS resulted in a temporary break between him and Fini, thus creating some confusion among their electorates. Finally, the decision to provoke the fall of the "technical government," despite its relative popularity, and the often hostile attacks on the government, pushed Dini into an alliance with the left. Dini's centrist formation cost the right between 2 to 3 percent of the electorate.[42]

The Future of the Italian Right

That the Italian right lost the 1996 elections only two years after their triumph in the 1994 national elections indicates that they were unable to overcome their divisions (see table 5.6). In addition to their internal divisions as an electoral coalition, the right miscalculated the effect of a broader center-left alliance. Berlusconi and Fini assumed that with the support of the small Christian Democratic partners they had a sufficient center-right base to win the elections. They were wrong. Bluntly put, the right was out-maneuvered by the left. In particular, Massimo D'Alema, leader of the PDS, succeeded in putting together what appears to be a more stable center-left coalition than had been the case with Berlusconi. With Bossi's decision to eschew any electoral alliances, the left did not have to worry about forming a government with an unpredictable partner. Also, the left could count on the League taking votes away from the right, which is what happened.

The right's defeat, however, was not only due to their internal divisions and strategic miscalculations. It also stemmed from the right's lack of ideological coherency. Quite literally, the right was all over the place.

On one hand, Berlusconi sought to champion FI and the right as the supporters of free enterprise and lower taxes. While he was prime minister, however, he did little to promote these principles. On the other hand, the National Alliance appeared to advocate the continuation of a centralized state apparatus with extensive involvement in the Italian economy. As part of the government, Fini wasted little time in getting individuals close to the party appointed to important parastatal bodies. Even before coming to power, the party had adopted a recalcitrant position toward privatization.[43] Indeed, Bossi argued that one of the key reasons the League left the coalition was that Fini's statist approach to government conflicted with the League's federalist position.

While all of the parties on the center-right supported European integration and the Maastricht Treaty, the AN-MSI expressed reservations about the loss of national sovereignty and some of the neoliberal policies of the community. In particular, AN-MSI feared that European Union demands to further liberalize the Italian economy, accelerate the process of privatization, and dismantle much of the welfare state would hurt its electorate, especially in the south.

Moreover, once in power, the center-right coalition proved incapable of developing a coherent strategy to reform the Italian state, cut public spending, and reduce the nation's huge public debt. This failure arose not only because of mobilization on the left; it was also due to opposition from supporters of the center-right. Pensioners, in particular, viewed Berlusconi's proposed budget as an attack on their standard of living. After a series of mass protests throughout Italy in 1995, the government backed down on many of its proposed reforms and cuts. In this respect, the Italian center-right was not able to unify around a set of neoliberal policies.[44] Indeed, many of these policies undermined an already fragile center-right coalition.

Whether or not the center-right will come to power again in Italy in the short-term depends on how long Romono Prodi's center-left government can stay together. Like Berlusconi's center-right government, Prodi's center-left government has its internal and ideological divisions. In the lower house, he relies on the Communist party for votes. Within his government, he has to consider the centrist positions of Lamberto Dini. So far, these divisions have not provoked a crisis; however, it could still happen. Without the collapse of the left, the right is likely to be in opposition for the next five years.

This presents a number of challenges to them. First, it is far from clear how effective FI is as an opposition party, since it still lacks a solid and effective institutional base outside of Parliament and beyond Berlusconi's personal appeal. Second, at some point, the uneasy relationship between Berlusconi and Fini will probably come to a showdown. While there have only been minor skirmishes so far, there is an implicit conflict over who is the leader of the right. Third, the small centrist parties might be tempted at some point to merge with the centrist parties on the left. If this happens, it is unclear what the effect will be on the right and for Prodi's government. Finally, the right needs to develop a more coherent ideological agenda that effectively mediates between the different constituencies that they represent and, in the future, the ones they would like to attract. This will be difficult since territorialization of voting will not disappear any time soon. Since social scientists are good at predicting events *post factotum,* I will wait until things have transpired before providing an assessment of what has happened to the Italian right in the future.

Notes

1. Gianfranco Pasquino and Patrick McCarthy, eds., *The End of Post-War Politics in Italy: The Landmark 1992 Elections* (Boulder, CO: Westview Press, 1993); Leonardo Morlino, "Crisis of Parties and Change of Party System in Italy," *Party Politics* 2:1 (1996): 5–30.
2. Piero Ignazi, *Dal Pci al Pds* (Bologna: il Mulino, 1989). The decision to change its name and move away from its communist past resulted in a split. Members of the party who still identified with the communist tradition and ideology created a breakaway party—*Rifondazione Communista.*
3. Richard S. Katz, "Electoral Reform and the Transformation of Party Politics in Italy," *Party Politics* 2:1 (1996): 31–53.
4. Stefano Bartolini and Roberto D'Alimonte, "Les Elections Parlementaires de 1994 en Italie: Competition majoritaire et realignement partisan," *Revue Française de Science Politique* 45:6 1995): 915–953.
5. Paolo Farneti, *The Italian Party System, 1945–1980* (New York: St. Martin's Press, 1985.)

6. Robert Leonardi and Douglas A. Wertman, *Italian Christian Democracy: The Politics of Dominance* (New York: St. Martin's Press, 1989).

7. Giorgio Galli, *Mezzo Secolo di DC: 1943–1993 da De Gasperi a Mario Segni* (Milano: Rizzoli, 1993).

8. Mario Caciagli, "The Mass Clientelism Party and Conservative Politics: Christian Democracy in Southern Italy," pp. 288–9, in *Conservative Politics in Western Europe,* Zig Layton, ed., (New York: St. Martin's Press, 1977); also, see Alan S. Zuckerman, *The Politics of Faction: Christian Democratic Rule in Italy* (New Haven, CT: Yale University Press, 1979).

9. Robert Leonardi, "Political Power Linkages in Italy: The Nature of the Christian Democratic Party Organization," p. 26, in *Political Parties and Linkages: A Comparative Perspective,* Kay Lawson, ed. (New Haven, CT: Yale University Press, 1980).

10. Edmondo Berselli, "The Sunset of Christian Democracy," pp. 237–238, in *Deconstructing Italy: Italy in the Nineties,* Salvatore Sechi, ed. (Berkeley, CA: University of California Press, 1995).

11. Roberta Cartocci, *Lega e chiesa: L'Italia in cerca di integrazione* (Bologna: il Mulino, 1994).

12. Galli, *Mezzo Secolo di DC . . . ,* pp. 35–40.

13. Ibid., pp. 11–12.

14. Bartolini and D'Alimonte, "Les Elections Parlementaires de 1994 . . . ," pp. 915–916.

15. Roberto Cartocci, 1987. "Otto risposte a un problema: la divisione dell'Italia in zone politicamente omogenee," *Polis,* 1 (1987): 481–514.

16. Gabriele Calvi and Andrea Vannucci, *L'elettore sconosciuto: Analisi socioculturale e segmentazione degli orientamenti politici nel 1994* (Bologna: il Mulino, 1995), p. 52.

17. Ibid.

18. Cartocci, *Fra Lega et Chiesa . . . ,* p. 6.

19. Renato Mannheimer, "Questions and Answers About the Lega Nord," in *Deconstructing Italy: Italy in the Nineties,* Salvatore Sechi, ed., (Berkeley, CA: University of California Press, 1995).

20. Umberto Bossi, *Vento del nord: le mia Lega, la mia vita* (Milano: Sperling & Kupfer Editori, 1992), p. 190.

21. Carlo E. Ruzza and O. Schmidtke, "Roots of Success of the Lega Lombarda: Mobilization Dynamics and the Media," *West European Politics* 16:2 (1993): 1–25.

22. Bossi, *Vento del nord . . . ,*" pp. 192–195.

23. Renato Mannheimer, "Forza Italia," in *Milano a Roma: Guida all'Italia elettorale del 1994,* Ilvo Diamanti and Renato Mannheimer, eds., (Roma: Donzelli Editore, 1994), pp. 37–38.

24. Patrick McCarthy, "Forza Italia: The Overwhelming Success and the Consequent Problems of a Virtual Party," *Italian Politics: The Year of the Tycoon* (Bologna: Cattaneo 1996), pp. 43–45.

25. Further evidence of FI inability to mobilize an electorate at the regional and local levels was demonstrated in the regional elections in Sicily. These elections occurred two months after the national elections. FI had done quite well in Sicily during the national elections but was overtaken by the CCD and CDU in the special regional elections there. See *Corriere della sera,* "Sicilia al Polo, ma crolla Forza Italia," June 18, 1996.

26. Morlino, "Crisis of Parties . . . ," p. 16.

27. Marco Maraffi, "Forza Italia dal governo all'opposizione," *Political in Italia* (Bologna: Il Mulino, 1996).

28. Richard S. Katz and Peter Mair, "Changing Models of Party Organization and Party Democracy: The Emergence of the Cartel Party," *Party Politics* 1 (1995): 5–28.

29. Bartolini and D'Alimonte, pp. 933–936.

30. Marcello Veneziani, *La rivoluzione conservatrice in Italia* (Varese: Sugarco Edizioni, 1995).

31. Piero Ignazi, *Postfascisti: Dal movimento sociale italiano ad Alleanza nazionale* (Bologna: il Mulino,1994), p. 11; Marco Tarchi, *Dal Msi ad An* (Bologna: il Mulino, 1997).

32. Roberto Chiarini, *Destra italiana dall'Unitè d'Italia a Alleanza Nazionale* (Venezia: Marsilio Editori, 1995), pp. 94–95.

33. Ignazi, *Postfascisti . . . ,* p. 19.

34. Ibid., pp. 34–38.

35. Goffredo Locatelli and Daniele Martini, *Fini: La biografia del presidente di AN* (Milano: Longanesi, 1994) p. 52.

36. This does not mean that MSI has not undergone important changes in relation to its fascist past. It has. See Piero Ignazi and Collette Ysmal, "New and old extreme right parties: The Front National and the Italian Social Movement," *European Journal of Political Research* 22 (1993): 101–121.

37. Ignazi, *Postfascisti . . . ,* pp. 105.

38. *La Repubblica,* "Ma dov'e finita la destra sociale," April 24, 1996.

39. Calvi and Vannucci *L'elettore sconosciuto . . . ,* p. 18.

40. *La Repubblica,* April 23, 1996, p. 4.

41. Giacomo Sani, "From Berlusconi to Prodi: Electoral Alliances and Voting Behavior in Italy 1994–1996." Paper Presented at the Annual Meeting of The American Political Science Association, San Francisco, August 1996, p. 8.

42. Istituto CIRM, *L'opinione degli Italiani: Annuario 1996 attraerso i sondaggi* (Milano: Sperling & Kupfer Editori, 1995).

43. Orazio Carbini, "Fame di sottogoverno a destra," *Il Mondo* 18:25 (1994): 23–24; Gennaro Schettino, "La Destra all'assalto dell'Iri," *La Repubblica,* July 26, 1994, p. 38.

44. Patrick McCarthy, *The Crisis of the Italian State: From the Origins of the Cold War to the Fall of Berlusconi* (New York: St. Martin's Press, 1995), p. 175.

CHAPTER SIX

Ups and Downs on the Right: The VVD and CDA in the Netherlands

Galen A. Irwin

If it were up to the political parties themselves, there would probably be no chapter on the Netherlands in this volume. No party advertises itself as a conservative party or would wish to be called one. The term conservative has a strong negative ring to it and in the Netherlands it is virtually synonymous with "old-fashioned," "outmoded," "cramped," and "reactionary."[1] The *Volkspartij voor Vrijheid en Democratie,* generally known as the VVD, and translated into English as the Liberal party, is the most concerned not to have this label applied to it. In 1990 the Telders Foundation, the think-tank arm of the party, held a symposium in which a number of leading intellectuals were invited to discuss and debate the characteristics and merits of liberalism and conservatism and their importance for the Netherlands in general and for the VVD in particular.[2] Frits Bolkestein, who was later to become the party leader, drew a distinction between conservatives and socialists on the one hand and liberals on the other:

> Socialists and conservatives hold the collective in high regard. They place little value on the revolutionary power of the principle of competition, which respects no societal position. Liberals wish to raise people to be competitive individuals who find their way in the world and are able to resist the state. For the former stability is the ideal, for the latter dynamism.[3]

If conservatism is seen as a political method, characterized by incrementalism and "trial and error," then, according to Klaas Groeneveld,[4] all the major Dutch parties are conservative. If conservatism, however, is associated with a feeling that things might have been better in the past, then certainly the VVD is conservative when it wishes to improve society by undoing negative developments. But the Christian Democrats also often evidence a desire to return to a more "caring society," structured as it was in the 1950s, whereas the social-democrats long for the income distribution policies of the 1970s[5] and rue the destruction of the social welfare state.

If conservatism is defined in terms of the conservation of norms and values, the VVD can hardly be viewed as a conservative party, according to Groeneveld. With such a definition, it would be better to call the Christian Democratic Appeal (CDA) the conservative party in the Netherlands. It is, however, unlikely that Christian Democrats would be pleased with this conclusion. How Christian democracy is related to conservatism is also a matter of debate. Lucardie states that outsiders generally attempt to reduce Christian democracy to some more familiar concept: a variety of conservatism, a variety of liberalism, a sort of Christian socialism, or a synthesis of these.[6] Insiders tend to reject such attempts to classify it in terms of other ideologies and see it as a separate and equal type. In the Netherlands there have at times been groups that see themselves as progressive Christian Democrats, but few would ever call themselves conservative.

How then are we to conclude that these parties should be included in a volume on conservative parties? A more fruitful approach might be to think in terms of the left-right dimension. However, a new difficulty immediately arises. Although it may be difficult to define "conservatism," it at least has some substantive content. The terms "left" and "right" are essentially devoid of such content and must be filled in according to the context.[7] When members of the Second Chamber of Parliament were themselves asked in a 1990 survey to indicate what they meant by the term, 47 percent indicated that "right" meant conservative, whereas 18 percent said it meant retaining differences in incomes and uneven distributions, and 16 percent equated it with free-market principles.[8] Without going into a lengthy discussion of whether one can equate the right with conservative, it would seem that they are sufficiently similar to examine the parties in terms of left-right placement.

We must recognize, however, that remnants of a second definition of the distinction between left and right can still be found. In the nineteenth century the right was defined in terms of those drawing their ideological inspiration from the Bible (in the Netherlands called "confessional.") Even today evidence of this interpretation of the terms can be found. In the same survey, 8 percent of the MP's defined "right" as confessional and in the 1994 Dutch National Election Study, 6 percent of the responses defined "right" in terms of religion or religious parties. Thus, though dying in importance, this dimension still exists in the Netherlands. Nevertheless, it remains important, since it is on this dimension that the CDA is clearly the party of the right.

Although at times it can prove useful to maintain a distinction between these two definitions of left-right, it cannot be denied that both the electorate and members of parliament are quite comfortable with placing themselves and the various parties on a single left-right scale. Figure 6.1 indicates how the members of the Second Chamber and the electorate place the various parties. The values are average placements and are subject to a number of cautions, but do provide useful information. With possibly minor exceptions concerning the ordering of the small religious parties, both MPs and voters are in agreement over the ordering of the parties on the left-right scale. The Center democrats are on the far right, followed by the cluster of small religious parties. Because of their small size and their extreme positions, they are not considered in this chapter. For the larger parties, the CDA is placed somewhat to the right of center, with the VVD more to the right. This provides reasonable justification for including both of these parties in the discussion here.

History and Development

It has been said that conservatism in the Netherlands died on March 13, 1848. At least it was on this day that King William II admitted that he changed from being ultraconservative to ultraliberal. Fearing that the revolutions that were sweeping Europe would arrive in his kingdom, the king decided to seize the initiative and commissioned a revision of the constitution.[9] The new constitution marked the triumph of liberalism by establishing the predominance of Parliament over the monarchy. It introduced the doctrine of the infallibility of the king, but coupled it with the principle of ministerial responsibility to Parliament. The Lower House (Second Chamber) was henceforth to be elected directly and obtained new powers, such as the right of amendment. Annual budgets were introduced and basic rights were extended.[10] Liberal attitudes on religion also made it possible for the Catholic Church to reestablish its hierarchy in 1853. One can therefore hardly conclude that the current VVD has its roots in conservatism or conservative principles.

For that matter, neither does the CDA, whose roots lie in the Catholic and Calvinist emancipation movements of the nineteenth century. Since the sixteenth century, Catholics had had second-class status in the

Figure 6.1   Placement of Political Parties by Members of Second Chamber (1990)

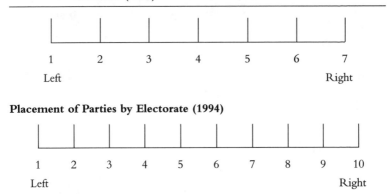

Placement of Parties by Electorate (1994)

Table 1.   Placement of Parties on Left–Right Scale

Party	Placement by Members of Second Chamber (7 point scale)	Placement by the Electorate (10 point scale)
GreenLeft	1.5	2.62
PvdA	2.7	3.72
D66	3.8	4.94
CDA	4.9	6.45
VVD	5.7	7.25
SGP	6.7	7.52
GPV	6.2	7.59
RPF	6.6	7.50
CD	6.9	8.11

Netherlands. Although Catholicism was never forbidden outright, the Church hierarchy was disbanded and many of the outward symbols, such as religious processions and clerical dress, were not allowed. At times, mass could only be held in "hidden" churches. Catholics were not accorded equal political rights and often could not hold public office.

The Dutch Reformed Church was the dominant religion in the country, but within this church there were those who felt frustrated and thwarted socially, politically, and religiously. Many were craftsmen or shopkeepers; *kleine luyden* ("little people") as they were called, were organized into a major emancipation movement. One of their strongest leaders, Abraham Kuyper, organized the first mass political party in the Netherlands in 1879.

It is in the choice of the name for this party, the Anti-Revolutionary Party (ARP), that one might see conservative elements within the movement. The party rejected the principle from the French Revolution that sovereignty belonged to the people. "Against the Revolution, the Gospels," the earlier leader G. Groen van Prinsterer had written. Sovereignty was given by God and could best be exercised through the hereditary monarchy of the House of Orange. Disagreement within this party over the expansion of suffrage led to the establishment of the Christian Historical Union (CHU) in 1908.

Not only did Kuyper organize a political party, he brought groups that had broken away from the Dutch Reformed Church together in the *Gereformeerde Churches*, set up a newspaper, and founded the Free University. Catholics followed the lead and also established organizations for their believers in virtually all sectors of society—schools, media, trade unions, employers, health care, etc. With the addition of socialist organizations and numerous neutral organizations, the basis had been laid for the segmentation of Dutch society that has been called the *verzuiling* (literally, "pillarization"). The segments provided organizations for virtually all aspects of life from the cradle to the grave, such that members needed to have little contact with each other.[11] The related political system has been called by Lijphart "consociational democracy."[12]

The four pillars and the five associated political parties dominated social and political life through the first half of the twentieth century. The Liberals declined in importance after the introduction of universal suffrage in 1917, but were saved from extinction by the change from a district system of election to proportional representation. The Catholic party and the two Protestant parties dominated the political scene and at times together held a majority in Parliament.

Events in the 1960s led to a reversal of fortune. For reasons that are still not fully understood, "election winds"[13] swept through the Netherlands and led to major losses of votes for the Catholic party and the CHU. Discussions were begun that eventually led to the establishment of a single Christian Democratic Appeal (CDA) in 1980.[14] The merger stemmed the loss of votes for several elections, but in 1994 the new party suffered dramatic losses and for the first time since the introduction of universal suffrage did not participate in the new cabinet.

One party that profited from the decline of the religious parties was the VVD. A young, dynamic new leader, Hans Wiegel, made the party more popular, but he also made it more conservative. He presented a kind of populist conservatism that helped the party jump from 10.3 percent to 17.9 percent of the vote between 1971 and 1977. In 1994 it also made major gains and at the provincial elections of 1995 gained the largest percentage of the vote. Table 6.1 presents the electoral results for all parliamentary elections since 1977.

Given this short description of the major political parties, it is hardly surprising that until the 1970s, voting behavior could best be understood in terms of a "structured model."[15] This model was first proposed by Arend Lijphart[16] and relates social groups to the vote. About 85 percent of Catholics supported the Catholic party. Almost that many of the *Gereformeerde* church members voted for the Anti-Revolutionary Party, and most of the rest supported the Protestant splinter parties. Church-going members of the Dutch Reformed Church supported the CHU. Among the less and nonreligious, votes split heavily along class lines, with the working class supporting the Labor Party and the middle class (to a lesser extent) supporting the VVD. Lijphart estimated that in 1956, 72 percent of the electorate cast its votes along these lines, and in 1977 this percentage was still 52 percent, but by 1994 it could account for only 36 percent.[17] This decline in importance can be seen in the figures in table 6.2.

Party Organization

Despite a lack of legislation regulating political parties, there is considerable similarity in the organizational structure of most Dutch political parties, which tends to parallel the territorial structure of the Dutch state. The Netherlands is organized in some 700 municipalities, 12 provinces, and the national government. At each of these levels, representatives are elected to legislative bodies. Complicating matters somewhat is the fact that elections for the Second Chamber are carried out in 19 electoral districts, which thus do not parallel the provinces. The parties therefore tend to have organizations that relate to both the province and these electoral districts.

For both the CDA and the VVD, the basis for the party organization is the local party affiliate. In most cases the geographical area covered by the affiliate will coincide with the municipality. However, when a municipality consists of a number of villages, these units may coincide with the lowest party level. In larger cities, there may also be subdivisions, corresponding to recognized areas within the city. Above the municipal affiliates, both parties also have organizations at the provincial and electoral district level. Representatives from the local level are selected for these levels, who in turn select representatives to the national Party Council. The Party Council of the CDA is the highest decision-making body of the party, having essentially reduced the Party Congress to an organ for discussion and motivation of party workers. The Party Council of the VVD serves as the highest decision-making body during the periods between General Meetings of the party.[18] Decision making here should be seen as

Table 6.1 Election Results 1977–1994 (in percentage of votes cast)

	1977	1981	1982	1986	1989	1994
CDA	31.9	30.8	29.4	34.6	35.3	22.2
VVD	17.9	17.3	23.1	17.4	14.6	20.0
PvdA	33.8	28.3	30.4	33.3	31.9	24.0
D66	5.4	11.1	4.3	6.1	7.9	15.5
Other left	4.3	6.7	6.5	3.1	4.1	3.5
Small religious right (SGP, GPV, RPF)	3.1	4.0	4.2	3.6	4.1	4.8
Extreme right	.8	.1	.8	.4	.9	2.5
Other	2.6	1.8	1.4	1.5	1.2	7.6
Total	99.8	100.1	100.1	100.0	100.0	100.1

Table 6.2 Voting in Accordance with Structured Model of Voting Behavior

	1956	1968	1977	1986	1989	1994
Catholics (practicing) voting Catholic or CDA	95	72	66	66	72	52
Dutch Reformed (practicing) voting CHU or CDA	63	55	52	58	53	43
Gereformeerd (practicing) voting ARP or CDA	93	78	75	58	59	56
Secular working class voting PvdA	68	65	67	60	63	41
Secular middle class voting VVD	32	25	30	28	23	30
Total voting structured model	72	60	52	44	42	36
N	982	1491	1265	1255	1385	1725

Sources: 1956 and 1968, Lijphart, 1974, p. 250; 1977 through 1994, Dutch National Election Study

setting out the general policy lines for the party. These party councils can meet between one and ten times per year.[19]

Both parties have bodies that meet more often and are more concerned with the day-to-day activities of the party. A national party administrative board (*partijbestuur*) is elected by intermediate level organizations. Finally, a party chairman and the executive board (*dagelijks bestir*) are elected.

Both parties hold national conventions, called the General Meeting for the VVD and the Party Congress of the CDA. This meeting is more important for the VVD, for it is here that internal policy debates are held. The Party Congress for the CDA has recently resembled American party conventions in that the selection of the leader is confirmed rather than decided and the meeting is more important for rallying the party workers than for actual substantive debate. The delegates for these conventions are selected in the local divisions of the parties.

Ideological Background

"Liberalism strives for the greatest possible freedom for the individual," begins Andreas A. M. Kinneging in his search for the philosophical bases for liberalism. Liberalism is defined in terms of three basic principles: (1) belief in the ultimate worth of the individual, (2) belief in self-regulating processes in the interactions between individuals and groups of individuals, (3) belief that government and the state should be organized on the principles of representative democracy, the rule of law, and countervailing powers.[20] The name of the party, People's Party for Freedom and Democracy, cleverly combines these fundamental elements of liberalism.

Classic liberalism has been suspicious of the role of the state. The state should fulfill the role of night watchman, protecting the possibility for the individual to develop himself. After the World War II, some liberals first joined with former socialists in founding the Labor Party (PvdA). However, the desire for greater economic freedom and a distaste for the new party's tendency toward governmental intervention and regulation led to a break, and in 1948 the VVD was founded. It recognized that the classic liberal principles of night watchman state and individualism were no longer tenable. The party accepted that the state must occasionally intervene for the general good, but this should be limited to temporary and general measures to stimulate economic development. Wage and price levels should be left to the free market. Social insurance programs were accepted, but warnings were issued concerning the rise in premiums and taxes.[21]

It is in these areas of social and economic policy that the VVD is now seen as conservative. At the beginning of the 1970s, party leader Hans Wiegel attempted to make political gain out of the losses that were being suffered by the Christian Democratic parties by taking a more polarized stand against the progressive Labor Party. Wiegel and his party objected strongly to the attempts of the government, led by the Labor leader Joop Den Uyl, to achieve more equal distributions of income, knowledge, and power. They argued that low income differentials had reduced the motivation and desire of individuals to work harder and perform more efficiently. They opposed attempts to give workers greater influence in the companies in which they were employed.

Since then the conservatism, or at least rightist tendencies, of the VVD are seen in various issue areas that will be discussed in more detail below. One of the most important goals has been the reduction of the size of government and, above all, the budget deficit. To achieve this it is necessary to scale down or eliminate many of the social programs that formed the backbone of the social welfare state. Another goal, which, although it can be claimed is based upon liberal principles, but now seems rather conservative, is the drive for deregulation and privatization. Most recently, the current leader, Frits Bolkestein, has made statements concerning social issues such as immigration, and stressed traditional values in ways that have more of a conservative than liberal ring to them.

Similar to freedom for liberal philosophy, Paul Lucardie has outlined four basic principles upon which Christian Democratic thought is based: justice, responsibility, solidarity, and stewardship.[22] For liberals, justice means equal rights to freedom, education, employment, and income based upon performance. For social democrats, justice tends to mean equality, most of all in terms of income, knowledge, and power. Both are concerned with the justice of distribution. For the CDA, justice is broader and includes not only how rights and opportunities are distributed, but also the role of the government in protecting and guaranteeing law and order, fundamental rights, and the position of the weak in society. Responsibility in society is spread across both individuals and their social organizations and involves not only responsibility for oneself, but for others, the society, and the environment. This principle is related to the organic view of society that has traditionally been important in Catholic political philosophy, but in its more collective view it is more similar to conservative thought than liberal philosophy. The organic view is in contradiction to the radical individualistic view taken by some liberals. Christian Democrats reject the idea that individuals have the right to determine what to do with their lives and bodies (suicide, euthanasia, abortion).

The principle of responsibility leads to rejection of total freedom for market mechanisms. The desire for profit is accepted, but there must also be a sense of responsibility for the social and ecological consequences. There is also a fear that commercial and market interests may come to dominate in areas where they are less desirable, such as culture, education, media, and health care. Responsibility, cooperation, and controlling excesses lead to development of a type of neocorporatism in which unions, employers, and government are seen as partners.[23]

The Christian Democratic view of man concerns the relation between the individual and society and between the individual and God. Man was created by God and made steward over His creation. He has responsibility for this creation, which includes a concern for one's fellow man. Christian Democrats have in recent years stressed the need for a more caring and concerned society. There is need for the support provided by family and surroundings. It is particularly in this emphasis upon traditional values that the CDA has been labeled a conservative party.

Issue Positions

If the VVD and CDA can, at least to some degree, be seen as conservative or rightist, this should be reflected in the stands they take on various issues facing the country. Ideology is often seen as either an underlying force driving the stand taken on an issue, or a unifying force that brings such viewpoints together in a coherent manner. Either a conservative ideology determines the positions the parties take on issues, or the issue positions taken make up a conservative ideology. In either case, it is necessary to examine what stands are taken by the parties on important political issues, especially those that are related to core aspects of a conservative ideology. In this chapter, four issue areas will be considered. As indicated above, many members of Parliament define the terms "left" and "right" in terms of views on the distribution of income and power in society. Such issues are therefore considered first. Closely related to this are issues dealing with the social welfare state. Since it was also argued that an older definition of the left-right dimension was related to a religious-secular division, viewpoints on social and ethical issues are then examined. Finally, European and foreign-policy issues are considered.

As it is not possible to treat all areas within these four issue areas, it will be necessary here to concentrate on those specific aspects that best illustrate the viewpoints of the parties and the divisions between them. The choice will be guided in part by the choices that other researchers have made when faced with similar dilemmas. In the 1990 survey the members of Parliament were asked to express their opinions on some of these most crucial issues. This information is highly important in determining where the parties stand on such issues. In 1994, as with each parliamentary election, a National Election Study was carried out in the Netherlands. Respondents were asked where they felt the parties stood on some of these issues. These two surveys, together with the party election platforms for the 1994 election, serve as the main sources for understanding where the parties stand.

Distribution of Income and Power

During the 1970s introduction of important income transfer programs and other government policies produced an equality in income levels that was quite high in comparison with other countries.[24] Such policies were at the time particularly important to the Labor Party, which was greatly concerned with achieving greater equality in income, knowledge, and power. The VVD feared that such equality was thwarting individual development and had destroyed the initiative of the individual to work harder and be more efficient and productive. Its view was stated clearly and prominently in the first section of the 1994 election program:

> On the one hand there is too little difference between the level of wages and of governmental benefits, on the other hand, differences in wage levels are too compressed. The VVD is of the opinion that differences in effort should lead to differences in income. It is not fair that these differences are to a great extent taxed away by the government.[25]

Not surprisingly, the CDA is not nearly as outspoken on this question and never treats the aspect of differences in incomes directly. Instead it presents a somber picture for all income groups:

> The development of incomes in the coming years must be subservient to concern for more employment, a better environment, and more safety. Must pay a real price for solidarity and stewardship. . . .
>
> Given financial-economic developments as well as the necessity for new balancing mechanisms and the reestablishment of responsibility, the government can give no guarantees for buying power during the upcoming term of office.
>
> All income groups must share the burden of the somber expectations, taking each persons ability to bear responsibility into account. Special attention must be given to the weaker in society. . . . [26]

Reading these election platforms, it seems clear that the VVD has the more conservative or rightist position, with the CDA taking a more centrist position. Voters certainly perceived such differences in 1994 and they were evident in the responses of the members of parliament for these parties in 1990. The VVD members of parliament clearly place themselves farther to the right on this issue than any of the other parties (see figure 6.2).

Figure 6.2   Average Placement on Issue of Income Differences by Party's Members in Parliament (1990)

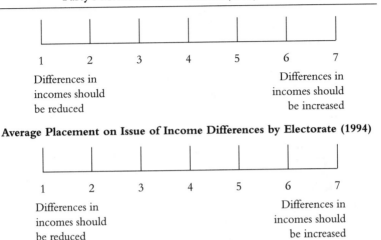

Average Placement on Issue of Income Differences by Electorate (1994)

Table 2.   Average Placement on Isssue of Income Differences. Seven-point scale: 1 = differences in incomes should be reduced, 7 = differences in incomes should be increased.

Party	Placement by Voters 1994	Placement by Party of Party's Members of Parliament 1990
GreenLeft		1.00
Labor party	2.57	2.02
D66	3.56	3.41
CDA	4.40	4.08
VVD	5.41	5.10

The CDA members, on the average, take a more centrist position, just slightly right of center. The average perceptions of the voters are amazingly similar to the average placements by the members of the parliamentary parties. At least in the aggregate, the voters have quite accurate perceptions of where the parties stand.

The social welfare state.   Income transfer policies must be seen in a more general context of the welfare state. Between the postwar period and about 1975 the Netherlands built up a welfare system that was one of the more extensive in the world. Governmental insurance programs were initiated for unemployment compensation, old age pensions, care for widows and orphans, child payments, compulsory medical insurance, major medical expenses, and disability. In some cases, particularly unemployment and disability, the number of persons receiving benefits became far larger than had ever been anticipated. Costs for both employers and employees rose dramatically, adding significantly to the total wage costs. Today, insurance premiums add roughly 50 percent to the before-taxes wages of employees in terms of costs to employers. To insure that recipients of benefits did not fall behind the working population in terms of purchasing power, the amount of the benefit was "coupled" to rises in wages in the private sector. Thus, as wages went up, so did welfare benefits.[27]

Financing these programs led to one of the largest public sectors in the world, rising to over 70 percent of the nation's GDP at the beginning of the 1980s. Although tax revenues have remained steady at about 30 percent, social insurance premiums reached 24 percent of the net national income in 1983. Even with these increases, the revenues were insufficient to keep up with expenditures and the gap had to be filled by nontax revenues and borrowing. One source of revenue was the reserve of natural gas, and using them to pay for such programs rather than for investment was described as a symptom of the "Dutch disease." The national debt doubled between 1982 and 1991 so that yearly interest payments have risen from 2 percent to almost 6 percent of GNP. Whereas economists view a financing deficit in the government budget of between 4 and 5 percent as tolerable, a peak of 10.7 percent was reached in 1982.

It was the VVD that led the way in pushing for change in governmental policy. In 1982 a "no-nonsense" Cabinet of CDA and VVD began taking fairly drastic measures. Salaries of government employees were cut, welfare benefits were "uncoupled" and scaled down, and subsidies for all sorts of activities were reduced. Although the Labor party often watched wistfully as the welfare state was dismantled, the recognition of the necessity for such financial measures transcended ideology. In 1989 the Labor party leader Wim Kok assumed the position of minister of finance in the new CDA/Labor coalition in part to convince voters that his party did not deserve its free-spending image and could make needed, though painful, financial decisions. Most painful was the decision to restructure the disability insurance program.[28] Despite a loss of voter support,[29] Kok continued to move the party toward the center of the political spectrum. By 1994 it was no longer impossible for VVD and PvdA to cooperate, and both joined the governmental coalition.

The 1994 election platform of the VVD reveals that the party has not let up the pressure in these areas. "In the coming governmental period, the collective [tax and insurance premium] burden must be reduced to maximally 50 percent of the net national income." The goal of the party is to eliminate governmental borrowing except for infrastructural investments.[30] The party proposed reducing welfare benefits to a basic level, requiring individuals to insure themselves if they wished to have higher levels of protection. Before benefits were given, the government would first check to determine whether work was available for the individual.[31] The party would further reduce wage costs by lowering the legal minimum wage level and the associated insurance premium levels.

The party program of the CDA also spoke of reduction of the collective burden to the 50 percent level. However, the party is less stringent in its demands with respect to the financing deficit, speaking of a reduction to 2 percent of the gross domestic product. The party also shows a reluctance to lower social benefits, stressing that the rise in costs was caused more by the number of persons receiving benefits than the increase in amounts received. Thus better control and imposition of sanctions on those who misused the system are a better answer than benefit reduction.[32] Rather than immediately lowering the minimum wage, a trial period would be initiated in which those without work experience could be paid at a lower level. If this experiment proved successful in producing jobs, a general reduction of the minimum wage could be considered, but this should not be allowed to affect the minimum level of a socially acceptable standard of living.

The VVD seems to be more conservative, or to the right, on these issues than the CDA. Unfortunately, no questions were posed in either the parliamentary survey or the national election study that could provide more insight into the position of the two parties or how the parties were perceived in the electorate.

Social issues.   There is probably no issue area for which the Netherlands has received more international publicity during recent years than social issues. Foreigners often have the idea that drugs, prostitution, abortion, and euthanasia are completely legal and totally out of control. It is hard to explain to foreigners that all four are actually highly restricted or outright illegal, but that the government chooses not to prosecute offenders under certain conditions. Prostitutes will not be prosecuted if they solicit in specially designated areas. Soft drugs may be purchased in small quantities in designated "coffeeshops." Abortion is legal if an "emergency" situation exists and then only after a five-day cooling off period, although there are indications that there is considerable leeway with regard to the definition of emergency.[33] Euthanasia is not legal, but the courts are determining under what circumstances doctors will not be prosecuted.

Of course, not every voter and party is in total agreement with what is legal or illegal and with what is permitted. The progressive parties,

GreenLeft, Labor, and D66 tend generally to be more permissive and tolerant. For example, D66 has taken the initiative in the debate over euthanasia. However, these are not the parties under consideration here. The more intriguing question is what position the parties that have been identified here as the more conservative or rightist parties take on such issues. For the CDA we might expect that reliance upon traditional, religious values would lead to a conservative viewpoint. For the VVD the matter is less clear. It is in this area that the liberal-conservative dichotomy within the party is put to a test. If the party is at all faithful to its liberal roots, we might find that it would be reluctant to impose state control on the individual.

Such information cannot, however, be gleaned from the party platform of the VVD. The 1994 electoral program of the party is totally silent on all of these issues. We could, of course, obtain such information from other sources, but a good indication will be found below from looking at the information from the survey of parliament and the national election study.

Even the CDA has little to say about such issues in its election manifesto. On abortion, the party is concerned about medical developments that create multiple pregnancies and then selectively abort some of the resultant fetuses; this is not in accord with the law on abortion that permits abortion only in emergency situations.[34] Implicitly, of course, the CDA thereby supports the legislation on abortion, which it helped to pass. On euthanasia the party simply states that the practice of having doctors report instances of euthanasia should be evaluated regularly and that special attention should be given to the position of those who are unable to express their will in such matters.[35] On drugs, the CDA favors action to reduce the number of coffeeshops, and is concerned that the Netherlands not become isolated internationally and within the European Union. Yet rather than opposing policies completely, the party is concerned that "a more active and consistent presentation" of policy is necessary.[36] Prostitution is not mentioned in the CDA electoral program; presumably this is seen as a matter to be handled by local authorities.

Neither of the party programs presents the picture of a strongly conservative party on social issues. There is certainly no emphasis on such issues in an attempt to win votes. If one is looking for conservative statements, they are to be found in the programs of the small, religious parties, such as the Reformed Political Federation (RPF):

> A government in which abortion, euthanasia, traffic in and use of drugs, public blasphemy, prostitution, pornography, attacks on public virtue, disturbance of the sabbath, and gambling, are looked upon with a blind eye or even legalized, contributes to a normlessness and moral decay.[37]

Two of the social issues—abortion and euthanasia—were included in the surveys that can provide us insight into the position of the parties.

The responses from the survey of members of parliament (see figures 6.3 and 6.4) reveal why abortion is no longer a political issue in the Netherlands. The members of the progressive parties place their parties in a cluster at or near the most leftist pole on the scale representing the standpoint that a woman should herself have the right to decide about abortion. The VVD sees itself as only slightly more toward the center, certainly not in a conservative position. The CDA members see their party to the right of these parties, but this is only relative. In fact, on average the CDA parliamentarians place the party almost exactly in the middle of this seven-point scale. The issue has lost so greatly in salience that it has not been asked in the National Election Study since 1986, so that we have no recent information on how voters view the positions of the parties.

In the National Election Study, abortion has been replaced by a question on euthanasia, so that on this issue a comparison of voters and members of Parliament is possible. The placements in figure 6.4 indicate that the

Figure 6.3 Average Placement on Issue of Abortion by Party's Members in Parliament (1990)

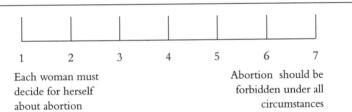

| 1 | 2 | 3 | 4 | 5 | 6 | 7 |

Each woman must decide for herself about abortion

Abortion should be forbidden under all circumstances

Table 3. Positioning of the Parties on the Issue of Abortion (average placements; 1 = each woman must decide for herself about abortion, 7 = abortion should be forbidden under all circumstances)

Party	Placement as Perceived by Voters 1994	Placement as Perceived by Members of Party in Parliament
GreenLeft		1.00
Labor party		1.56
D66		1.08
CDA		4.02
VVD		2.00
Small religious		6.6

Figure 6.4 Average Placement on Issue of Euthanasia by Party's Members in Parliament (1990)

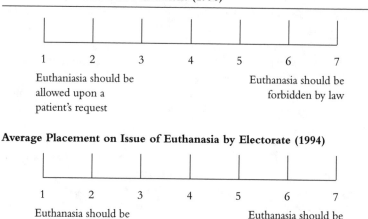

Average Placement on Issue of Euthanasia by Electorate (1994)

Table 4. Positioning of the Parties on the Issue of Euthanasia (average placements; 1 = euthanasia should be allowed upon a patient's request, 7 = euthanasia should be forbidden by law)

Party	Placement as Perceived by Voters (1994)	Placement as Perceived by Members of Party in Parliament (1990)
GreenLeft		1.83
Labor party	3.00	2.12
D66	2.72	1.92
CDA	5.13	5.22
VVD	3.05	2.89
Small religious		7.0

voters and members of the CDA in parliament are in agreement that, with the obvious exception of the small religious parties, this party has the most conservative stand among the political parties. Both place it clearly to the right of center. Nevertheless, this placement is at some distance from the small religious parties, indicating that neither see the CDA as strongly conservative even on this issue. Neither the voters nor the VVD members of Parliament see the VVD as a conservative party on the question of euthanasia; the placements hardly differ from the placements for the Labor Party. D66, which has been perhaps the most outspoken party for liberalization of euthanasia legislation, is seen as somewhat more to the left, as is the GreenLeft.

In summary, on these social issues involving the position of the individual and the role of the state, the VVD genuinely follows its liberal traditions. The CDA is clearly the most conservative of the major Dutch parties, but this position is more centrist than extreme. Only the small religious parties in the Netherlands take a truly conservative position on these issues.

A new issue, which also might be classed as a social issue, may possibly be emerging. The Netherlands has had a century-old tradition as a place of refuge for religious and political dissidents, including British Separatists, French Huguenots, and Portuguese Jews. However, this tolerance has been put to a test in the 1990s when refugees began to pour in from Africa and the former Yugoslavia. When added to the increasing numbers of Turkish and Moroccan "guest" workers who clearly had decided to stay and bring along their families, and the number of citizens from the former colonies in South America and the Caribbean, the Netherlands was becoming more of a multi-ethnic society than it had anticipated. For a time the major parties silently agreed to keep the issue out of politics, but as the extreme right began to gain in support, by 1994 the assimilation of immigrants had become an issue that could not totally be avoided in the election.

How issues associated with the infusion of new immigrants is related to the ideologies of liberalism, conservativism, or Christian democracy is not immediately evident. Perhaps it is an indication of the conservative leanings of the VVD that this party seemed to have the most reservations.

> The VVD concludes that the effectiveness of policy to encourage the integration of minorities has become endangered by the major rise in immigration. Immigration must therefore, within the requirements of treaty commitments, be tied to certain conditions . . . Cornerstone [of this policy] remains that political refugees should continue to be considered for refugee status and that economic refugees gain no admittance to the Netherlands. The Netherlands is not a country of immigration.[38]

One aspect of this issue was included in the 1994 National Election Study, where respondents were asked to indicate where the parties stood on the question of whether new arrivals in the country should be allowed to keep their own culture or should adjust fully to Dutch culture. The respondents placed all four major parties near the center on the issue, perhaps because views had not become highly polarized. Nevertheless, Labor, D66, and CDA are, on average, placed slightly left of center, whereas the VVD is placed clearly right of center. Respondents were not asked to place the Center Democrat party, which would surely have been placed far to the right of the VVD. We have no comparative figures from the members of parliament, since in 1990 this question was not yet an issue. If the issue continues to occupy a place on the political agenda, it seems likely that the VVD will take the most rightist stand and could compete with the Center Democrats for votes (see figure 6.5).

Foreign policy.   Following the World War II, the Netherlands abandoned its traditional policy of neutrality and joined the North Atlantic Treaty Organization (NATO). During the early postwar period, the Netherlands took the Atlantic Alliance as the cornerstone of its foreign policy and was one of the staunchest allies of the United States.[39] The Vietnam War placed strains on this relationship, and although the CDA foreign minister Joseph Luns remained loyal to the United States, many on the left became more critical. During the 1970s opposition to NATO and to American policies became more vociferous. More than 1.2 million people signed a petition to oppose the neutron bomb. In 1981 about 400,000 people and in 1982 500,000 people demonstrated against the deployment of cruise and Pershing II missiles on Dutch territory.[40] The fear that the Netherlands was returning to a policy of neutralism led to a diagnosis of "Hollanditis."[41]

The VVD had few problems in sustaining its support for NATO and the United States during this period. The CDA, however, experienced greater difficulties. Church groups, particularly the Interchurch Peace Council (IKV), were among the most active opponents of the new missiles. Within the party, especially just after the CDA was formed in 1980, pressure was brought on the party leadership and cabinet ministers. Only by postponing decisions and a clever ploy by Prime Minister Lubbers were major problems avoided until arms reductions agreements were reached.[42]

After the end of the cold war, the Netherlands enthusiastically sought new tasks for its military forces. Peacekeeping was an activity that appealed to the Dutch. However, after the controversy surrounding the Dutchbat contingent in the abandonment of Srbrenica, this enthusiasm has cooled considerably. The VVD and CDA are now saying the country must be more careful before entering into any new peacekeeping activity.

The integration of Europe has never been an issue in the Netherlands. The country was one of the founders of the European Community, pushed for the entry of Great Britain, and has maintained strong support for the movement toward economic and political union. All the major parties are on record in their election programs as being in favor or strongly in favor of European integration. Only the small religious parties show concern about a loss of national sovereignty. However, al-

Figure 6.5 Placement by Electorate on Issue of Adjustment by Immigrants to Dutch Culture

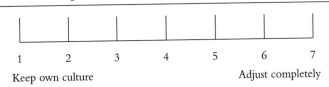

Table 5. Positioning of the Parties on Issue of Adjustment by Immigrants (average placements; 1 = keep own culture, 7 = adjust completely)

Party	Placement as Perceived by Voters
Labor party	3.20
D66	3.83
CDA	3.91
VVD	5.09

though certainly minor in comparison with other countries, there are nevertheless signs of emerging "eurocynicism," particularly within the VVD. The most important source of potential disagreement among the parties is the decision that must be taken in the spring of 1998 concerning the European Monetary Union. The Netherlands satisfies the criteria for entry, but other countries, particularly Germany, are having difficulties reducing their budget deficit to less than 3 percent. There are indications that the Labour Party, D66, and the opposition CDA might be willing to be forgiving, but the VVD holds solidly to the position "three is three." Since the decisions must be taken just before the Dutch elections of 1998, the possibility emerges that it could become a campaign issue. However, the Dutch Minister of Finance (also VVD) stated that it was not an important political question in the Netherlands.[43] Warnings by the European liberal leader, Gijs de Vries (also VVD) that the Netherlands should not run away from its responsibilities, thereby publicly disagreeing with his national party leader, indicate that the issue may be more of an internal VVD issue than an election issue.[44] For the moment, the ripples are relatively minor. On January 1, 1997, the Netherlands assumed the chairmanship of the Union. It was assumed that a Dutchman, Wim Duisenberg, would become the first president of the European Central Bank, and optimism and support was high in all circles.

Issues and voting.   Discussion of these four issue areas has led to the conclusion that it is not possible to align the parties on a single left-right dimension. On an economic left-right dimension, the VVD is to the right, but on a social-ethical left-right dimension, this position is held by the CDA (excluding minor parties in both cases). Although some authors, principally Cees Van der Eijk and Kees Niemoller,[45] contend that a single dimension is sufficient, this author has long contended that both dimensions are necessary to understand voter choice.

As the importance of the social bases for voter choice has declined, issues become more important in understanding how voters determine their vote. These two ideological issue-dimensions can be combined to produce an issue space that helps understand issues and voting. In 1989, together with a colleague, this author borrowed the terminology of a "heartland"[46] and applied it to the Netherlands. By combining the two seven-point scales on income distributions and euthanasia (in 1989 abortion was used), a matrix of 49 possible cells is created. In figure 6.6 "heartlands" for the three major parties are defined. A heartland reflects the issue position of a party on the two dimensions. For example, Labor is in favor of reducing differences in income and for extending possibilities for euthanasia. Heartlands are defined only for the three largest parties. Most of the minor parties would be subsumed within one of these heartlands. For D66 it has not been possible to define a clear heartland. The heartland of the Labor Party contains the largest percentage of voters (27 percent). The two possible conservative parties have smaller percentages—20 percent for the VVD and only 12 percent for the CDA.[47] If there is a correspondence between issue positions and voting, we may expect voters in these areas to vote for a heartland party. However, the largest percentage (41 percent) of voters are situated in areas of the figure that cannot be clearly associated with a party heartland. This area has been called the "battlefield" to indicate that it is here that the parties must fight for votes.

In a multiparty system such as the Netherlands, parties must compete even within their own heartland. This can be seen from table 6.3, containing the choices of voters in the four areas. In each case it is the major party in the heartland that receives the largest percentage of the vote. The election of 1994 was a lean year for both the Labor Party and the CDA, as revealed by the fact that they fell below the 50 percent level in their heartlands. Competition from D66 was especially strong for both Labor and the VVD, and the party did quite well in the battlefield area. The CDA has considerable competition within its heartland from the other religious parties, but also from the PvdA. The latter has

Figure 6.6 Distribution of the Electorate over the Parties' Ideological Heartlands and Battlefield

	Reduce income differences 1	2	3	4	5	6	Increase income differences 7
Permit euthanasia 1							
2	Labor (PvdA) heartland 1989 29% 1994 27%				Liberal (VVD) heartland 1989 14% 1994 20%		
3							
4			Battlefield 1989 40% 1994 41%				
5							
6			Christian Democratic (CDA) heartland 1989 17% 1994 12%				
Forbid euthanasia 7							

1	2	3	4	5	6	7

Vrouw beslist over   Vrouw beslist
eigen abortus   niet zelf

(continues)

Figure 6.6 *(continued)*

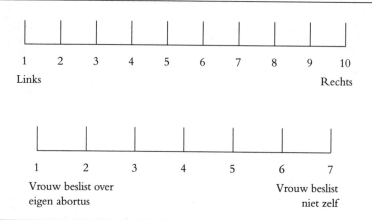

Table 6.3 Party Choice in Electoral Heartlands, 1994

	Labor (PvdA) Heartland	VVD Heartland	CDA Heartland	Battlefield
PvdA	**42**	9	19	23
CDA	8	13	**45**	24
VVD	8	**54**	5	20
D66	18	18	6	22
GreenLeft	13	1	2	4
Religious right	0	—	18	1
Old Persons parties	6	3	3	4
Socialist Party	3	0	1	—
Center Democrats	—	1	1	1
Other	2	1	1	1
Total (%)	100	100	101	100
N =	359	277	137	562
Row %	27	21	10	42

competition in its heartland from the GreenLeft and from D66. In general one can conclude that the heartland model is useful in understanding issues and voting in the Netherlands. The major party is largest in each heartland and competition seems to be more within the heartland than from parties outside the heartland. The battlefield is an area in which all major parties can win votes.

COALITION-BUILDING

Although two dimensions may be required to understand voting behavior, until recently only one was needed to understand cabinet formation. One of the basic characteristics of the Dutch multiparty system is that no single party has ever come close to obtaining a majority of the vote; the highest percentage ever achieved was for the CDA in 1989 with 35.6 percent of the vote. Government has therefore always been by coalition. With the exception of the participation of the Radical party (one of the parties that later merged into the Green Left), coalitions have always consisted of combinations of CDA, Liberals, Labor, and D66 (or their predecessors).

Between 1917 and 1967 the Catholics generally controlled just under one-third of the seats in Parliament. Together with the two Protestant parties, they at times held a majority. Because of the size of this combination and the fact that they were in the center of the economic left–right dimension, they tended to control the coalition formation process. The Catholics and later the CDA participated in all government coalitions between 1917 and 1994, almost always in combination with either the Liberals or Labor.

After an unfortunate incident in 1918, in which a Labor leader called for a proletarian revolution, the predecessors of the Labor party were excluded from government until 1939. Even thereafter, Daudt has argued that Labor was included in a coalition "only as a last resort."[48] He has argued that the Christian Democrats should never be considered a true party of the center, but a party of the right. His definition of "left" would include those parties committed to a radical change of society, whereas the "right" includes those parties who want to keep things pretty much as they are. As such the Christian Democrats belong on the right and have a natural preference for governing with the VVD. They would therefore only opt for the Labor party as a last resort, that is, when they did not have sufficient seats for a coalition with the Liberals or when possible social unrest meant that it could be important to include Labor. Daudt's theory can be disputed for the full postwar period, but became more accurate as the CDA moved more clearly to the right after 1980.[49]

Whether or not they were centrist or rightist, the Christian Democrats were able to play Labor and the Liberals against one another. The were assisted in this by a resolution adopted by the VVD in 1958 that the party would not participate in a government with the Labor party. Labor quickly reciprocated. All understanding of coalition formation in the Netherlands was thrown overboard in 1994. For several years some prominent members of the VVD and Labor parties had been conducting secret talks to try to bring about the elimination of the blockade that both had thrown up. As the 1994 election approached, it hardly seemed likely that such cooperation was likely, but at least the formal blockade was dropped. Had the CDA not lost so dramatically at the election, this would probably have had little effect. But when the CDA lost 20 seats to only 34 and Labor lost 12 to drop to 37 an entirely new situation developed.

With this loss of seats, the CDA had become too small to form a majority with either Labor on the left or the VVD on the right. Moreover, it no longer held sole control of the center. The substantial gains made by D66 (from 12 to 24 seats) made it a major rather than a minor player in the game. The CDA would have needed D66 for any combination with Labor or the VVD, but D66 also controlled sufficient seats to allow for the possibility of coalition formation along the social left–right dimension.

In part because of frustration with how they had been treated by the Christian Democrats during the cabinet formation in 1989,[50] D66 now had a strong preference for a coalition *without* the CDA. To the surprise of virtually all observers (although based upon the results of the 1990 survey of parliament Ron Hillebrand and Jacqueline Meulman had shown that such a coalition was possible[51]), all the ingredients were brought together and a totally new coalition of Labor, D66, and VVD eventually emerged. Although some thought it might be quite short-lived, at the time of writing it has been in office more than two years and internal relations between the members in the cabinet have seemingly become better rather than worse.

This coalition will undoubtedly provide some problems for both the parties and the voters at the coming election. Dutch voters have long understood that what parties say in the platforms and call for during the campaign cannot be realized without compromise. Yet it is entirely new that the parties that were for so long seen as polar opposites are apparently able to cooperate quite successfully in a coalition. What meaning do concepts such as "progressive" and "conservative" or "left" and "right" have if the ideological differences are so small that such cooperation becomes possible? How voters will react to this new situation makes the next elections quite intriguing.

Prospects for the Future

What the future holds in store is an intriguing question for both of the political parties discussed here. In 1994 the Christian Democrats lost the dominant position in Dutch politics that they had held throughout the century. As the next century approaches, a major question is whether this party can recover from this loss or whether it will decline to the status of a minor party. On the other hand, the VVD made substantial gains at the 1994 elections, and the question is whether this growth can be maintained or even increased.

As explained above, for many years the voting behavior of the Dutch electorate could be understood quite well with a simple model based upon religious activity and social class. The Christian Democratic parties drew their support from the church-going adherents of their religious domination, whereas the VVD gained its votes primarily from the secular middle-class. In table 6.2 we have seen that this model is losing its importance and in 1994 could account for only 36 percent of the vote.[52] Table 6.4 shows that, in addition to actual voting change, demographic changes are taking place that affect the relative positions of the two conservative parties. Two important trends are revealed in this table. One is the decline in the number of practicing religious adherents in the Netherlands. The percentage of the population who described themselves as practicing adherents of one of the three major religious denominations had declined from 52 percent in 1956 to only 30 percent in 1989. The second is the dramatic rise in the size of the secular middle class. Just under a majority of the population described itself as secular middle class in 1989.

These changes have far-reaching implications for the two more conservative parties. The social base for the CDA is declining, whereas that of the VVD is increasing. For the CDA, matters are made worse by the fact that the size of its heartland also seems to be declining. Although changes in the questionnaire make figures not completely comparable, there are indications that the size of the Christian Democratic heartland has declined from 28 percent in 1977 to 12 percent in 1994.[53] If current trends continue, the Christian Democrats will slowly fade to a minor position. It is not easy to indicate what the party can or should do to produce a revival. Even winning votes away from the small religious parties in the heartland will not

Table 6.4   Distribution of the Population According to the Structured Model of Voting Behavior

	1956	1968	1977	1986	1989	1994
Catholics (practicing)	30	30	24	16	14	13
Dutch Reformed (practicing)	12	16	9	8	8	6
Gereformeerd (practicing)	10	12	9	5	8	5
Secular working class	33	25	28	26	22	21
Secular middle class	15	18	30	45	48	54
Total (%)	100	101	100	100	100	101
N	982	1491	1199	1192	1370	1725

Sources: 1956 and 1968, Lijphart, 1974, p. 250; 1977 through 1994 Dutch National Election Study

be sufficient to provide restoration of earlier glory. The party could attempt to produce a religious revival that would increase the number of religious adherents that might then support the party, but it is not easy to see how this can be accomplished. Emphasis on conservative, traditional values does not have great potential at the moment, since most Dutch voters have rather liberal views on social issues. Barring a religious or moral revival, the only option open is to profit from its position as opposition party and to produce a popular political leader. However, at the moment the party is still trying to adjust to this new position and a new, charismatic leader has not emerged.

This contrasts sharply with the picture for the VVD. Not only has the size of its social base, the middle class, increased over the last decades, public opinion is shifting slowly in its direction. The losses in the CDA heartland have, in the aggregate, been shifting slowly to the VVD heartland, which almost doubled between 1977 and 1986, from 8 percent to 17 percent.[54] In the new operationalization the size had increased from 14 percent in 1989 to 20 percent in 1994.[55] In the past the VVD seems to have suffered from a stuffy, elitist image. Upwardly mobile, new members of the middle class hesitated to support the party and the party did poorer in its heartland than did the other two major parties. The latter changed in 1994, when the VVD had the greatest success in its heartland. Perhaps the image has changed sufficiently, or older working-class identifications are becoming forgotten so that earlier hesitations have been overcome.

Whereas the social conservatism of the Christian Democrats is losing support, the economic conservatism of the VVD has wide support. Even the Labor party has become sufficiently converted to support reductions of the budget deficit and cutbacks in governmental welfare programs that it is possible for the party to govern in a coalition with the VVD. Some more traditional social democrats have the feeling that their party is carrying out the VVD agenda. Even though it has moved to the center, the PvdA has regularly lost votes in recent elections, even though it emerged as the largest party in 1994. Nevertheless, whereas for many years it was Labor that was the innovative party in Dutch politics, whether in government or not, this impetetus seems to have shifted to the VVD. If the VVD can develop a less elitist image and can hold onto recent gains, it has the possibility of becoming the dominant party in the Netherlands.

Notes

1. K. Groenveld, "Hoe liberaal is de VVD?, " in K. Groenveld and G. A. Van der List eds., *Liberalisme en Conservatisme: Verslag van een symposium* (The Hague: Teldersstichting, 1990), pp. 104–109.

2. Groenveld and Van der List, eds., *Liberalisme en Conservatisme.*

3. F. Bolkestein, "Liberalen, conservatieven en socialisten, " in Groenveld and Van der List, pp. 27–36.

4. Groenveld, "Hoe liberaal is de VVD," p. 105.

5. Ibid., p. 106.

6. Paul Lucardie, "De ideologie van het CDA: een conservatief democratisch appel?," in Kees van Kersbergen, Paul Lucardie, Hans-Martien ten Napel, eds., *Geloven in macht: de christen-democratie in Nederland* (Amsterdam: Het Spinhuis, 1993), pp. 39–40.

7. Giovanni Sartori, *Parties and Party Systems* (Cambridge: Cambridge University Press, 1976), pp. 78–79.

8. Ron Hillebrand and Jacqueline Meulman, "Afstand en nabijheid: verhoudingen in de Tweede Kamer," in J. J. A. Thomassen, M. P. C. M. van Schendelen, and M. L. Zielonka-goei, eds., *De Geachte Afgevaardigde* (Muiderberg: Coutinho, 1992), pp. 98–128.

9. Rudy B. Andeweg, "Institutional Conservatism in the Netherlands: Proposals for and Resistance to Change," in Hans Daalder and Galen Irwin, eds., *Politics in the Netherlands: How Much Change?* (London: Frank Cass, 1989).

10. Hans Daalder, "Consociationalism, Center and Periphery in the Netherlands," reprinted in J. Th. J. Van den Berg and B. A. G. M. Tromp, eds., *Politiek en Historie* (Amsterdam: Bert Bakker, 1990), p. 32.

11. See, for example, Rudy B. Andeweg and Galen A. Irwin, *Dutch Government and Politics* (Houndsmills, Basingstoke, Hampshire and London: Macmillan, 1993), pp. 27–33.

12. Arend Lijphart, *The Politics of Accommodation: Pluralism and Democracy in the Netherlands* (Berkeley: University of California Press, second edition, 1975), p. 209.

13. Rudy B. Andeweg, *Dutch Voters Adrift* (Leiden: Leiden University dissertation, 1982), pp. 207–211.

14. Hans-Martien T. D. Ten Napel, *"Een Eigen Weg": De totstandkoming van het CDA (1952–1980)* (Leiden: Leiden University dissertation, 1992).

15. Galen A. Irwin and Joop J. M. Van Holsteyn, "Decline of the structured model of electoral competition," in Daalder and Irwin, eds., 1989, pp. 21–41.

16. Arend Lijphart, "The Netherlands: Continuity and Change in Voting Behaviour," in Richard Rose, ed., *Electoral Behavior: A Comparative Handbook* (New York: The Free Press, 1974).

17. Galen Irwin and Joop Van Holsteyn, "Where to From Here: Revamping Electoral Politics in the Netherlands," *West European Politics,* 20:2 (April 1997): 93–118.

18. Ruud Koole, Paul Lucardie, and Gerrit Voerman, *40 Jaar Vrij en Verenigd: Geschiede nis van de VVD-partijorganisatie* (Houten: Uitgeverij Unieboek, 1988), p. 113.

19. Ruud Koole, "Politieke Partijen," in H. Daalder and C. J. M. Schuyt, eds., *Compen dium voor politiek en samenleving in Nederland* (Alphen aan den Rijn:

Samsom). This article is part of a large compendium of political and social information that is published in looseleaf form and continually updated. These pages were published in November 1996, April 1997, and December 1997.

20. Andreas A. M. Kinneging, *Liberalisme* (The Hague: Teldersstichting, 1988).

21. Paul Lucardie, "Liberalisme," in D. Th. Kuiper, M. Brinkman, and A. P. M. Lucardie, eds., *Drie stromen land* (Leiden: Stichting Burgerschapskunde, 1993), p. 51.

22. Paul Lucardie, "De ideologie van het CDA . . . ," pp. 41–49.

23. See, for example, Steven B. Wolinetz, "Socio-Economic Bargaining in the Netherlands: Redefining the Post-war Policy Coalition," in Daalder and Irwin, eds., *Politics in the Netherlands.*

24. Wilfred Uiterhoeve, Geert Franssen, Arie Mens, Lodewijk G. Moor, Ben de Pater, and Otto Verkoren, eds., *Staat van Nederland* (Nijmegen: SUN, 1990), p. 170.

25. I. Lipschits, ed., *Verkiezingsprogramma's 1994* ('s-Gravenhage: Sdu Uitgeverij Koninginnegracht, 1994), p. 389.

26. Lipschits, *Verkiezingsprogramma's 1994,* pp. 348–349

27. See overview in Andeweg and Irwin, pp. 194–211.

28. R. Hillebrand, "Changing Strategies: The Dutch Labour Party, 1884–1991," paper presented for the workshop "Party Behaviour, Party Organisation and Democracy," University of Essex, March 22–28, 1991.

29. Galen A. Irwin, "Tussen de verkiezingen," in J. J. M. Van Holsteyn and B. Niemöller, eds., *De Nederlandse kiezer 1994* (Leiden: DSWO Press), pp. 9–26.

30. Lipschits, *Verkiezingsprogramma's 1994,* p. 393.

31. Ibid., p. 392.

32. Ibid., p. 346.

33. "Artsen zouden abortuswet overtreden," *de Volkskrant,* January 17, 1997, p. 1.

34. Lipshits, *Verkiezingsprogramma's 1994,* p. 340.

35. Ibid., p. 35.

36. Ibid., p. 337.

37. Ibid., p. 196.

38. Ibid., p. 401.

39. Alfred Van Staden, "The Changing role of the Netherlands in the Atlantic Alliance," in Daalder and Irwin, eds., *Politics in the Netherlands.*

40. See summary in Andeweg and Irwin, pp. 214–220.

41. Walter Laqueur, "Hollanditis: a new stage in European neutralism," *Commentary,* August 19–26, 1981.

42. See description in Andeweg and Irwin, p. 217.

43. Cees Banning, "EMU mogelijk verkiezingsthema Nederland," *NRC Handelsblad,* April 7, 1997.

44. Ben Van der Velden, "Nederland moet niet weglopen," *NRC Handelsblad,* April 5, 1997.

45. C. Van der Eijk and B. Niemöller, *Electoral Change in the Netherlands* (Amsterdam: CT Press, 1982).

46. A. Heath, R. Jewell, and J. Curtice, "Attitudes, Values and Identities in the British electorate," paper presented at the annual meeting of the American Political Science Association, the Palmer House, Chicago, September 3–6, 1987.

47. Irwin and Van Holsteyn, op. cit., pp. 104–105.

48. Hans Daudt, "Political Parties and Government Coalitions in the Netherlands since 1945," *The Netherlands Journal of Sociology* 16, pp. 1–24.

49. See also, Andeweg and Irwin, pp. 121–122.

50. See Andeweg and Irwin, p. 122.

51. Hillebrand and Meulman, "Afstand en nabijheid," pp. 98–128.

52. Rudy Andeweg, "Afscheid van de verzuiling," in J. J. M. Van Holsteyn and B. Niemöller, eds., *De Nederlandse kiezer 1994* (Leiden: DSWO Press, 1995), p. 117; and Irwin and Van Holsteyn, "Where to From Here?"

53. Galen Irwin and Joop Van Holsteyn, "Towards a more open model of electoral competition," in Daalder and Irwin, eds., *Politics in the Netherlands,* p. 115; and figure 6.

54. Ibid.

55. Irwin and Van Holsteyn, "Where to From Here?"

CHAPTER SEVEN

The Center-Right Parties in Norwegian Politics: Between Reformist Labor and Radical Progress

Lars Svåsand

The Norwegian political system has been characterized as containing "cross-cutting cleavages,"[1] implying the presence of multiple parties. By the end of the 1930s the politicization of the various cleavages had resulted in a seven-party system, which from left to right consisted of: the Communist party (NKP), the Labor party (DNA), the Liberals (V), the Agrarians (B), the Christian People's party (KrF), the Conservatives (H), and the Fascist party (NS). With the end of World War II, the NS was eliminated, and the remaining six parties held all parliamentary seats until 1961.

The genealogy of the party system is outlined in figure 7.1.[2] In 1957 the Communist party lost its last seat in parliament (Storting), and in the following election a left-wing defection from Labor formed the Socialist People's party (SF—*Sosialistisk Folkeparti*). In the turbulence following the first referendum on Norwegian membership in the EU in 1972, this party, together with other leftist anti-EU groups and individuals, formed the Socialist Left party (1973, SV—*Sosialistisk Venstreparti*).[3] Another fall-out from the EU debacle was the split of the Liberals. A pro-EU splinter group formed the Liberal People's party (DLF—*Det Liberale Folkeparti*), which proved unsuccessful and declined rapidly. What was left of it reunited with the Liberals in 1988. Finally, a new right-wing populist party, the Progress party (FRP—*Fremskrittspartiet*)[4] burst onto the political arena, emphasizing

Table 7.1 Percentage of Votes for Major Parties in Parliamentary Elections, 1961–1993

	1961	1965	1969	1973	1977	1981	1985	1989	1993	1997
Socialist										
Left	2.4	6.0	3.5	11.2	4.2	5.0	5.5	10.1	7.9	6.0
Labor	46.8	43.1	46.5	35.3	42.3	37.1	40.8	34.3	39.9	35.0
Liberals	8.9	10.4	9.4	3.5	3.2	3.9	3.1	3.2	3.6	4.5
Christian										
People's party	9.6	8.1	9.4	12.3	12.4	9.4	8.3	8.5	7.9	13.7
Center party	9.3	9.9	10.5	11.0	8.6	6.6	6.6	6.5	16.8	7.9
Conservative	20.0	21.1	19.6	17.4	24.8	31.8	30.4	22.2	17.0	14.3
Progress party	—	—	5.0	1.9	4.5	3.7	13.0	6.3	—	15.3

Sources: Author's file.

drastic reduction in taxation and bureaucracy. In the 1980s this party became increasingly identified with opposition toward immigration.

In this multiparty system it is fairly easy to characterize parties on the left, from the social democrats to the Marxist-Leninists, and on the far right the Progress party maintains a distinct policy profile. The rest of the parties are more problematic to characterize by a common denominator. In Norwegian politics they are usually referred to as what they are not—nonsocialists—rather than what they have in common.

The only party that identifies itself, and is also identified by others, as a conservative party is *Høyre* (H—literally "right"). Its origin as one of the first political parties (1884) in Norway goes back to the period known as the struggle for parliamentarism, a principle Høyre opposed.[5] The party leaders and MP's were mainly higher civil servants and in effect the governing class in Norwegian society. Thus, the background for the Conservative party is the state apparatus itself—rather than in a rural aristocracy as in so many other European countries. In this century, the party gradually became the party of the business community, with a concentration of electoral support in urban areas in general, and particularly in the central eastern part of the country.

Its opponent from 1884 through the early part of this century was the Liberals (V—literally "left"). This party began as a rather broad coalition of farmers, craftsmen, and urban intellectuals united in their opposition to the Conservative regime.[6] As figure 7.1 indicates, as a broad coalition it has been fragmented repeatedly over its century-long history. Almost immediately after winning the struggle for parliamentarism, a religious group, the Moderate Liberals (MV), defected, and at the turn of the century a business-oriented group, the National Liberals (FV), left. Both of these ended up in the Conservative party. By 1920, the Farmer's Union decided to organize into a party, the Farmers party (B—*Bondepartiet*).[7] Although the new party was not a split from the Liberals in a formal sense, the Liberals were more affected than other parties. The Christian People's party (KrF—*Kristelig Folkeparti*) split off from the Liberals in 1933, protesting against the increasing secularism in the Liberal party.[8] These three parties see themselves as "centrist" and would certainly object to being classified as "conservative," although both the Christian People's party and the Center party (formerly the Agrarian party) share cultural perspectives often identified as conservative. The emphasis in this chapter will be on the Conservative party, although comparisons and references will be made to the other parties. The nature of nonsocialist party politics in Norway is such that it is hardly possible to discuss one party without also taking neighboring parties into consideration.

The nonsocialist parties have some features that make it meaningful to deal with them as a group. In terms of economic policy, they have traditionally opposed the comprehensive governmental involvement in the economy espoused by socialist ideology. They also have in common an emphasis on the individual in society, rather than the collectivity. On the whole they also share a stronger affection for religion and national culture than either the far left or the far right. However, they are based on different groups and orientations. The Christian People's party's main focus is on preserving religious values in society. The Center party has its stronghold among farmers and in rural areas in general, while the Conservatives are particularly strong in urban areas and among people employed in the private sector. The Liberals are the least distinct party in terms of ideological orientation or links with particular groups. The electoral heterogeneity among the four parties enhances the possibilities for cooperation between them, yet also limits the extensiveness of such cooperation. On the one hand, because the parties have, to some extent, "saliency issues" that are distinct from each other, cooperation is possible as long as each party's issues do not conflict too much with the priorities of the others. However, at times their preferences cannot be reconciled, hence the limits to their relationship.

Electoral Support

Prior to 1961, the Labor party enjoyed a parliamentary majority in parliament (Storting) although they have never had a majority of the votes. Labor has, however, remained the largest party by far also after 1961 (see table 7.1). The Conservatives have traditionally been the largest nonsocialist party and were usually supported by a fifth of the electorate. The 1977 election ushered in a period referred to as the "wave from the right," which coincided with the electoral success of Conservative parties and politicians in other countries.[9] In the 1990s the party has again declined to its previous level. The success of the Conservatives in the late 1970s and first half of the 1980s must be seen against the backdrop of the significant changes in Norwegian social structure during the reign of the Labor party. Even if voting intentions in various social and occupational groups had remained constant, Labor would be likely to lose. Employment in manufacturing declined from 25 percent of the workforce in 1960 to 16 percent in 1990, while the service sector expanded from 43 to 69 percent. Agricultural employment dropped from 22 percent to 7 percent in the same period.[10] During the three decades following World War II, social and geographic mobility increased tremendously, as witnessed by the growth of the educational system and the concentration of population in central regions.[11] All of these shifts increased those segments of the electorate that had been the core of the Conservative party:

urban voters, middle- and upper-level functionaries employed in the private sector and self-employed persons, and voters with higher education. Among white-collar employees, Conservative voting increased from 29 percent in 1969 to 41 percent in 1981, the peak year of support for the party. Among the self-employed, the Conservatives' share increased from 40 to 54 percent. During the "wave from the right" period the party was also able to reach beyond its traditional electorate. Among blue-collar workers, only 6 percent had voted Conservative in 1969, but 15 percent did in 1981, and among farmers the party's share increased from 9 to 22 percent. Within these "untraditional" groups the party benefited particularly among voters with higher education, high income, and weak integration in the working-class culture.[12]

At one point, Norwegian political analysts were predicting the emergence of the "two-party system," as Labor and Conservatives approached the same size. In 1981 the gap in the share of the votes for the two parties had narrowed to 5.3 percentage points, compared to 26.8 percentage points two decades earlier. However, at the end of the decade, the new conservative electoral coalition started to fall apart in spite of continuous social change that should have been to its benefit. Both from the left and the right political challenges appeared. The "wave from the right" not only increased support for the Conservatives but led to a general right turn in several policy areas in the Labor party as well. In addition, the Progress party's appearance and the increased saliency of the "immigration" issue pulled parts of the Conservative electorate toward the right, while the party itself tried to cooperate with the parties to its immediate left. Finally, the question of Norwegian EU membership reappeared on the political agenda in 1992, again blocking nonsocialist cooperation.

The multidimensionality of Norwegian politics includes the left-right cleavage, as evidenced in the distribution of occupational and educational groups in the parties. In addition, three cultural variables have traditionally been significant: religion, teetotalism, and language.[13] Finally, geographically based conflicts, such as among regions, and between urbanism and rural life, account for differences in voting strength between parties. (Only rural-urban differences are shown here.) Gender and age also show some variation between the parties.

The composition of the electorates of the nonsocialist parties in the 1989 election is displayed in table 7.2.[14] In spite of its effort to become a party with an appeal to the electorate in general, there is still a fairly skewed recruitment of voters to the Conservative party, as table 7.2 displays. Private functionaries are the most overrepresented occupational category, as are voters with post - high school education and higher income. Its stronger urban base is reflected in the language preference of its voters,

Table 7.2 Voter Profiles of the Conservative, Center, Christian Peoples Party, and Liberals 1989 (in percentages)[*]

	Conservative	Center Party	Christian People's Party	Liberal Party	All Voters
Occupation					
Workers	17	22	27	23	32
Public function	23	6	24	26	21
Private function	29	17	20	19	19
Self-employed	12	4	9	10	8
Farmers/fishermen	10	41	9	4	7
Education					
College level	33	7	25	47	20
Less than college	67	93	75	53	80
Gender					
Male	49	51	56	41	50
Female	51	49	44	59	50
Age					
Less than 30	31	18	14	32	26
31–50	39	38	30	45	40
51+	30	43	56	23	34
Teetotalism					
Yes	7	19	62	10	14
No	93	81	38	90	86
Language					
Rural	6	32	26	18	15
Urban	94	68	74	82	85
Religious activity					
Active	24	38	79	24	29
Passive	76	62	21	76	71
Residence area					
Urban	54	22	40	50	55
Rural	46	78	60	50	45

Source: This table has been constructed from information in Henry Valen and Bernt O. Aardal: *Endring og kontinuitet,* op. cit. pp. 102–107. Some categories have been aggregated.
[*]Tables do not necessarily add to 100 percent because of rounding and also because some minor categories have been left out.

but on cultural variables like religion and teetotalism the Conservative party is fairly representative of the electorate in general. Class remains the most important barrier in preventing the party from becoming a rival to Labor again.

The Conservatives' ups and downs were partially mirrored in the fate of the other nonsocialist parties. The combined votes of the three center parties declined from 27.8 percent in 1961 to 20 percent in 1981. The 1972 referendum on EU-membership split the Liberal party in two. In 1985 the party lost its last two seats in parliament and although it reunited with its splinter party in 1988, it was barely able to win one seat in 1993.

The main problem for the Liberals has always been the lack of an ideologically or socially defined segment in the electorate. The party is overrepresented among people with higher education (37 percent of its voters vs. 20 percent for the whole electorate), among high income people (39 percent vs. 26 percent), and among voters in the southwestern part of the country (45 percent of its voters, vs. 27 percent of the whole electorate).

The two other center parties have fared much better in part due to a fairly distinct political profile. At times, the parties have benefited from the intense mobilization of the anti-EU forces in the Norwegian electorate. The Christian People's party is strongly embedded in that segment of the electorate that is mostly concerned with religious and moral values. As a consequence, the class dimension plays little role in shaping its electorate, and the party is from a socio-economic point of view the most representative party in Norway.[15]

The Christian People's party deviates from the electorate in general in terms of age and gender. It is particularly strong among older women. The southwestern part of the country has historically been a stronghold for the so-called counter-cultural movements.[16] In this part of the country, the Lutheran lay movement, the rural-language movements, and teetotalism are stronger than elsewhere in the country. Thus, among its voters, 62 percent declared themselves to be teetotalers, versus 14 percent of all voters. A similar difference exists with regard to membership in religious associations. Although less marked, support for the "rural language" was also strong among voters for the Christian People's party: 26 percent versus 15 percent for all voters. This identification with a specific set of cultural and moral values is a strong buffer against turbulence in the electorate. The party's ability to maintain its current strength lies in this "ideological" field. Secularization and movement of the population to urban areas followed by "new" social habits shrink the party's electorate.

The Center party, formerly the Agrarian party, enjoys a similar entrenchment in an electoral segment as the Christian People's party. However, this segment is primarily defined in terms of support for an economic sector—agriculture—and for rural areas in general. In spite of its change of name in 1959 from Farmers' party to Center party, it is still perceived to be a party for the rural areas: 41 percent of its 1989 voters were farmers, compared to 7 percent of the total electorate. A consequence of this is that the party is strongly overrepresented, by 33 percent, in rural areas: more than three-quarters of its voters live in sparsely populated districts. Thus, for the Center party, the concentration of population in cities is a "creeping" hazard to the party, at least in terms of the share of the vote.[17] It has yet to gain a strong foothold in urban areas, as its Swedish sister party managed to do in the 1960s.[18] The extraordinary increase in votes for the party in 1993 was linked to the EU- membership conflict in which the party was the main opponent of membership.[19]

As the nonsocialist parties share to some extent a common ground in at least opposing the socialist parties, there is naturally some exchange of voters between them. Yet, because they cater to different clienteles, this exchange is limited (see table 7.3). Although the 1993 election may be "exceptional" in the sense that it was impacted heavily by the pending EU issue, the exchange of voters between nonsocialist parties and other parties nevertheless is revealing. First, it demonstrates the more closely integrated electorate of the Center and Christian People's party than of the Conservative party and the weakness of the Liberal party. The latter was able to keep only slightly more than a third of its 1989 voters in 1993, with the other two-thirds almost equally divided between parties to the left and the right. Second, the Conservative party lost as many voters to the socialist parties as it did to the other nonsocialist parties (not counting Progress). On some issues, like EU membership, support for industrialization, and some larger infrastructure projects, Labor and Conservatives find themselves in agreement.

Party Organization

The nonsocialist parties have often been perceived as having a much weaker party organization than the Labor party. This impression is, however, only partly true and is primarily based on the traditionally greater independence of the nonsocialist parliamentary groups from control exercised by the extraparliamentary organization.

It is true that in the Conservative party the party organization was not considered important.[20] During the late 1960s this changed and a new leadership imposing its mark on the party in the early 1970s envisioned it as a well-organized mass movement. Their model was their traditional adversary—the Labor party.[21] This organizational model implied three elements: the establishment of a nationwide network of local party organizations, the mobilization of members, and a party structure in which the organization was given an enhanced role within the party.

From its beginning the Conservative party had been particularly strong in urban areas in general, but in rural areas it was absent from large parts

Table 7.3   Nonsocialist Party Voters in 1989, by 1993 Vote (in percentages)

| | Voted in 1989 | | | |
Voted in 1993	Liberals	Center	Christian Party	Conservatives
Socialist parties	31	6	6	15
Liberals	35	—	4	5
Center	16	82	8	8
Christian Party	6	2	69	2
Conservative	6	2	4	54
Progress	—	—	2	3
Others	—	1	2	—
Did not vote	6	7	5	13

of the country, except for the Oslofjord region.[22] In the 1960s the party was without local branches in most of the rural municipalities in the southwestern part of the country. By the mid 1980s local branches were established in every municipality. The formation of the local branches was a precondition for the second objective in the organizational transformation: membership mobilization. Membership enrollment surged, from about 90,000 in 1972 to almost double that figure in 1983, the peak year. Whether the growth in members reflected or caused the increase in electoral support is difficult to determine,[23] but it appeared that although successful in terms of mobilizing new members, the party did not succeed in integrating its new members. Just as electoral growth correlated with the organizational expansion, so also with the reverse process from the last part of the 1980s. Conservative party membership figures took a nosedive, dropping to 71,000 in 1995—less than in the premobilization period. Electorally the party was replaced by the Center party as the largest nonsocialist party. In part the exodus of members is related to the frustrating attempts of the party to battle with its coalition partners on the one side and the Progress party on the other. However, declining party membership has also become the norm among the other parties. The strong correlation between membership enrollment and increased electoral support in the Conservative party had no parallel in the other nonsocialist parties.

The Liberals, always weaker in membership mobilization than the other parties, collapsed organizationally when they split in 1973. Since then, the membership figures have declined to 7,000. The Christian People's party parallels the Conservatives in having a strong mobilization of new members in the late 1970s and 1980s. Membership increased from about 50,000 in 1970 to 67,000 in 1982, but declined again to 54,000 in 1995. However, contrary to the experience of the Conservatives, there was no corresponding surge in voter support. It appears that the Christian People's party succeeded in incorporating voters it already had into the party organization, while the Conservatives mobilized new voters and new members almost simultaneously. Finally, trends in membership for the Center party show a different trajectory. In 1957 the Center party claimed 38 percent of its voters as members, the highest share among all Norwegian parties.[24] The party membership figure increased to 70,000 in 1970, but then declined slowly to 48,000 in 1994. The Center party benefited strongly in electoral terms from opposing Norwegian EU membership and was also able to increase its membership to some extent.[25] The slow decline in the number of members in the two center parties contrasts with the ups and downs of the Conservative party and is probably related to how well the members are integrated into the party. A survey among party members in 1990 by Knut Heidar[26] (table 7.4) shows that the Conservative party had more passive members than the other nonsocialist parties and also more members likely to be less involved in the party in the future.

Structurally, the four nonsocialist parties are very similar and in general the nonsocialist parties have not changed their basic structure—except for the Conservatives who have been through a turbulent period since 1970. The reforms in the Conservative party did not so much change the type of organizational elements of the party structure as they changed the composition of party bodies and the relationship between them.

The structure of the parties is adapted to that of the political system itself.[27] The organizations in Norwegian parties are complex, with three main dimensions. First, there is the hierarchical dimension. The base organization is at the municipal level, with some of the larger municipalities

Table 7.4 Percentage of Party Members, by Activity Level

	Co	C	CCP	Li	All Party Members
Did not attend any meeting previous year	69	53	45	48	53
Expect less involvement in the future	23	3	9	22	14

Source: This table has been extracted from Knut Heidar, *The polymorphic nature of party membership*, op. cit., pp. 68, 83.
Note: Co: Conservative party, C: Center, CPP: Christian People's party, Li: Liberals

divided into ward branches. The municipal branches recruit members, nominate candidates for local elections and formulate party policies for this level of government. The nonsocialist parties were often without strong local branches in many municipalities in the 1950s and had to present joint slates of "nonsocialist" candidates for local elections. A local government reform in 1965 reduced the number of municipalities from 732 to 465. An effect of this was to merge smaller municipalities without party branches with larger ones in which parties were established. This reorganization of local government made it possible for the parties to present their own lists of candidates at elections.

All municipal branches are included in the province level organizations (*fylkesorganisasjon*). The province level nominates the candidates for parliamentary elections[28] and for provincial elections (which were introduced in 1975). This unit is the link between the national party organization and the local branches and thus occupies a central place in the party machinery. It is this organizational level that sends delegates to the national convention and that is represented at the national committee, the most representative organ functioning between conventions.

It is important to notice that the line of command is from the top down. The national party organization is not a federation of local or province-level units. The latter are subdivisions of the national organizations. This fact implies that the local and province levels have limited autonomy, not only in terms of how they organize but also in terms of political maneuverings. The rules regulating local and province organizations are decided upon nationally. If a province-level unit would prefer to nominate joint candidates with other parties for the Storting election (which sometimes is done to benefit from the electoral system), it must obtain permission to do so from the national committee. This committee can also impose on province organizations to engage in joint lists of candidates.

This hierarchical dimension is at the same time a geographic dimension. Thus, the ever present center-periphery conflict in Norwegian politics runs within parties as well as between them. When the Conservative party succeeded in expanding its organizational network in the 1970s and had electoral success in the 1980s it was also affected by the conflicting demands from various regions in ways it had not previously been used to.

At the national level, the national convention meets annually in the Conservative party and biannually in the three other parties. In the Conservative party, the province organizations are guaranteed a number of delegates equal to the total number of seats a constituency is *allocated* in parliament. In addition, province-level organizations are allocated additional delegates for every 15,000 votes in the last parliamentary election.[29] Prior to the 1970 reform of the party statutes, the number of additional delegates was limited to the number of seats the party had won. In 1970 this was changed to 25,000 votes and in 1979 to its current level of 15,000. The rule changes altered significantly the composition of the convention. The numerical role of the MPs and other office holders was reduced as the party expanded electorally.

The national convention is a significant event in both parties. The party leadership is elected at the convention and during election years the convention adopts the party program. The party statutes can only be amended at the convention. In the nonsocialist parties the national conventions include all members of parliament as well as any members of the government and leaders of the province councils. The strong presence of public office holders sets these parties apart from the socialist parties, in which office holders are significantly less represented. In each party the party leader is elected at the convention for a two-year period, together with one or two deputy leaders and an executive committee that also includes representatives from auxiliary organizations for women and youth. Effective leadership of the party organization remains with this group, and with a smaller working committee in the Center and Christian People's parties. Between national conventions there is also a national committee, with representatives from each province association that function as liaisons between the party leadership group and the membership organization.

The second dimension of the party organization is interorganizational relations. The parties are complex compositions of independent but mutually related organizations. The youth and women's organizations are represented at all levels in the party hierarchy.[30] In the Conservative party, the pensioners' organization is also represented at the national level, in the convention, and in the national committee. The party reform of 1970 improved also the position of these auxiliary organizations. Prior to 1970 the National Committee decided itself how many delegates the auxiliary organizations could send, but the reform gave these organizational units a fixed number of delegates. The auxiliary organizations operate largely independently of the party proper. Thus, attempts to reform them must be accepted by these organizations themselves—and they usually resist. However, in 1993 the Conservative party pushed through a new reform whereby the women's organization, which had been in numerical decline for years, was stripped of its representation and replaced by a special officer for women affairs in the party. As a consequence the women's organization dissolved "itself." The Center party has twice in the last 15 years attempted a similar reform, which the women's organization has successfully resisted.

The third dimension in the party organization is the linkage between the party as such and the party representatives in parliament and other offices. The parliamentary group has its own rules and elects its own officers, but the party organization is linked to the party's parliamentary group through representation of the latter in the party organs and the attendance of organizational representatives in meetings of the parliamentary group. However, an even more important link is the strong personnel overlap between the parliamentary and organizational leadership. The party leader is always a senior party politician with a seat in parliament.[31] In the Conservative party in the postwar period the parliamentary chair and the chair of the party organization have more often than not been held by different persons. All parliamentary groups have an executive committee and usually also among these are found members who also serve on one of the top organizational committees. Thus, although the parliamentary group is largely autonomous in formal organizational terms from the party, in reality the two branches of the party are tightly knit together. As we have seen, the nonsocialist parties give ample representation in the convention for this group and in the Conservative party the MPs were clearly the dominant faction in the organization. This was not just an organizational device in itself but conformed to the party's conception of the importance of the role of the elected representatives in parliament. The 1970 reform undercut the MP's dominance. In the new organizational model the right of the party's MPs to attend meetings of the national committee was removed and replaced by a fixed number of seats. Thus, the relative dominance of the parliamentary group was reduced and regional and auxiliary organizations gained influence.[32]

The turbulence in the Conservative party also had repercussions for the leadership as well. During the two first decades after World War II the party was dominated first by Carl J. Hambro and later by John Lyng. Neither was elected chair of the party organization but both functioned as chairs of the parliamentary group. When the first opportunity arose in 1963 for a nonsocialist coalition government it was self-evident that Lyng would be the prime minister. The division of labor between the party organization and the parliamentary group ended in 1980 when Jo Benkow assumed both positions, although for only four years. In 1986 Rolf Presthus, followed by Jan P. Syse in 1989, also occupied both offices. When Kaci Kullman Five occupied the party chair, Anders Talleraas headed the parliamentary group. Since 1994, Jan Pettersen has occupied both offices.

From the resignation of Erling Norvik as party chair in 1980 until the election of Jan Pettersen in 1994, the Conservative party has had six chairs of the party organization. This high turnover must be seen against three developments in this period.[33] First, after the peak of electoral success in the mid-1980s the party has sustained considerable setbacks. Rightly or wrongly, the party leadership has assumed part of the blame for this. Second, the rise of the Progress party as a competitor to the right, combined with the problems of finding a broad and lasting political consensus with the center parties, pulled the party in various directions. Finally, the organizational reforms and the expansion of the party as a mass movement made it increasingly difficult for one person to successfully manage both positions.

Governmental Experience

The electoral results for the 1961–1993 period (see table 7.1) bring out two facts that underline the possibilities and the limitations of the nonsocialist parties in Norwegian politics. First, although Labor has lost its dominating position, it is still the largest of the Norwegian parties. Second, until 1993 the Conservatives have been the largest of the nonsocialist parties, but not large enough to replace Labor alone. Thus, for the Conservative party to be a governmental alternative to Labor it has to form a single-party minority government or be part of a nonsocialist coalition.

Since 1961 minority governments have been the norm in Norwegian politics (see table 7.5). In the summer of 1963, when the Labor party government lost a vote of confidence, the Conservatives took the initiative to build a coalition with Liberals, the Christian People's party, and the Center party. Although the new government survived for only two weeks, its political impact was significant as it demonstrated that the four nonsocialist parties could work together and be a governmental alternative to Labor. During the last half of the 1960s, the four parties even had a parliamentary majority until the government resigned in 1971. The 1981 election brought a clear nonsocialist majority in parliament, and a particularly strong representation for the Conservative party. The Conservatives formed a minority government—the first single-party Conservative government since 1927. Two years later the government was reorganized as a majority coalition government with the Center and Christian People's parties.[34] Following the 1985 election the coalition continued as a minority government until it lost a critical vote in parliament and resigned in March 1986. The three parties again formed a minority coalition in 1989 but fell apart a year later.

The pattern of coalition formation and termination illuminates the problems of nonsocialist cooperation. First, it is instructive to see which coalitions that have *not* been formed: Labor never engages in any formal coalitions. When the Conservative party is in a coalition government, it is always with more than one of the other nonsocialist parties since neither of them wants to be a junior partner in a government dominated by the

Table 7.5   Norwegian Governments, 1961–1996, by Status and Party Composition

| Period | Party(ies) in Government | | Government Status |
	PM's Party	Other Parties	
Sept. 1961–July 1963	L		Minority
July 1963–Sept. 1963	Co	Li, C, CPP	Minority
Sept. 1963–Oct. 1965	L		Minority
Oct. 1965–March 1971	C	Co, Li, CPP	Majority
March 1971–Oct. 1972	L		Minority
Oct. 1972–Oct. 1973	CPP	Li, C	Minority
Oct. 1973–Jan. 1976	L		Minority
Jan. 1976–Feb. 1981	L		Minority
Feb. 1981–Oct. 1981	L		Minority
Oct. 1981–June 1983	Co		Minority
June 1983–Sept. 1985	Co	CPP, C	Majority
Sept. 1985–May 1986	Co	CPP, C	Minority
May 1986–Oct. 1989	L		Minority
Oct. 1989–Nov. 1990	Co	CPP, C	Minority
Nov. 1990–Oct. 1996	L		Minority
Oct. 1996–present	L		Minority

Note: C: Center, Co: Conservatives party, CPP: Christian People's party, L: Labor, Li: Liberals

Conservatives. The Progress party has so far never been a governing partner, even though it could have provided a majority for a nonsocialist coalition government in 1985 as well as in 1989. That party is considered by the Christian People's party and the Center party to be so extreme as to be an impossible coalition partner.[35]

When coalition governments have fallen, it has twice been due to the EU issue (1971, 1990) and once (1986) due to Progress voting together with the socialist parties in a crucial parliamentary vote. These two ways of ending nonsocialist governments[36] capture more than anything the strategic dilemma for the parties, and in particular for the Conservative party. Both in 1971 and 1990 the coalitions fell apart when the Conservatives' preference for EU membership met with resistance from the other parties. In both cases Labor took over. In 1986 the Progress party, holding the balance between the coalition and the two socialist opposition parties, demonstrated its independence from the nonsocialist parties by voting together with the socialist parties (for different reasons) in a critical parliamentary vote. Thus, for the Conservative party, governing with the Center and Christian People's parties means keeping its distance from Progress.

However, by doing so it alienates parts of its electorate that prefer a more right-wing policy.

Policy Profiles of the Nonsocialist Parties

The prime minister in the first elected nonsocialist coalition government (1965–1971), Per Borten from the Center party, compared the challenge of leading a coalition government of four parties to " . . . carrying a bundle of poles pointing in all directions." His characterization has become an integral part of the Norwegian political vocabulary and is constantly referred to in explaining the fragility of nonsocialist coalitions.

Kaare Strøm and Yørn Y. Leihart's analysis of Norwegian party manifestos found that although there are significant differences in the policy sectors that parties emphasize, it is often a matter of degree rather than of opposite preferences.[37] By means of a factor analysis they identify four factors in the party programs: social welfare, economic liberalism and free-enterprise conservatism, traditional religion, and technological efficiency. They conclude that until the early 1970s party programs were characterized by policy convergence.[38] Thus, even the Conservative party, which supposedly should represent a completely different view of society to that of the Labor party, has presented policies that do not contradict Labor in many policy areas. A reason for this is that the only way for the Conservative party to challenge Labor as a governing party has been to work with parties to its left. To break out of the 17 to 20 percent share of the electorate, the party had to present policies suitable to larger parts of the electorate. When Sjur Lindebrække was elected chairman of the party in 1962 he initiated a modernization of the party program to make it more credible in the eyes of the electorate, leading some commentators to characterize it as "socialistic."[39] Thus, when finally coming into government office, the nonsocialist parties and the Conservatives among them effectively maintained the work of preceding social democratic governments. The Conservative party has been under constant pressure to tone down its conservatism in order to build a broad political coalition.[40] The appearance of the Progress party seems to have pulled the Conservatives in a more right-wing direction in the post-1973 period, particularly on the first two factors, which correspond closely to the left-right axis.[41]

On the third factor, which taps support for traditional moral-religious issues, the Conservative party appears rather neutral, neither negatively nor particularly positively associated with the issues. Finally, the fourth factor is identified with regional economic development and education and includes the vital center-periphery concerns in Norwegian politics, again with diminishing differences between the parties.

From 1973—when Progress first appeared—a "political swing door" opened between the Conservatives and the new party. Strøm and Lijphart's article was written prior to the explosion of support for the Progress party in 1989, when the party increased its parliamentary representation from 2 to 22 seats. In that election, 18 percent of the Conservative party's 1985 voters shifted to Progress.[42]

We may look closer at three policy areas to see where the three larger nonsocialist parties now agree and where they disagree: economic policies and the role of the public sector, cultural policies, and foreign policy. It may also be fruitful to contrast the policies of the Conservative party with that of the Progress party, as the Conservative party is struggling to find a balance between its traditional partners in the political center and the populist Progress party.

Economic Policy and the Role of the Public Sector

In the field of economic policy, the Conservative party favors deregulation and privatization together with lower overall taxation as means both to reduce the size of the public sector, which the party identifies as a hazard to individual freedom, and to deal with what the party identifies as the greatest challenge facing the Norwegian society: unemployment. But there is still a long distance between the Conservatives and the Progress party. The Conservatives do not favor privatization of governmental agencies like the railways, the mail, and telecommunications, but would rather see them reorganized as government shareholding companies. The public-sector role is still stressed in the program: "An efficient market requires a strong state to regulate the limits of the market." Also, the Center and the Christian People's parties emphasize private ownership as essential, but the former has lately taken a completely different perspective of the role of the public sector. The Center party stresses the importance of political involvement in the economy to achieve a better distribution of resources in society. A dominant perspective for the party is to maintain the distribution of population in the Norwegian territory. In order to achieve this aim, the public sector must be actively involved in supporting local government as well as in protecting economic enterprises from the forces of market liberalism. The party sees a pure capitalist market as incompatible with the need for an ecologically sustainable development. This is a rather different view of economic policy than the one promoted by the Conservatives. The Christian People's party is somewhere between these two extremes. The contrast between the Center and the Conservative parties is particularly marked in agricultural policy. The Conservatives favor a greater role for the market in the heavily regulated and subsidized agricultural sector, including removing import barriers. The Center party takes the exact opposite view: the structure of the agricultural sector in Norway is seen as the backbone of the regions and localities. Rather than leaving the sector to the market, the party favors extensive support schemes and protection from international markets.

The disagreement between the parties over the public sector's responsibility for health and social welfare is more of degrees than of kinds. Though the Conservatives " . . . will protect the core of the public health, education and social welfare provisions,"[43] at the same time the party now advocates a much more significant role for the private sector and individual choice. The individual is seen as a consumer, rather than as a client. Efficiency and freedom to choose suppliers of medical services are stressed by the party program in clear contrast to the programs of the socialist parties and the Center party, and more in line with that of the Progress party.

Cultural and Moral Issues

All three parties emphasize the Christian basis for their view of society, but nowhere is this as pronounced as in the Christian People's party, where the Christian perspective runs like a red thread through all of the party program. Although conservative parties are usually associated with a positive view of religion, the Norwegian Conservative party has a rather low-profile religious perspective. The role of the church is described in positive but not very strongly committed formulations, except that the church must have " . . . independence in theological issues, which the state can not overturn."[44] This muted commitment to religion is reflected in the party's electorate. Conservative voters are not religiously active. In 1993 only 5 percent reported membership in religious associations, while the Conservative party's coalition partner, the Christian People's party, 58 percent of its membership were affiliated with religious associations. Also, 87 percent of Conservative voters report they have not attended any church service for a year, while in the Christian People's party more than half report at least one attendance.

Another strong cultural tradition in Norway is teetotalism. Again, the Conservative party is rather neutral on this issue. The party advocates close supervision of sale and service licenses and claims that " . . . preventive efforts is the best investment against excessive alcohol consumption."[45] On this issue Conservative voters are at opposite ends from the Christian People's party: 5.5 percent of Conservative and 63 percent of the Christian People's party voters are teetotalers. Also, when it comes to belief in traditional societal institutions there is a distinct "conservatism" in the Conservative party. The family's role in socialization and care are seen as vital and should therefore be strengthened. Greater economic resources (i.e., less taxes) and more freedom to choose services are ways to achieve this goal, but the party also acknowledges that " . . . for some people marriage is not possible or the proper framework for family life."[46]

Finally, on the abortion issue the Conservative party is divided; hence abortion is not mentioned at all in the party program. When abortion was liberalized in 1980 the party was so divided internally that it let each MP vote as he or she preferred. Among the party's electorate 58 percent of the voters agree with the current free abortion law, the highest percentage of all the nonsocialist parties and almost the same as among Labor party voters. The Christian People's party is, however, united in its opposition to the law and favors its repeal. When the party takes part in nonsocialist coalition governments it declines to lead the Ministry of Social Affairs because the abortion law belongs to that ministry's portfolio, although the rest of the ministry's portfolio covers policy areas that are at the heart of its concern, such as welfare policy and alcohol policy.

Support for the cultural sector in general is where the Conservative party—and the other parties—is furthest away from the Progress party. Where Progress wants to privatize virtually everything in the cultural sector and withdraw most public financial support, the Conservative party takes the opposite view: " . . . the government must have the responsibility for the widespread diffusion of culture."[47]

Foreign Policy

With the exception of Norway's relationship to the EU, there has been a strong consensus on foreign policy issues among the nonsocialist parties and also with the Labor party. Two aspects seem to be particularly relevant here. First, all parties are strong supporters of Norway's membership in NATO with its self-imposed limitations.[48] Second, Norway's development aid programs have been backed by a broad political consensus. The differences between parties have been over the specific orientation of such programs toward certain countries and for certain program activities, but rarely over the policy in general. This includes a substantial level of governmental aid, now 1.2 percent of the gross national product. Among the nonsocialist parties, indeed among all parties in Norway, the Christian People's party has development aid programs as one of its top priorities, in sharp contrast to the Progress party, which favors a total abolition of such state-funded policies. Third, all parties favor extensive Nordic cooperation, although in the early 1950s there was considerable skepticism. However, there are different motivations. For the Conservatives, the Nordic level became a stepping-stone to closer relationship with the EU, while for the

Center and Christian People's party Nordic cooperation assumed the role of a substitute for wider European integration. Finally, in international trade policies, the consensus among the parties has been limited to trade in industrial goods and partly to secure a favorable international regime for shipping—a major economic sector in Norway. However, when the primary sectors of the economy—agriculture and fisheries—are involved, the Center party in particular withdraws from the international orientation while the Conservatives have been more favorably inclined to international competition.

Immigration

The immigration issue has become a relevant issue in Norwegian politics since the late 1980s, and has been the most important issue for the supporters of the Progress party in the recent elections. Progress is the most vocal party opposing both the scale of immigration as well as protesting against what the party perceives as too liberal ways of dealing with immigrants already in Norway. The Conservative party on the other hand takes a different position. It emphasizes the responsibilities of the Norwegian society to take care of refugees and asylum seekers. It contends that immigrants must be allowed to practice their culture and religion and that "refugees and asylum seekers shall have the same rights and duties in society as Norwegians." The party explicitly "rejects the nationalistic feelings now spreading in Europe."[49] The contrast between the Progress party and the Conservatives on this issue is significant, and among both Conservative voters and politicians the anti-immigration views of Progress are seen as incompatible with the Conservative party's policies. Among Conservative party voters, there are rather weak expressions of nationalism. Oddbjørn Knutsen[50] has analyzed the linkage between party preference and a series of indicators tapping national feelings. He constructs five indices of national identity. On the index called "nationalism" Progress party voters score the highest, 7.7. The Conservative party voters score 5.8, which place them between the Labor party and Socialist Left party. Only on one index, "pride in the welfare state," are Conservative voters among the three top parties.

In a comparative perspective, the conservatism of the Conservative party is therefore clearly limited to some sectors of society and politics. In defense policy, the economic sphere, and attitudes on individual rights and obligations, the party is a typical conservative party. But in terms of cultural aspects there is a greater variance. Cultural policy, as a form of preserving and expressing Norwegian and international art forms, is seen as an important arena for the state. But in aspects of traditional culture, such as religion and teetotalism, and on moral issues like abortion, the party is hardly conservative at all. Also, the international orientation of the party is more typical of other northern European parties rather than of British or American conservatism. In sum, economically it is conservative, culturally modernized, and politically internationalized.

The EU Issue in Norwegian Politics

The EU-membership issue is the Achilles' heel of Norwegian politics. Twice the electorate has voted on the issue in specially arranged referenda;[51] twice membership has been rejected in spite of substantial parliamentary majorities in favor, and twice it has created internal problems in several parties and toppled nonsocialist governments. On this issue the Conservative party finds itself in opposition to its partners on the nonsocialist wing and in alliance with its traditional opponent, the Labor party. Thus, each time the EU has appeared as an issue (1971 and 1990), and a highly salient one, the nonsocialist coalition fell apart.

The Conservatives have been the only party more or less solidly united in favor of EU membership.[52] After membership was rejected in 1972, Europe became a non-issue in Norwegian politics for almost 20 years. Partly as a result of the vitalization of European integration in the 1980s and fuelled by the transformation in Eastern Europe, the issue reappeared in 1989. By that time, the Conservative party had exhausted the possibilities of unseating the Labor party minority government by a nonsocialist coalition in the fall of 1986.[53] Inside the party, the strategy of "leaning over backwards" to please the centrist parties was replaced by the demand for a distinct party platform: the EU-membership issue was again taken out of the political closet. In spite of this, a successful attempt was made to rebuild the nonsocialist coalition, provided that EU membership was not on the government's agenda. This time the Conservatives and the Center party— the strongest opponent of EU membership—shared an interest in forming a government, but for opposite reasons. For the Conservatives, the government might bring Norway closer to the EU, while for the Center party being in the government might prevent or delay closeness to the EU. A difference from 1972 was the ongoing negotiations about the European Economic Area (EEA). After a year, the government fell apart and Labor completed the EEA negotiations—which caused further conflicts between the nonsocialist parties. Forced by the sudden and quite unexpected EU-membership applications from Finland and Sweden, the membership issue was pushed onto the Norwegian political agenda sooner than many had preferred. From being an issue for the Conservative party, it became an issue for every party. In the build-up to the 1994 referendum, the positions of the parties were like this:

	EU Membership—For	EU Membership—Against
EEA-treaty—For	Labor[55] Conservatives Progress	Christian People's Party Liberals
EEA-treaty—Against	—	Center Socialist Left

For the Conservatives, EU membership is seen as supporting traditional Norwegian foreign-policy positions, such as integration in multinational organizations, and conforming with their economic philosophy of market orientation and less governmental regulation. Even so, the party hardly embraces the vision of a deeply integrated Europe but subscribes to the subsidiarity principle: only issues that cannot be solved locally, regionally, or nationally should belong at the European level.

Although 52 percent of the electorate rejected membership, and the Labor party prime minister, Gro Harlem Brundtland, suffered her greatest political defeat, the referendum had no implication for the government as such. The constitution does not permit dissolution of parliament and the Labor party announced before the referendum that they would not resign even if the voters rejected membership.[55] The parliamentary balance therefore remained locked by the 1993 election results. In the postreferendum period the Conservative party has lingered in no-man's-land in parliament. Increasingly, the center parties have established de facto political cooperation with the Labor party in several policy areas. But in its efforts to accommodate Norwegian laws and regulations to the EEA treaty, the government has relied on support from the Conservatives and the Christian People's party. Here is an important difference from the post-1972 referendum period. At that time the European issue disappeared from the political agenda, but this time the EEA agreement has built a further barrier between the Center party and the right. In addition, the issue might reappear, pending the next expansion of the EU into Central and Eastern Europe and the revision of the Maastricht Treaty.

Left, Right, or Straight Ahead: The Conservative Dilemma?

While it is true that the Conservative party has moved to the right in economic policies, it is also true that other parties have done the same. The problem for the Conservative party is that the Labor government has already implemented several of the Conservatives' pet projects. Deregulation, reorganization, and partial privatization have become parts of the government's policy portfolio, preempting many of the Conservative arguments while leaving the Progress party to be a more vocal advocate by going even further. Thus, although the social and economic changes have increased the "natural" electorate for the Conservatives, they have only been partially successful in mobilizing it. With the right turn in the Labor party, the "ideological gap" between the two traditional adversaries has narrowed. In 1993 the Conservatives lost 14 percent of its 1989 voters to Labor, and of those still voting Conservative, 48 percent mentioned the Labor party as their second choice. This is three times more than Conservative voters preferring the Progress party and more than double those who prefer any of the centrist parties as second choice. The combination of the right turn of Labor in economic policy and the organization of the public sector, the rise of Progress as being the most "conservative" party, and the shadow of the EU issue, have locked the Conservative party in a corner: if it moves to the right, seeking to coopt or cooperate with Progress, as some parts of the party prefer, it will in the process burn bridges to the center parties. However, keeping its distance from Progress does not automatically mean an alliance with the center. In the post-EU referendum period, the Center party and the Christian People's party have positioned themselves much closer to the Labor party and the Socialist Left party in parliament, particularly on economic issues and on the central-local relationship. Time and again the Center party leadership has declared the old "left-right" division dead. Combined with the Center party's leftward orientation on economic issues and the structure of the public sector, Norway's future relationship with the EU represent serious obstacles against rebuilding the "center-right" alternative in Norwegian politics. Increasingly, the Conservative party has become isolated. The Progress party continues to attract considerable electoral support by mobilizing the anti-immigration sentiments in the electorate. The net effect has been to land the Conservatives in search of a message that will present it as a distinct political alternative to Labor and also as a credible alternative to a Labor government. This strategic dilemma has yet to be resolved and may come to depend as much on internal factors in the party, as on external ones. Internally, one faction advocates building a coalition with the Christian People's party and possibly a reinvigorated Liberal party. With the current left turning of the Center party, it seems unrealistic that a broad four-party government can be rebuilt. A second possibility is to continue in "splendid isolation," hoping that the parliamentary cooperation between Labor and the two center parties sooner or later will break down. A third, and the least likely alternative, is for the pro-Progress party wing in the

Conservative party to gain the upper hand. Its malaise has been very well captioned by the following quote from the Labor party newspaper: "The indecisiveness the last decade between the Progress party at one extreme and the Center party at the other has affected the Conservatives with the syndrome of the Liberals: one does not know where one wants to go. Therefore one never arrives anywhere."[56]

Notes

1. See Stein Rokkan, "Geography, Religion and Social Class: Cross-cutting Cleavages in Norwegian Politics," in S. M. Lipset and S. Rokkan, eds., *Party Systems and Voter Alignments* (New York: Free Press, 1967), pp. 367–444; and Henry Valen, *Valg og politikk* (Oslo: NKS-forlaget, 1981).

2. Parties that appeared independent of other parties early in Norwegian history or current smaller parties without any noticeable impact on national politics have not been included in the figure. A total of 25 parties were registered in 1996.

3. The party was first formed as an electoral alliance (1973) and transformed to a regular party in 1975. A Marxist-Leninist party, AKP-ml, had also been formed in 1973.

4. Originally named after its founder Anders Lange: "Anders Langes parti til sterk nedsettelse av skatter og avgifter og bekjempelse av offentlige inngrep" (Anders Lange's party for strong reduction in taxes and fees and prevention of public interference), renamed Progress party in 1976.

5. See Alf Kaartvedt, *Kampen mot parlamentarisme. Høyres politikk 1880–1884* (Oslo: Universitetsforlaget, 1967).

6. See Leiv Mjeldheim, *Folkerørsla som vart parti: Venstre frå 1880-åra til 1905* (Oslo: Universitetsforlaget, 1984).

7. See Tertit Aasland, *Fra landmannsorganisasjon til Bondeparti* (Oslo: Universitetsforlaget, 1974).

8. See K. Lomeland, *Kristelig Folkeparti blir til* (Oslo: Universitetsforlaget, 1971).

9. See Bernt Hagtvet and Tor Bjørklund, eds., *Høyrebølgen—epokeskifte i norsk politikk?* (Oslo: Cappelen, 1981); and B. Cooper et al., eds., *The Resurgence of Conservatism in Anglo-American Democracies* (Durham, N.C.: Duke University Press, 1988).

10. *OECD: Historical Statistics, 1960–1990* (Paris, Organization for Economic Cooperation and Development, 1992).

11. The number of post–high school students in 1950 was less than 10,000, while in 1990 it was ten times higher. In 1950, 52 percent of the population lived in densely populated areas, increasing to 72 percent in 1990.

12. Henry Valen and Bernt O. Aardal, *Et valg i perspektiv. Stortingsvalget 1981* (Oslo: Central Bureau of Statistics, 1983), p. 121.

13. Teetotalism refers both to membership in temperance organizations as well as declaration of temperance itself. The language issue refers to whether or

not the respondent in the survey uses "nynorsk" the version of Norwegian language spoken mostly in rural areas of the Southern and Western parts of the country, or "bokmål," the language version dominating in urbanized areas. Religious activity include membership in religious associations as well as self-declaration of "fairly active."

14. 1989 has been selected rather than 1993 because the later election was almost totally dominated by the approaching EU-membership issue and the results were highly atypical of Norwegian elections. Opinion surveys in 1996, as well as the local elections of 1995, indicate the exceptional nature of the 1993 election.

15. Henry Valen, Bernt O. Aardal, and Gunnar Vogt, *Endring og Kontinuitet. Stortingsvalget 1989* (Oslo: Central Bureau of Statistics in Norway, 1992), p. 103.

16. Stein Rokkan, "Geography, Religion, and Social Class"; and Henry Valen, *Valg og politikk.*

17. Urbanization of the electorate may have a less marked impact on the party's representation. This is because the number of seats per constituency, identical with the provinces, is skewed deliberately in such a way as to benefit peripheral areas. The number of seats per constituency is specified in the constitution, and changing the constitution is a cumbersome process.

18. See Dag Arne Christensen, "Fornyinga av bondepartia i Noreg og Sverige," in *Partiene i en brytningstid,* Knut Heidar and Lars Svåsand, eds., (Bergen: Alma Mater, 1994), pp. 327–355.

19. Already, in the province council elections of 1995, its support slipped to 11.8 percent and further declined in the polls in 1996.

20. The negative assessment of the local branches was expressed this way, by Mr. Sirkka, secretary to a 1968 committee on organizational structure: "The branches today are reduced to an unrepresentative discussion club . . . functioning as appeal instance for querulants and dissatisfied party members. . . . The branches are in reality no instrument for the party in communicating its message to groups of voters." (Cited in Asbjørn Brandsrud, *Lovdebatt og organisasjonsstruktur. Holdninger til organisasjonsarbeid i Høyre, ca. 1955–1977.* Unpublished dissertation in history, University of Oslo, 1983, p. 116).

21. See Francis Sejersted, *Opposisjon og posisjon. Høyre 1945–1984* (Oslo: Cappelen, 1984).

22. Bjarne Kristiansen and Lars Svåsand, "The Conservative Party in Norway: From Opposition to Alternative Government," in *Conservative Politics in Western Europe,* Zygmunt Layton-Henry, ed., (London: Macmillan, 1982), pp. 103–130.

23. See Sejersted, *Opposisjon og posisjon,* and Per Selle and Lars Svåsand: "Partiorganisasjon og valgresultat," in *Strukturer og prosesser. Studier i finske, norske og svenske partiorganisasjoner,* Gøran Djupsund and Lars Svåsand, eds., (Åbo: Åbo Academy Press, 1990).

24. See Stein Rokkan and Henry Valen, "The Mobilization of the Periphery," in Rokkan, *Citizens, Elections, Parties* (Oslo: Universitetsforlaget, 1970), pp. 169–180.

25. The party was also able to increase its membership, the only party to reverse the general trend of decline in party members.
26. See Knut Heidar, "The Polymorphic Nature of Party Membership," *European Journal of Political Research* 22:1 (1992): 61–89.
27. Data on the composition of the Norwegian party structures are available in my chapters on Norway, in *Party Organizations. A Data Handbook,* Richard S. Katz and Peter Mair, eds., (London: Sage, 1994), and in Lars Svåsand, "Change and Adaptation in Norwegian Party Organizations," in *How Parties Organize,* Richard S. Katz and Peter Mair, eds., (London: Sage, 1994).
28. See Henry Valen, "Decentralization and Group Representation," in *Candidate Selection in Comparative Perspective,* Michael Gallagher and Michael Marsh, eds., (London: Sage, 1988), pp. 210–235.
29. A similar delegate allocation principle applies also to the Center and Christian People's parties.
30. Additional auxiliary organizations may exist for students, the party press, and educational programs.
31. In 1962 Sjur Lindebrække was elected chair of the Conservative party without being a member of parliament. Today, it seems highly unlikely that a major party would choose a nonparliamentarian as party chair.
32. A former senior Conservative politician, Lars Roar Langslet, attributes the decline of the party to these reforms (Lars Roar Langslett, "Høyres svekkede stortingsgruppe," *Aftenposten,* February 27, 1991).
33. One leadership change was caused when Rolf Presthus suddenly passed away in 1988.
34. Initially, the Christian People's party had refused to join in a nonsocialist coalition government because of the law permitting abortion. The Liberals had lost their two last seats in parliament in 1985.
35. This has not prevented local alliances between parties, but attempts to form a city government in Oslo (1996) between Progress and the Conservatives created sharply opposing views in the latter party.
36. The first nonsocialist government formed in the summer of 1963 was defeated as it made its government declaration after only two weeks. In 1973 a three-party government of Liberals, Christian People's party, and the Center party, had been in office for a year, following the Labor government's resignation in 1972 when it lost its bid for Norwegian membership in the EU in a referendum. In these two cases, the nonsocialist governments were considered to be only intermediary and not lasting cabinets.
37. Kaare Strøm and Jørn Y. Leipart, "Ideology, Strategy and Party Competition in Postwar Norway," *European Journal of Political Research* 17:3 (1989): 263–288.
38. Ibid., p. 280.
39. See Sjur Lindebrække, *Tro og tillit* (Oslo: Aschehoug, 1983), pp. 148–150.
40. See Sten Berglund and Ulf Lindstrom, "The Scandinavian Party System in Transition," *European Journal of Political Research* 7 (1978): 187–204;

and Sten Ljunggren, "Conservatism in Norway and Sweden," in *The Transformation of Modern Conservatism,* B. Girvin, ed. (London: Sage, 1988), pp. 120–144.

41. This finding, has been confirmed by Harmel and Svåsand using a different method. See Robert Harmel and Lars Svåsand, "The Impact of New Political Parties: The Cases of the Danish and Norwegian Progress Parties," paper presented at the Conference on Party Politics Towards the Year 2000, University of Manchester, January 1995.

42. See Henry Valen, Bernt O. Aardal, and Gunnar Vogt: *Endring og kontinuitet. Stortingsvalget 1989* (Oslo: Central Bureau of Statistics in Norway, 1992).

43. *Conservative election program 1993,* p. 40.

44. Ibid., p. 52.

45. Ibid., p. 41.

46. Ibid., p. 34.

47. Ibid., p. 51.

48. No permanent foreign bases in peacetime, no nuclear arms stationed in peacetime. The Progress party is the only party favoring a rejection of these limitations.

49. *Conservative election program 1993,* p. 73.

50. Oddbjørn Knutsen, "Dimensjoner ved nasjonal identitet. Deres årsaker og konsekvenser," presentation at the Conference on National Identity, NSD/ARENA, Bergen, February 7–8, 1996.

51. The Norwegian constitution does not demand referendums on any issues, but parliament may decide to arrange "consultative referendums."

52. About 18 percent of Conservative party supporters voted "No" to EU membership in 1994. For a general overview of party positions on EU membership, see Ulf Lindstrøm and Lars Svåsand, "Scandinavian Political Parties and the EU," in *Political Parties and the European Union,* John Gaffney, ed. (London, Routledge, 1996), pp. 204–219.

53. For an excellent analysis, see Kaare Strøm, "The Presthus Debacle: Intraparty Politics and Bargaining Failure in Norway," *American Political Science Review* 88 (March 1994): 112–127.

54. A fraction within Labor opposed EU membership but favored the EEA treaty.

55. This was a lesson from 1972 when Prime Minister Trygve Bratteli said the government would resign in the event of a "No" victory. This move was perceived as a threat against Labor supporters and caused severe conflicts within the party.

56. Leading article in *Arbeiderbladet* (Labor newspaper, February 28, 1996).

CHAPTER EIGHT

Conservative Parties in Democratic Transitions: The Center-Right in Spain and Portugal

Maria Theresa Frain and Howard Wiarda

On October 1, 1995, the center-right Social Democratic party (PSD) of Portugal was voted out of office and replaced as the party of government by a revived, more centrist Socialist party (PS). The Portuguese PSD had been in power since 1985 and in and out of power in various coalition arrangements since 1979. On March 3, 1996, the Socialist Workers' party of Spain (PSOE) was narrowly defeated at the polls by the People's party (PP), a center-right party led by José María Aznar. Both these electoral shifts, although pointing in opposite ideological directions, serve to indicate how firmly democracy has been established in Spain and Portugal. Portugal has had several peaceful, democratic changes of administration since the "revolution of the carnations" in 1974 that overthrew the authoritarian *Estado Novo* regime of António de Oliveira Salazar and Marcello Caetano. But the recent victory of the PP in Spain marked only the second time since Generalissimo Francisco Franco's death in 1975 that there had been a democratic electoral shift from one administration to the opposition. Two such democratic changes of administration are usually considered by political scientists as a major criteria for establishing that a successful transition to democracy has occurred.[1]

The history and experience of the conservative parties of Spain and Portugal provide several unique and especially interesting variations on the topic of conservative parties in Western Europe:

1. Democracy in Spain and Portugal is a relatively new phenomenon, dating only from the mid-1970s. After only one generation, democracy has been consolidated in both countries through the establishment of parties, a party system, and party government.

2. The newness of the parties is complicated by a long history in both countries of anti–political party attitudes manipulated to their advantage by Franco and Salazar. Parties in Iberia were often viewed as diverse "factions" that detracted from the *grandeur* of the nation.

3. Because authoritarianism lasted so long in the Iberian Peninsula, conservative parties, or parties of the right—often identified with the discredited former regime—have had a particularly difficult time organizing, building a party base, and securing stable electoral support. Such parties must struggle to shake their identification with the defunct authoritarian regime. They also have had to organize a programmatic, mass-based political party to compete exclusively in the electoral arena.

4. The role of conservative parties in general in the transition to democracy literature has been almost completely ignored; hardly any serious theoretical literature exists on the topic. More than that, an ideological mindset may be involved. The assumption both politically and in some of the literature is that transitions to democracy often take place in two stages: first to moderate, middle-class democracy, and then to "full" economic and social democracy. So once there is a transition to left-of-center rule, little thought or attention has been devoted to conservative parties or to a reversion to conservative rule.

5. Because of their relatively recent entry into the European Union and the large subsidies they have been receiving, neither Spain nor Portugal—including their conservative parties—have so far devoted much serious attention to state downsizing, welfare reform, or the neoliberal economic agenda. But EU subsidies are winding down and both Spain and Portugal are struggling to meet the tough convergence criteria embodied in the Economic and Monetary Union (EMU) of the Maastricht Treaty.[2] The economies and social welfare systems of both Spain and Portugal are vastly overextended and in desperate need of reform. Hence, the conservative and neoliberal agendas will now, belatedly, be at the fore. Conservative parties are not the only ones having to deal with these issues, but because these are "their issues" the incidence and fall-out from this agenda—for good or for ill—are likely to resonate most strongly on the center-right.

6. One other theme merits mention in this preliminary list, and that is the parallels and divergences of changes in Spain and Portugal. To the extent the Portuguese revolution was peaceful and democratic, Spain wished to emulate it; but to the degree it verged toward violence, anarchy, and communism, Spain sought to avoid it. Similarly with political parties: the success of the Portuguese conservative government in power in the 1980s through the mid-1990s helped make a conservative comeback in Spain more palatable.

These factors make the subject matter of conservative parties in Spain and Portugal especially intriguing and significant. The discussion now turns to a more in-depth analysis of the conservative parties in Spain and Portugal, their electoral support, organizational bases, and positions on the main issues. In order to understand what conservatism means in these Iberian countries, we will examine how the parties behave in power (Spain) and out of power (Portugal), and their relations with other parties in the system, including parties to the far right. In the conclusion, we will return to some of the themes raised in the introduction.

The Conservative Parties of Spain and Portugal

The center-right parties of Spain and Portugal are of relatively recent vintage, dating only from the early-to-mid-1970s. However, conservative positions in Spain and Portugal, regardless of party name and even predating the formation of political parties, have had a very long history. In this section we will briefly identify the key center-right parties, look at the base of their electoral support, and examine party organization—including both internal unity and cohesion—and relations with other movements on the right.

Spain's People's Party

The Spanish PP was organized in 1988; only eight years later, on March 3, 1996, the PP won its first national election and became Spain's governing (though minority) party for the first time.[3] Results of Spain's elections are shown in table 8.1. The PP was organized to fill the large void that had existed on the center-right in Spain. The Spanish right had a long history going back to the eighteenth century—and even longer if one considers the long sweep of Iberian history. Following Franco's death in 1975, the Spanish right had been discredited and went into eclipse. This right consisted of a variety of monarchists, conservative Catholics, old corporatists (not of the "neo" variety), and even a handful of "francoists" left over from an earlier time. With its allies in the Church, the Army, and the elite, the right had seldom seen the need to organize as a political party and to contest elections. Even Franco's *Falange,* later rebaptized as the *Movimiento,* was viewed not so much as a political party but as a movement, a rally, a civic union. Political parties were viewed not only as divisive, but as part of the hated "liberalism" that both Franco and Salazar had repudiated in the 1930s.[4]

With Franco's death, the right reconstituted itself as the People's Alliance (AP), headed by Franco's ex-cabinet minister and intellectual Manuel Fraga. But in the immediate post-Franco euphoria for democracy and repudiation of the old regime, the AP had little electoral support. More important was the Union of the Democratic Center (UCD), the political machine put together by Adolfo Suárez, the young president chosen by King Juan Carlos to preside over the post-Franco democratic transition. The UCD consisted of over a dozen moderately conservative and bureaucratic groups whose chief purpose was to guide the transition in preferred directions while keeping Suárez (and themselves) in power. The UCD had no coherently defined political program or ideology and it showed a disturbing tendency to fragment into its component parts after Suárez's electoral victories in 1977 and 1979. Suárez grew tired of the constant feuding within the UCD and eventually resigned as president in January 1981. Leopoldo Calvo-Sotelo replaced him until the party literally disintegrated at the hands of Felipe González's Socialists in the October 1982 legislative elections. During the rest of the 1980s the UCD continued its decline until it all but disappeared from the electoral map. That conservative parties successfully emerged at the regional level—especially in Catalonia and the Basque Country—served to cut into any nationally organized conservative party's gains in those important areas. By the mid-1980s a huge gap existed on the center-right of the Spanish political party spectrum.

It was in this gap that the reconstituted PP under Aznar sought to find its political raison d'être. The PP pulled together remnants of the AP and UCD, monarchists, reformed francoists, conservatives, progressives, humanists, Catholics and liberals. But unlike other rightist parties, the PP was from the beginning a political party, committed fully to democracy and to contestation in the electoral arena alone. It was not just a political machine or a front for more extraconstitutional political machinations. It sought to build an electoral coalition to bring together the center-right as an avenue for winning elections. Its platforms (often vague, yet pragmatic) and indeed its entire political strategy (inclusive, nonconfrontational, nonthreatening, broadly based) was designed to oust González and the Socialists from power by electoral means. It gradually built up its

Table 8.1 Spanish 1993/1996 Election Results

Party	1996 % Vote	Seats	1993 % Vote	Seats
Popular Party	38.85	156	34.76	141
Socialist (PSOE)	37.48	141	38.76	159
United Left	10.58	21	9.95	18
Catalan Coalition (CiU)	4.61	16	4.94	17
Basque Nationalists	1.28	5	1.24	5
Canarian Coalition	.89	4	.88	4
Galician National Bloc	.88	2	.54	—
Herri Batasuna	.73	2	.88	2
Republican Left of Catalonia	.67	1	.80	1
Basque Solidarity (EA)	.46	1	.55	1
Valencian Union	.37	1	.48	1

Source: Ministry of Justice

strength in local, European Parliamentary, and national elections of 1993 (which it came close to winning). It subsequently won more local and European Parliamentary elections; since 1994 polls had consistently shown the PP favored over the Socialists by 8 to 12 percentage points. Its electoral victory in 1996, however narrow, was the culmination of these mobilizing and reconstituting efforts.

The PP has skillfully and steadily moved to capture the emerging broad center of the Spanish political system, as the country itself has become more affluent, middle class, and centrist. The party's social base of electoral support has become not the old political hacks and ideologues associated with the Franco regime, but young people, women, and the urban middle class. In the 1996 election, the average PP voter was male; from the middle to upper-middle classes; a businessman, agricultural worker, state-employee or a member of the liberal professions; an inhabitant of a city of more than 100,000 people; and between 30 and 60 years of age.[5] It used to be in Spain that conservatism was concentrated among the elites, the old, and the traditionally Catholic and conservative peasantry. But recently, the PP has been winning strongly in the northern industrial provinces and in the big cities where the Socialists have long been strong. Now, in a remarkable reversal of positions, it is the Socialists who are strong among the old and the farmers because of the large subsidies they have been receiving from state coffers. The PP has been steadily building support among the more modern and dynamic sectors of the Spanish population.

The PP is a national party, but in order to govern it will have to work out an arrangement—as González had to do in 1993—with the regional parties, especially the Catalans. Moreover, while the PP has overcome many of the problems of division that earlier plagued the UCD, there are still many fragments within its ranks that will need to be satisfied to hold the party together and enable it to govern effectively. At one level, there are the various political "families" (patronage groups) within the PP that will want to see their loyalty and efforts on behalf of the party rewarded. At another level in Spain's complex political system, there are the regional groups (with their powerful local "barons") who help deliver the vote in their districts but who do not consistently share the national goals of the party.

Nor is the party entirely unified ideologically. The historic right still professes adherence to conservative ideals of order, discipline, and Castilian centralism; the monarchists and conservative Catholics of various hues all have a place within the PP. *Opus Dei,* a vigorous but secretive Catholic group, is said to be strongly present among Aznar's close advisors and cabinet ministers. There are also various "Thatcherites" among the party elite who are libertarian on social issues and believers in government downsizing and privatization in the economic realm. Aznar had resisted identifying himself too closely with that or any other faction of the party. A reader of David Hume and Karl Popper, Aznar claims he is a European-style "liberal, not a Thatcherite." In office, the enigmatic and sometimes inscrutable Aznar must define his policies more clearly. Meanwhile, the battle of the different factions of the PP to capture his mind and policies goes on.

At this stage, Spain has no serious, separate party of the far right. The PP, therefore, has the entire center-right to itself. Moreover, Spain has changed so greatly since the 1950s that, while the traditional right still has some influence within the PP, it is not able to dominate it. Traditional conservatives will stay inside the PP and will continue to vote for Aznar, but they cannot control him. The new social bases of the party (young people, women, middle class), its new leadership (Aznar is a consensus person, not an ideologue), and the party platform (discussed below), all point to the fact that the PP is a new, democratic, European-style conservative party. It has successfully exorcised the ghost of Franco. Having never been in power before, however, it is still to be seen how the party defines itself as the party of "government" in specific policy areas.

The Social Democratic Party of Portugal

The revolutionary events of the April 25, 1974, which brought about the rapid demise of the *Estado Novo* in Portugal, caught liberal elements associated with the old regime off guard and not well prepared to deal with the dominant political enemy to the left.[6] The PSD—first christened the

Popular Democratic party (PPD)—organized as a political party in early May 1974. Informed by the country's political, social, and economic realities, PSD leaders formulated a sufficiently vague and moderate (non-Marxist) program that provided practical, not ideological, ways to bring democracy and modernization to Portugal. Given the radical tempo of the transition, the new party claimed its space was in the center/center-left of the emerging political spectrum; to have been considered anything else would have been an act of political suicide. Under the charismatic leadership of Francisco Sá Carneiro, the PSD developed into a populist, national mass-based political party.

The PSD drew support from a diverse range of moderate opposition forces formerly associated with the *Estado Novo:* liberals, university student movements, masons, Catholic associations, cooperatives, and other semilegal opposition groups. By staking its claim to the center of the political spectrum, the PSD hoped to garner support from the majority of non-Marxist "leftists" alienated by the radical rhetoric of the socialists and communists at the time. Looking to its right, the formation of a small, more conservative party, the Social Democratic Center (CDS) has continuously cut into the PSD's share of traditional voters on the right.

Denied access to state power and its patronage benefits (unlike the UCD in Spain), PSD leaders knew that in order to survive the revolutionary tempo of the transition they would need to develop a mass-based organizational structure. The formation of the CDS three months after the PSD gave Sá Carneiro and party founders an important head start in establishing a national, grass-roots organization. This was especially true in the islands (Azores and Madeira) and the northern, rural interior of the country where the PSD and CDS would continually compete for conservative votes. The PSD was successful in building a national party structure on the preexisting network of patron-client relations in these areas. However, party leaders found it difficult (then and now) to attract a broad constituency among urban industrial workers and tenant farmers of the southern Alentejo already dominated by communists and socialists.

Within a populist, "very Portuguese" party such as the PSD, charismatic leaders were not only important but vitally necessary. Leaders served as a common reference point given the party's diverse membership and electorate, ill-defined non-ideological program, and flexible political strategies. This personalization of politics, however, also became a source of party vulnerability. Competition among elites for power has been an underlying factor of internal conflicts throughout the party's history. The PSD's participatory organic structures created the conditions for the formation of "tendencies" led by powerful barons. But the PSD developed into more than a party of "barons" as it gradually achieved a nationwide structure linking party militants to the leadership. This ensured that the bases remained intact even when disgruntled local "barons" opted to abandon the PSD for personal, ideological, or opportunistic reasons. The party's leadership has ideologically been located in between its bases (more to its left) and its electorate (more to its right). In the initial stages of the party's evolution, Sá Carneiro's strong leadership and charismatic personality helped unite this eclectic party organization.

The PSD pursued different, often contradictory, policies and strategies during the transition period in order to win political power. Party choices were logically defined more by survival and power considerations than by any ideological or programmatic rigidity. In the first constituent elections of April 1975 the PSD garnered 26.7 percent of the vote, second to the Socialist party led by Mário Soares. Results of Portuguese elections are shown in table 8.2. PSD leaders cooperated—though begrudgingly—with the Socialists to write the country's new *magna carta*. The Portuguese Constitution embodied a semipresidential political system, gave important powers to the revolutionary forces in the military (MFA), and established as an objective the construction of a "socialist economy"—the product of close collaboration between socialists and communists.

The predominance of leftist political forces and the nature of the electoral system limited the PSD's political fortunes at the national level until the party decided to run in a conservative coalition—the Democratic Alliance (AD)—with the CDS and a small monarchical party (PPM). That the minority Socialist government from 1976–1979 became identified with the severe austerity measures imposed on Portugal by the International Monetary Fund (IMF), helped to advance the political successes of the center-right in Portugal. After the demise of Soares' governments and several failed attempts at presidentially supported governments, the AD won the early elections of December 1979. For the first time the democratic right had won power in postauthoritarian Portugal.

The AD parties set out to legitimize the ideology and politics of the right in their own liberal agenda; they supported private initiative, criticized state socialism, and wanted to limit presidential intervention in the legislative arena. The AD enjoyed continued electoral successes at the local level and managed to win even more seats in the regularly scheduled October 1980 election. The AD governing coalition faced many internal challenges after the untimely death of AD founders Sá Carneiro and Amaro da Costa, in a (sabotaged?) plane accident on December 4, 1980. PSD leader Francisco Pinto Balsemao took over the reins of power but lacked the necessary charisma and strength to keep the coalition and his own party united.

Table 8.2 Portugal's Election Results: 1975–1995

Party	1975	1976	1979	1980	1983	1985	1987	1991	1995
PCP	12.5	14.3	18.8	16.8	18.1	15.5	12.1	8.8	8.6
PSP	37.9	34.9	27.3	26.6	36.1	20.8	22.4	29.3	43.9
PSD	26.4	24.4	44.9	47.5	27.2	29.9	50.2	50.4	34.0
CDS	7.6	16.0	(AD)	(AD)	12.6	10.0	4.4	4.4	9.1
PRD*	—	—	—	—	—	17.9	4.9	—	—

Source: Ministry of Justice.
Note: *Democratic Renewal Party

Once the conservative alliance broke up, the PSD remained in government by allying with the Socialists in the "Central Bloc," lasting from 1983 to 1985. As a governing party, the PSD would continue to enjoy the fruits of power and oversee negotiations with the European Community on Portugal's terms of accession. Neither the PS nor the PSD was willing to jeopardize nearly ten years of arduous dealings with the EC. As soon as the treaty was signed in June 1985, however, the new PSD leadership under the charismatic Aníbal Cavaco Silva broke with the PS and the coalition government came to an end. In the early elections of October 1985 the PSD was the most voted party and it opted to form a minority government. During its two-year duration, Cavaco was seen as being a competent, efficient, and strong leader. That his government enjoyed the benefits of an improved international economic situation strengthened Portugal's domestic conditions. His government's concrete actions and pragmatism in modernizing the country through badly needed structural reforms gained the confidence of a people accustomed to governmental immobilism. A successful motion of censure in 1987 brought the minority PSD government to an end and the next elections gave Cavaco Silva the governing majority he had demanded.

The PSD's performance in the 1987 election presented the center-right with an unprecedented landslide victory, with 50.2 percent of the vote. Even more significant was the PSD's ability to increase its base of support in the 1991 elections to 50.4 percent. The PSD received these majorities because it managed to attract votes from all the other parties on its left and right. By reducing the role of the state in society (discussed in detail below), the PSD hoped to modernize Portugal's economy and strengthen its democratic institutions.

The October 1995 legislative election results marked the end of the PSD's hegemonic position in Portuguese politics. That the PSD returned to the opposition was no surprise. The final years of Cavaco's government were marked by a worsening domestic economic situation, charges of increasing corruption, and complications in the relations between the prime minister and President Soares. And as if these conditions were not tough enough, the PSD contested the elections with a new leader, Fernando Nogueira, who lacked the charisma and authority of his predecessor.

The PSD lost its broad electoral appeal as disgruntled voters in the center opted for the Socialists and those more to the right gave their vote of support to the rejuvenated CDS—now called the Popular party (PP). When compared to the PSD's level of electoral support before the "Cavaco phenomenon," the 1995 results are not all that catastrophic. The PSD enjoys a solid electoral base of 35 percent in Portugal. The average PSD voter is female (55 percent); practicing Catholic (68 percent); lives in a town with less than 2,000 inhabitants (60 percent); older than 45 (65 percent); and resides in the northern and central litoral (52 percent).[7] The electoral map today reflects how the left still dominates south of the River Mondego, in the litoral, and in the large cities; the right continues to prevail in the north, the interior, and in the countryside.

The PSD as a party in opposition already has survived its first internal crisis. Nogueira (linked to the party's social democratic wing) resigned as party leader when the PSD's former leader and presidential candidate, Cavaco Silva, lost his bid to become president to Socialist Jorge Sampaio in January 1996. The party's March congress elected Marcelo Rebelo de Sousa (associated with the PSD's liberal wing) as the strongman needed to lead the party in opposition and, most importantly, to prepare to win back power. Denied the benefits of state patronage, Rebelo de Sousa will have a tough time keeping the party "barons" in line with a coherent party strategy. The PSD remains a divided party ideologically (social democrats, liberals, and conservatives), but its real weakness lies in its many competing personalities.

Spanish and Portuguese Conservatism at the Turn of the Century

The failures of Marxism-Leninism and the end of the cold war, the resurgence of neoliberalism in the economic sphere, and the decay of the post – World War II consensus on mixed economies and the social welfare state have all had a profound effect on the established European conservative parties, including those in Spain and Portugal. The questions are: Is there a new, what might be called neoliberal, consensus on these issues among the European conservative parties? And to what degree has this emerging consensus impacted the center-right parties in Spain and Portugal?

Leading Spanish and Portuguese conservative party leaders and intellectuals are certainly aware of these emerging trends in Western Europe and have become part of them. There are now conservative think-tanks, conferences, foundations, and meetings of party leaders that reach across national boundaries and have an impact on individual country leaders— almost like a new *internationale*. On the other hand, the influence of these broader, pan-European trends on the Spanish and Portuguese political parties has often been limited. For one thing, since the mid-1970s, when their dramatic transitions to democracy began, Spain and Portugal have been far more focused on domestic internal developments than on larger, international currents. Preoccupied with their own crises and electoral difficulties, they have not had the time nor the political space to devote as much energy to the emerging party currents in the rest of Europe.

Second, the Spanish and Portuguese center-right parties are still very new, uncertain of their electoral bases, and unclear ideologically. The Spanish PP is less than a decade old and has not yet been fully tested in or out of power; it is still uncertain and feeling its way. The Portuguese PSD was a party born on the right but pragmatically moved to the center/center-left of the political spectrum in order to survive the radical transition. Because of its broad-based appeal, the PSD has been able to attract votes from both the left and right of the emerging political spectrum.

A third factor has to do with Spain and Portugal's admission into the European Community (now the European Union—EU) in 1986. Membership in Europe's elite club has helped to raise the Spanish and Portuguese standards of living up to approximately two-thirds the general European level. However, the economies of the Iberian peninsula have become dependent upon EU financial assistance for the poorer regions, and generous agricultural subsidies. Political leaders from both the left and right have postponed discussions of state restructuring, downsizing, and privatization. This is what might be called the IMF's neoliberal agenda—now widespread and perhaps the *dominant* agenda in Latin America and other areas. The major Spanish political parties have yet to mention the word "neoliberal" in their platforms, even though most agree major economic reforms are desperately needed. Under direct pressure from the PSD, the Portuguese have spent the last 17 years trying to eliminate the socialist features of their economy as defined in the 1976 constitution, watered-down in the 1982 version, and finally eliminated in the constitution approved in 1989. Prime Minister Cavaco Silva ran his government on a neoliberal policy of implementing necessary structural reforms of the Portuguese economy, including an ambitious and successful policy of privatization. The benefits of the welfare state, however, have not been limited. With their economies in serious trouble, corruption on the increase, and the challenges to meet EMU convergence criteria more pressing than ever, Spanish and Portuguese political leaders are being obliged to respond to the neoliberal agenda as never before.

In both Iberian countries there are strong internal party differences over these issues. The Spanish PP, for example, is divided between its liberal, "Thatcherite," Catholic-corporatist, and other wings; so far, President Aznar has defined himself as a classic liberal but not yet a "neoliberal." In office, however, he may decide that the economy's main structural problems—the tax system, labor market, welfare, unemployment, the lavish pension system, banks—are so severe that only vigorous action will have a chance of solving them. The neoliberal, free-market advocates within the party believe that Aznar is closer to them than he has let on. Moreover, they believe that once confronted with Spain's manifold problems, he will have no choice but to move in their direction.

Whether in power or in opposition, the PSD has sought to "normalize" Portugal's domestic economic situation by making it capitalistic and competitive, first constitutionally, then in practice. Once the PSD won a governing majority, Cavaco Silva and his team of liberal economic advisors implemented a series of structural reforms to align Portugal's economy with her European neighbors. Among the more important reforms included housing, labor, trade unions, tax revisions, and privatization of financial, service, and industrial sectors. Linked to these reforms was a rigorous economic plan to reduce inflation, decrease public-sector deficit, not allow public debt to grow, maintain the escudo stable against the German mark, and keep inflation as low as possible. His successor, António Guterres, has followed the same economic guidelines and—like it or not—is committed to continuing his version of the neoliberal agenda. It will be much easier "to be from the left" than to "govern from the left."

Let us look specifically at the parties' recent programs, to judge how closely they correspond to what may be an emerging broader, European conservative consensus on the neoliberal agenda.

The Spanish PP remained vague and imprecise during the 1996 campaign as to how it would respond to the country's serious economic problems. It mainly concentrated on criticizing Felipe González's government for its failures in such areas as unemployment (21.8 percent in November 1996) and corruption. It remained vague because the PP had smelled, even tasted, victory in 1993 and it did not want to do or say anything that would cost it votes in the months leading up to the early 1996 electoral contest.

But the PP knew that it would have to administer bitter medicine if the economy was to turn around and if Spain was to qualify for the new Europe of the Maastricht agreement. It would have to cut the budget deficit by about half over a three- to four-year period and reduce public debt by around 5 percent.[8] It would need to sell or dissolve many state-owned industries that were left over from Franco's earlier autarkic and corporatist policies. The PP would need to change Spain's labor laws which, because of earlier social pacts and the fear of instability during Spain's transition to democracy, are among the most prolabor in Europe. The state would need to be downsized, privatized, made more efficient, and corruption/patronage reduced. At various unguarded moments during the campaign, Aznar admitted he would have to preside over a severe austerity program; but for electoral purposes, the party sought to avoid any specifics. Meanwhile, virtually every social and economic sector in Spain—press, television, film industry, the arts—had been lining up to preserve its government subsidies and special privileges.

On welfare issues it is clear that leaders in Spain and Portugal were watching closely the efforts of French Prime Minister Alain Juppé to reduce state subsides and entitlements in December 1995. The issue resulted in violent protest marches that not only closed down the country, but nearly signaled the demise of the government and left Juppé the most unpopular politician in France. Cognizant of these lessons, Aznar indicated that he had "no plans" to cut pensions, education, and health benefits. Aznar believed that he lost the 1993 election because González had been able to "frighten" the electorate into thinking the PP would lower pensions, and he was determined not to make the same mistake again. Hence, in 1996, he argued that "if there is a main responsibility for the government, it is to maintain and guarantee the pension system."[9] Again, because of the fears of destabilization during the transition phase, Spain has elaborate entitlement programs especially for old people, labor groups, and farmers that the country cannot afford. But during the campaign, Aznar said these areas would be "exempted" from any possible austerity program. He argued they would be paid for through the extra revenues generated by his plan to reduce taxes, a wildly unrealistic (as Aznar well knew) expectation that bore a striking resemblance to the "voodoo economics" of another time and place.

The PP took a very forceful stand on environmental issues and was generally seen in 1996 as stronger on the environment than González's PSOE. The PP's stand on the environment attracted and reinforced the party's appeal among young and better-educated voters—precisely those who voted for the PSOE during the 1980s.

Immigration is a very different issue in Spain; the Straits of Gibraltar are often referred to as "Europe's Rio Grande." There is a lucrative traffic of boats and people, often at night and illegal, across the Straits. At the same time, many of these are "pass-through" immigrants who view Spain as a "turnpike" to carry them elsewhere in Europe. As of 1996 there were 400,000 legal immigrants, mostly from Morocco, living in Spain; in recent years (and as Spain has become more prosperous and with often lavish social services) what had been a trickle of immigrants has become not a flood but at least a flowing stream. *All* the parties have urged a crackdown on illegal immigration and greater limits on legal immigration; the PSOE government began sending immigrants back. Opinion polls, however, show the Spaniards are not overly exercised by the immigration issue; the sensitive "racism" charge is frequently raised. Aznar's stand on immigration has not been noticeably different from that of the PSOE government.

Aznar has sought to make an issue out of terrorism, especially after terrorists tried to kill him in a car-bomb attempt in April 1995. Here the main issue is the long-running Basque (ETA) problem. Both the socialist government and its conservative opposition have taken strong, anti-terrorist positions. Aznar blamed the previous government for breaking the "anti-terrorist consensus" when it was revealed that the Socialists were holding secret talks with the terrorists, releasing some terrorists from jail without consultation, questioning the independent work of the Civil Guard in its anti-terrorist campaign, and negotiating with the terrorists at the expense of more moderate Basque political groups. He was also critical of the government for not keeping the PP fully informed of anti-terrorist policies.[10] The revelation that the Socialists had organized their own state-sponsored terrorist group (GAL) to kill suspected Basque terrorists in southern France and Spain—several of whom were erroneous targets—did little to reinforce any preexisting political consensus on how to deal with the ongoing problem of terrorism.

Beyond the problem of terrorism in the Basque country, the regional issue remains an important one in Spain. The 1978 constitution—distinct from Franco's tight centralism—gives considerable autonomy to the regions, making Spain a quasi-federal system. Through negotiations with the regional parties (because the PP needs their support in the Congress) the Aznar government has been expanding some important financial aspects of regional independence. Many Spaniards—including the PSOE and some historical members of the PP—are now fearful that the budget favors and grants of even greater autonomy to the "nationalists" have gone too far, thereby threatening the integrity of Spain as a nation-state.

Church-state issues have not been a major bone of contention in recent Spanish elections. On the one hand, the PP is widely thought of as having a strong Catholic constituency and of being more favorable to Catholic positions; on the other hand it is not a confessional or even Christian democratic party. Besides, Spain is by now (like France or Italy) a predominantly secularized society with some anticlerical sentiments lingering on from days past. Only about ten percent of all Spaniards attend mass on Sundays or have any connection with the sacraments; divorce and abortion (in limited cases) are both now legal. In recent times the Catholic Church has generally refrained from overt interference (which might backfire anyway) in political affairs.

Both main parties have supported Spain's full integration into European affairs. In Spain, this issue has in the past been more political and psychological than economic and strategic. To be in favor of "Europe" during the Franco era was to be in favor of democracy. In the early post-Franco years integration into Europe was preeminently a way of cementing Spain's place in the Western, first world, democratic camp. But now "Europe" as a vision has faded somewhat, or else Spain has begun to take its democracy and hence its "Europeanness" for granted. Now that we are reduced to concrete economic realities (with subsidies getting smaller), "Europe" has somewhat lost its luster. The current government (supported by the PSOE) is committed to meeting the Maastricht convergence criteria in order to make the first phase of EMU. Spain's European ambitions need to be brought into accord with harsh economic realities.

On other foreign-policy issues, the PP had expressed "reluctance" on the subject of Spanish participation in the Rapid Reaction Force in Bosnia. The PP has stated that it favors closer ties to the United States. There have been expanded contacts between political parties in the United States and the PP, as well as between conservative think-tanks in both countries. But neither Aznar nor his party are particularly close to the United States, and there are long traditions of both left- and right-wing anti-Americanism in Spain. Despite Spanish public opinion, the PP and PSOE voted on Spain's full integration into the military arm of the North Atlantic Treaty Organization (NATO).[11] The PP supported the appointment of socialist Javier Solana as Secretary General of NATO. As the West's defense alliance adapts to new exigencies in a post–cold war world, so too will the PP. On Cuba, the PP has said that it wishes to keep its relations at a minimum and that they should be "strictly humanitarian." The PP has been less inclined than the PSOE was to champion Cuba's cause in various international fora. The PP government, however, has challenged the United States' recently passed Helms-Burton law which could adversely affect Spanish investments in the Caribbean island.

The economic situation in Portugal changed dramatically under the PSD's majority governments. The PSD emphasized competition, efficiency, and private initiative as ways to make the economy larger and stronger. Quality of life improved as GDP per-capita levels went from 53.1 percent of the EC average in 1985 to 64 percent in 1994.[12] Public-sector debt went from 12 percent of GDP in 1985 to 5.8 percent in 1994. Inflation rates which topped 19 percent in 1985, had come down to 4.3 percent when the PSD left office—the lowest rate in 25 years. The escudo stayed within the European Monetary System (EMS) and the currency has maintained a credible and stable exchange rate.

The new Socialist minority government will have to deal with many of the same issues that had plagued the PSD during its last years in government. Similar to the initial economic policies coming out of Spain's new PP government, no government—be it of the left or right—wants to admit the urgency of reducing social programs in order to bring deficits down. That means cutting into pensions, universal health care, education, generous social services, and the jealously protected worker's rights. The Socialists have announced reductions in some areas (judicial, defense, and administration), but none significant enough to reduce the looming public-sector deficit. Enjoying their honeymoon period of government, the Socialists will not likely make any significant cuts soon in welfare programs generously supported by a state that can no longer afford to do so.

Both the PS and the PSD support an active voice for Portugal in the European Union. Portugal's economic health still depends on generous EU agricultural, regional, and cohesion subsidies that no political party wants cut. Consequently, the PS and PSD recognize the importance of Portugal meeting EMU criteria in a timely fashion. If a peripheral and poor country like Portugal fails to do so, it will miss out on a lot more than a single currency. Portugal will need to have its voice heard in Brussels as the EU prepares another enlargement to include central European countries.

While the logo "neoliberal" is far from the mouths of the Socialist leadership, Guterres and his government will have to continue down the liberal path of economic modernization if Portugal is going to make EMU. Inflation rates have continued to drop; public-deficit targets of 3.7 percent of GDP by 1997 now seem more credible; public debt will not likely fall below its current 72.2 percent of GDP, well above the 60 percent target for EMU. This year the PS will be selling off $2.5 billion of state holdings that—ironically enough—is the largest annual amount since the PSD began to privatize a decade ago. Revenues generated from these sales will go largely toward reducing the debt burden. Potential for greater economic growth has been further limited by rigid labor laws and a stable escudo policy. Unemployment four years ago was 4.5 percent and today it has risen to 7.2 percent. The Portuguese economy must become more competitive either by lowering inflation and interest rates—or via the less attractive alternative of currency devaluations.

Portugal has been a country of emigrants and immigrants. Many have left their homeland to find greater personal and economic opportunities outside their country's boundaries—be it in France, the United States, or Brazil. The money these emigrants send home in the form of remittances has helped balance many a payments schedule for governments long before there was democracy in Portugal. Legal immigration also has affected the sociopolitical map of Portugal. The colonial wars and the later process of decolonization resulted in internal civil battles in Angola and Mozambique. As a result, many *retornados* (generally conservative voters) have returned to the metropole.

Most illegal immigrants in Portugal come from the Portuguese-speaking African Countries—PALOP. The PSD began an active amnesty campaign in the early 1990s for these illegal immigrants to "normalize" their working and living situation in Portugal. Official statistics note that 38,000 of the estimated 80,000 illegal immigrants have since become legal.[13] The PS will continue with this process and it hopes to legalize the situation of about 40,000 immigrants. Compared to neighboring Spain, the immigration issue has not been as politicized in Portugal.

Church-state issues do not divide the major parties in Portugal. One can find practicing Catholics in the PP, the PSD, and the PS—and all of these parties depend on the "Catholic vote." In fact, Prime Minister Guterres is a church-going Catholic and some even claim he has links to *Opus Dei*. Like many modernizing societies, Portugal has become increasingly secularized with only about 25 percent of the population practicing their faith on a regular basis. Divorce is legal, but abortions can be performed legally only under very limited circumstances. This means that many Portuguese women cross over to Spain to have an abortion. Nor does the Church enjoy the lavish financial support from the state as is the case in Spain. The PSD did, however, award the Church one of the two private television channels airing in Portugal (and currently suffering from a severe economic crisis). Portuguese Church leaders have traditionally not taken public political positions. However, during the last couple of years of the PSD's government, several bishops voiced sharp criticisms against the government's policies that increased hunger, homelessness, and growing poverty.

The Portuguese have never had to deal with the traumatic issue of regionalism like their Spanish neighbors. Portugal continues to be a relatively homogeneous society with little historical justification for devolving power to the regions. After the revolution, a special autonomous status was granted for the Azores and Madeira. Portugal is currently going through a political debate surrounding the next constitutional revision, and regionalism has come to the top of the Socialists' political agenda. Prime Minister Guterres has claimed that the proposed regionalization plan would not increase state costs and bureaucracy. However, common sense dictates that any form of regionalization will cost Lisbon some of its already limited resources at a time when it cannot afford any extra expenses. The PSD has been in favor of developing administrative, not political, decentralization as a way to bring the state closer to the citizen. Only time will tell how the regionalization issue is resolved in Portugal.

Full integration into Europe has been an important objective of successive governments in this small Iberian country. Both the PS and PSD have envisioned Portugal's political and economic modernization as inextricably linked to the successful realization of the European Union project. Euroskeptics exist in both parties as Portugal struggles to meet the stiff convergence criteria on EMU. Only the PP and PCP are generally anti-Europe. The social costs of realizing these European-imposed standards may disillusion even more Portuguese.

Portugal has always been Atlanticist in its foreign-policy orientation and it continues to enjoy good relations with both the United States and Great Britain. In one of its last foreign-policy acts, the PSD government renewed the Azores base agreement with the Americans in 1995. Unlike their Iberian neighbor, the Portuguese still find benefits in the bilateral base agreement with the Americans. In a post–cold war world, the Portuguese want to reserve a special place for the Americans in the defense and security of Europe.

The Portuguese have been full and active members of NATO since its inception, and NATO houses its Iberian command center in Portugal. As Spain becomes fully integrated into NATO's military command structure, the Portuguese fear that the Spanish will severely limit their country's influence on the Alliance's southern flank. Many in Portugal were less than enthusiastic about the selection of a Spaniard as the Secretary General of NATO, even though a Portuguese (Jose Cutileiro) is currently the Secretary General of the West European Union (WEU). They have used this position to initiate a closer approximation between the WEU and the United States. The Portuguese have actively participated in UN peacekeeping and NATO (Rapid Reaction Forces and IFOR) operations in Bosnia.

The European Union serves as an important forum in which Portugal can emphasize its commitment to former colonies in Africa and Asia. The PSD engineered peace plans in Mozambique and Angola in order to end decades-long civil wars. The political and economic situation of Mozambique is now "stable" thanks to the Portuguese intervention; Angola still remains war torn and problematic. The Socialists have continued with the PSD's efforts to reverse Indonesia's invasion of East Timor in 1975 and to highlight the flagrant violations of human rights on the former island colony. Both the PS and PSD will have their eyes on what happens with Hong Kong's integration into China—especially concerning the question of human rights. The PSD signed the agreement that schedules Macao to be handed over to the Chinese in 1999 following the "one country, two systems" model adopted for neighboring Hong Kong. Here the foreign-policy strategy will be one of "wait and see" for whoever is in power in Portugal at the turn of the century.

The Right and Political Power

The victory of the Spanish PP in March 1996 was a major turning point in the consolidation of democracy in Spain. The Socialist Party was now out of office for the first time in 14 years. The PP victory demonstrated that a reformed, modernized, conservative party could win an electoral contest in Spain. The PP's triumph in a climate of peaceful voting and normalcy, however, was the best evidence yet of the strength of Spanish democracy. It demonstrated that the country could go democratically from the right to the left and back to the right again with no violence or handwringing.

But the PP's victory was less decisive than had earlier been thought likely. Pre-election polls had rather consistently shown the PP to be 10 to 12 percentage points ahead of the Socialists. However, when the votes were counted, the PP received only 38.8 percent of the vote, a razor-thin margin of 1.4 percent over the PSOE—a difference of a mere 400,000 votes of the more than 25 million (78 percent turnout) cast. In the Congress the PP secured 156 seats out of a total of 350—20 short of the majority needed to govern.

The slim margin of victory and the absence of a majority for his party meant that Aznar had to search for coalition partners among the other parties. After arduous negotiations, the PP struck an important agreement with the Catalan Convergence and Union (CiU) coalition whose leader is Jordi Pujol. The CiU is a moderate, regional, and nationalist coalition whose ideological orientation and social bases (center-right, pro-business, with Christian-democratic and liberal components) are not all that different from the PP. But Pujol, whose party also held the balance of power in the recent PSOE minority government, is a wily politician who seeks to extract the best deal possible for his party and region. This means that he has the power even with only 16 seats to make or break Spanish governments. While the PP tried to undermine the CiU's hold on Catalonia by emphasizing "pluralism" during the campaign, the PP also sought to reach out to and better its relations with CiU. Other agreements were signed with the Basque Nationalist Party and the Canarian Coalition.

Lacking a decisive mandate and having to compromise with other minority parties, Aznar and the PP will find it harder to carry out their goals of cutting government spending, reducing the bloated bureaucracy, privatizing state-owned industries, rooting-out corruption, dealing more effectively with terrorism, reducing taxes, and balancing the budget. *All* of this ambitious program, vaguely expressed during the election campaign, has been attempted by the PP government and its coalition partners. However, the requirements of coalition bargaining (such as a 30 percent return of taxes collected to certain autonomous regions) complicate the possibility of carrying out the financial reforms necessary for Spain to qualify for the EMU.

Portugal's PSD in opposition needs to realize several important short-term objectives. The first involves internal party dynamics. Rebelo de Sousa's immediate goal will be to revitalize internal party discussion and debate (limited by Cavaco) so the PSD can get back in touch with its "Portuguese soul."[14] After being in power at the national level for so long, the PSD became too dependent on the government and its privileges to quell internal party dissent. Some historical party leaders observed that even though the PSD was responsible for creating the conditions which helped Portugal change, the party failed to change with the country by adapting to a new political reality. If the PSD is to survive as a political entity, this goal must be realized quickly.

The second challenge concerns how the PSD will react to the PS government. The party must be strong in opposition, but it cannot be perceived as being a stumbling bloc for the further modernization and Europeanization of Portugal. The PSD has to check governmental power, abuses, excesses, and choices, but it cannot only be a naysayer. The PS and PSD share many of the same economic objectives for their country, most of which are imposed by Brussels. A revitalized PSD could reap significant political benefits in opposition. Assuming the PS begins to downsize the state, the Socialists—and not the PSD—will be held politically responsible for the difficult and costly economic reforms necessary for Portugal to fulfill its European vocation.

The PSD has also been engaging in a critical reevaluation of the party's political links to Europe. The PSD became associated with the European Liberal, Democratic, and Reformist Group in the late 1970s. Denied admission into the Socialist International by the Portuguese PS after the revolution, the PSD negotiated its admission into the European family of "liberals" on the condition that the term "reformist" also be included in its label. When the European Popular party (Christian democratic) group expelled the Portuguese PP/CDS because of its anti-Europe stance in 1993, the PSD began thinking about joining the EPP.[15] The party made this new association formal in November 1996. Several reasons informed this change: (1) the deputies in the liberal group had become dominated by central European parties unsympathetic to the special needs of Europe's "southern flank;"[16] (2) the PSD would be more likely to exert whatever limited influence it had within the stronger EPP grouping (173 deputies); (3) the PSD could still maintain its "reformist, nonconfessional" political identity; and (4) as the leader of the PSD in opposition, Rebelo de Sousa would enjoy direct contact with Germany's Kohl, Britain's Major, and Spain's Aznar. The PSD may have also been interested in securing badly needed funds from the German Adenauer-Stiftung and Ebert Foundations. That the EPP is more federalist in its positions on Europe than the PSD did not serve as a stumbling block for the party's admission.

At home, the PSD will have to define its position vis-à-vis the PP to its right. The 1995 election results breathed new life into this small conservative party, which has represented the "radicalization of the right." For the first time since 1975, the PP surpassed the communists with its third-place showing. However, public disagreements among party elites on strategies, close cooperation with the PS government, and an anti-European stance will do little to attract (and keep) conservative voters from a born-again PSD. The PP recently helped Guterres' government pass the 1996 budget by abstaining in return for small and insignificant tax reductions. If it continues to support the Socialists' social and economic agenda, the PP may alienate its more conservative base of support. Assuming the PP remains a viable political actor, the party's 10 percent of the vote will limit the PSD's opportunities for defeating the Socialists next time around.

Some PSD elites have resurrected the idea of establishing a formal alliance with the PP, a "neo-AD" or "AD-revisited." Most PSD leaders agree that any possible alliances with the PP would depend on a strong and independent PSD. This means the party needs time to regroup. Portuguese election laws favor the formation of alliances. The PSD has already said that it would collaborate with the PP for the local elections slated for December 1997, especially in the larger cities. Even after 20 years of existence, the PSD continues to fight a two-front war on the political battlefield—against the PP to its right and the PS to its left—to ensure its own survival.

The Mainstream Parties and the Far Right

Spain has long had a far right. As early as the eighteenth century the country was divided between the "Party of Order" and the "Party of Change." These two "parties" fought a series of civil wars, known as the Carlist Wars, in the nineteenth century, culminating in the Spanish Civil War of the 1930s, which was won by Franco and the right. This long-term conflict not only tore Spain apart repeatedly and polarized the country (the two main protagonists took radically different ideological positions and also had distinct social bases), but the violence and instability further retarded Spain's economic, social, and political development well into the twentieth century. Dominance by the far right also lasted longer than in other European countries, until Franco's death in 1975.

The Spanish PP is a political party that brings together diverse ideological constituencies. These include monarchists, conservative and moderate Christians, traditionalists, *Opus Dei* members, technocrats, liberals, progressives, reformists, and many bureaucratic and machine-politics interests. The PP has a nationally implanted party organizational structure closely controlled by the national party leadership. Unlike the UCD, which was a coalition incorporating many diverse parties and important personalities, the PP has been able to organize its diverse membership within accepted structures and rules. The PP has capitalized on the general discontent and malaise that has accompanied the democratic opening since the mid-1970s: rising crime, uncensored pornography, dirty streets, rising divorce rates, unruly teenagers, unchecked terrorism, increasing drug and alcohol abuse at all ages, vandalism and graffiti, a lack of order and discipline, and increasing corruption. None of these traits were present, or at least publicly acknowledged, under francoism, and there is undoubtedly a certain nostalgia for the romanticized old regime.

But Spain is a far different country than it was in 1975 and the PP is not a francoist party. The PP—and those conservative elements which support it—have modernized, democratized, and undergone a remarkable social transformation. Those who knew Spain or its reputation for "francoism" in the 1960s would hardly recognize the country today. Spain has become a truly European country in all of that term's dimensions: economically, politically, socially, culturally, morally, and psychologically. And the PP reflects those significant changes: a party of diverse factions and constituencies in which the ghosts of the past have been erased and where a dynamic, pluralistic, new generation of democrats representing a different social base is now governing the country. Spain and the PP have undergone a similar transition: its conservatism is modern, enlightened, close to the center, and devoid of any connection to the right's francoist past. According to Aznar, "In Spain, the far right no longer exists."[17]

The PSD remains the leader of the right in Portugal. Much like its Spanish counterparts, the right in Portugal has been rehabilitated and the far right is nonexistent. All system actors respect the democratic rules of the game, and the idea of returning to some form of authoritarianism is unthinkable. The PSD is a modern, European-oriented, and democratic political party. It attracts the support of different, often contradictory, ideological groupings. These include liberals, social democrats, Catholics, traditionalists, and conservatives. The PSD enjoys a strong, nationally established organizational structure in which powerful local "barons" are able to make their voice known. Charismatic and strong party leaders help keep these barons in line with party policies.

The PSD must promote lively internal debate in order to articulate clearly what its vision of Portuguese society should be. The party has to reestablish lost contacts with businesses, banks, cultural actors, and agricultural sectors in its society. The survival of a strong, cohesive, and innovative PSD will strengthen the consolidation of Portugal's democratic institutions.

Prospects for the Right at the Turn of the Century

Parties have come to make a major difference in Spain and Portugal. At a time when the demise of political parties in other European democracies is being lamented, the increasing importance of political parties in these countries is being celebrated.[18] Having been deprived of democracy for so long, people in these Iberian countries now look on democracy and political parties as something valuable, to be cherished.[19] The parties have been the main beneficiaries of the transition away from authoritarianism to a new political system where democracy—not coups or revolutions—enjoy virtually unquestioned legitimacy. To answer the question posed long ago by Richard Rose, and recently by the editor of this book, political parties *do* make a difference in these two countries.

The center-right parties of Spain and Portugal had several unique problems that they needed to overcome in order to make their transitions to democracy successful. Among these were the newness and weakness of still young democracies, the lack of a center-right political party tradition historically, the long Franco and Salazar dictatorships that prevented the growth of democratic political parties, and the fear tactics (fear of the far right) that their oppositions have been able to use against them. These are the "local issues" that often make the PP and the PSD different from their conservative European counterparts.

But the center-right parties now have advantages as well. Among these are (since the 1980s) a web of think-tanks, foundations, and support from like-minded parties in other nations that have begun to match the solidarity of the socialist movement. The generous development assistance funds from the EU have enabled *all* the parties in Spain and Portugal to largely avoid thus far the politically damaging policies of austerity, budget balancing, government and social programs downsizing, and general belt-tightening. This last factor helps explain why the Spanish and the Portuguese center-right parties have so far been able to resist defining themselves too unambiguously with the neoliberal position.

In both countries, the center-right parties came to power after a period of postauthoritarian upheaval and decompression. These parties on the center-right entered office after a time of hopeful, but in the end disappointing, Socialist rule; the PSD in 1979 and then again in 1985, and the PP in 1996. But recall also that the Portuguese transition from authoritarianism occurred in a context of revolution and upheaval, while the Spanish transition, observing and learning from the Portuguese experience, was peaceful and evolutionary. Hence, the Portuguese transition unfolded in a sometimes disruptive and telescoped time period, while the Spanish one was gradual and built on broad consensual agreements. The result is that the Portuguese PSD already has had a long experience in government, in both coalition arrangements as well as by itself. The Spanish PP has only just recently won power and is still inexperienced and uncertain as a governing party.

Another important question in Iberia is whether the switch in the political agenda from a social-democratic and even socialist consensus on a larger state sector and advanced social welfare state to state downsizing and neoliberalism will have a major impact on the center-right political parties. We believe that in the short term it will have such an impact—mainly negative for the parties carrying out this agenda—but in the long term less so. In Portugal after the early socialist stages of the 1970s revolution, the PSD from the mid-1980s began a campaign of reducing the state sector and implementing austerity. Although these reforms helped stimulate Portuguese economic growth, the PSD paid a price for these changes when it lost the 1995 elections. But then the PS began implementing much the same policy, paving the way we believe for an eventual PSD comeback.

In Spain the socialists dominated from 1983 until 1996. Moreover, within the left there has long been a certain sense, until widespread government corruption and inefficiency made the handwriting on the wall of a future PSOE defeat clear to all but the most devout true believers, that socialism would simply go on to ever new and greater triumphs. So, in this sense, Spain is behind Portugal. The PP government in Spain is carrying out a program of state downsizing and greater budgetary discipline just like the PSD did earlier in Portugal. Doubtless the PP, at least initially, will suffer for this electorally. But when and if the PSOE comes back to power, it will likely have to carry out the same agenda—as the PS is doing in Portugal—and this will pave the way for the PP eventually to return, as the PSD will, for a new term in office.

Spain and Portugal have both successfully completed their transitions to democracy; by this time, they have also satisfied all the criteria of consolidated democracies. It would be unthinkable for either country to revert to some form of government other than democracy. In these successful transitions, the center-right parties have come to play a crucial role. Indeed, it can be said that the resurgence of a center-right movement after the earlier discrediting of the right and the sometimes teleological attitudes on the part of the postauthoritarian left is perhaps the best evidence for the triumph of democracy on the Iberian peninsula. For instead of the usual reliance in the past by the right on the armed strength of the military, the blessings of the Church, and the financial power of economic elites, the electoral triumphs and failures of these center-right parties are the best indications of their commitment to the democratic process.

At the same time, the weaknesses ought also to be remembered. Spain and Portugal still lag behind European levels of social and economic modernity. Their primary challenges are economic in scope, which have more to do with their retarded and slow development than with their newly consolidated democracies. Spain and Portugal suffer from internal challenges—be it in the form of terrorism, the federalism/regionalism question, or uneven economic development—that may complicate, but not reverse, their young democratic systems. In both countries, the center-right parties (as well as others along the political spectrum) share common weaknesses—electoral bases, exaggerated dependence on strong leaders, competition among party barons for power within parties, eclectic ideological compositions, and oftentimes ill-defined (bordering on catch-all) party appeal. Both the PP and the PSD have demonstrated their commitment to working at the international level in our increasingly interdependent and global economy.

So while these conservative parties have now become an established part of the functioning democracies and the political spectrum in Spain and Portugal, the parties' debilities and uncertainties of policy direction make the positions and futures of these parties no more certain than those of their leftist counterparts at home and in Europe.

Notes

1. See the four *Transitions from Authoritarian Rule* volumes edited by Guillermo O'Donnell, Philippe Schmitter, and Lawrence Whitehead (Baltimore: Johns Hopkins University Press, 1986); and Samuel Huntington, *The Third Wave: Democratization in the Late Twentieth Century* (Norman, OK: University of Oklahoma Press, 1991).
2. The EMU economic convergence criteria embodied in the Maastricht Treaty are: (1) public-sector deficit must not exceed 3 percent of GDP; (2) public-sector debt must not exceed 60 percent of GDP; (3) inflation rates may only be 1 percent above the three best rates; (4) exchange-rate stability within EMS; and (5) interest rates may be only 1.5 percent above the three best European rates.
3. "Vista a la Derecha," *El País Semanal,* June 9, 1996, pp. 32–60.

4. Howard Wiarda, *Corporatism and Development: The Portuguese Experience* (Amherst: University of Massachusetts Press, 1977).

5. Information from a study by Luis Pérez as cited in *El País Semanal,* June 9, 1996, p. 42.

6. For an analysis of the right after April 25, see Jaime Nogueira Pinto, *A Direita e as Direitas* (Lisbon: Difel, l996).

7. Statistics cited from Mario Bacalhau, *Atitudes, Opiniones e Comportamentos Politicos dos Portugueses: 1973–1993* (Lisbon: Heptagono, 1994), pp. 113–114.

8. The following statistics illustrate each country's situation at the end of 1996 on the convergence criteria. Spain: budget deficit of 5.7 percent of GDP; public debt of 67.1 percent of GDP; long-term interests rates are 8.3 percent and inflation is 3.6 percent. Portugal: budget deficit of 5.4 percent; pubic debt of 70.5 percent; long-term interest rates are 8.3 percent and inflation is at 3.2 percent. Statistics from Banco de Espana and Banco de Portugal.

9. WEU–95–052, *Foreign Broadcast Information Service,* March 17, 1995, p. 24.

10. *El País,* August 19, 1994, p. 15.

11. *El País,* November 15, 1996, p. 1.

12. Statistics cited from the National Bank of Portugal.

13. Statistics from the Portuguese Ministry of the Interior and the Service for Foreigners and Frontiers (SEF).

14. Commented by Angelo Correia.

15. The PP/CDS joined the European Alliance of Democrats (RDE), whose primary members include the French Gaullists and the Irish Fianna Fáil.

16. The majority of the members of the Liberal Group voted against the Delors II plan which provided special community funds for Portugal until 1999. The EPP group approved the plan unanimously.

17. *New York Times,* March 6, 1996, p. 3.

18. See B. Guy Peters, *European Politics Reconsidered* (New York: Holmes & Meier, 1991); Peter Mair, "Continuity, Change and the Vulnerability of Party," *West European Politics* 12 (October l989): 181; Angelo Panebianco, *Political Parties: Organization and Power* (Cambridge: Cambridge University Press, 1988); and Peter Mair, "Political Parties, Popular Legitimacy and Public Privilege," *West European Politics* 18 (July 1995): 55.

19. A number of observations justify this generalization: political parties played a key role in the transition to and consolidation of democracy; voters think parties are important for democracy and vote for parties closest to their ideas; parties serve to link the electorate to the state in the absence of strong interest groups; and the party system has remained relatively stable with the overwhelming majority of votes concentrated in the center. For statistical data on these issues for Portugal, see Bacalhau, *Atitudes, Opiniones e Comportamentos Politicos.*

CHAPTER NINE

Sweden's Nonsocialist Parties: What Difference Do They Make?

M. Donald Hancock

An assessment of the political role and policy contributions of Sweden's three principal nonsocialist parties—the agrarian-based Center, the Liberals, and the Moderates (conservatives)—compels a juxtaposition between Francis Castle's notion of a prevalent Social Democratic "image of society" in Scandinavia[1] and Richard Rose's leading question: "Do Parties Make a Difference?"[2] Castles, in his comparative study of the extraordinary strength and policy success of Social Democratic parties in Sweden, Norway, and Denmark, argues that long years of Social Democratic governance have led to the "permeation of the state and, even to some degree, the industrial structure, by the representative of the organised working class. . . ." This permeation, he continues, "makes it inconceivable that temporary election losses by the Social Democrats will have any impact on either the existing level of welfare state provision or the impetus for this type of reform."[3] Two interregna of nonsocialist rule in recent decades in Sweden constitute a solid empirical test of Castles' thesis. From 1976 to 1982, and again from 1991 to 1994, the Center, the Liberals, and the Moderates displaced the Social Democrats in cabinet office, thereby offering the center-right parties an opportunity to enact an alternative policy agenda to the long-term Social Democratic commitment to social reform and the extension of citizen rights.

The short-term question my chapter addresses is: To what extent did the bourgeois parties succeed in their efforts to modify central policy tenets? A larger question concerns the dialectical effects of alternating phases of socialist and nonsocialist governance for the future of the

Swedish welfare state: Have successive periods of nonsocialist executive leadership contributed to the erosion of what Castles has depicted as a distinctive Social Democratic reformist "image of society"?

The "Swedish Model" and Social Democratic Hegemony

The Scandinavian states in general, and Sweden in particular, are distinctive within the broader context of comparative politics. One reason is their deeply rooted legacy of constitutionalism, which predates that of England. A second is their largely peaceful transition in the early decades of the twentieth century to stable forms of parliamentary democracy.[4] At a time when much of Central and Western Europe succumbed to political dictatorships during the 1920s and 1930s, Scandinavia remained a bastion of democratic stability.[5] A third reason is the long-term political ascendancy of Social Democratic parties throughout the region.

The Social Democratic Workers' Party (*Socialdemokratiska arbetarepartiet*, or SAP) became Sweden's largest political party as early as 1917 when it mobilized 31.1 percent of the popular vote (compared to 27.6 percent for the Liberals, 24.9 percent for the Conservatives, and 8.4 percent for the Agrarians). SAP strength fluctuated during the 1920s but edged gradually upward until it achieved "realigning" proportions in the 1932 general election, when the party amassed 41 percent in response to the debilitating domestic consequences of the Great Depression.[6] Already a significant factor in Swedish politics for nearly three decades, the SAP thereby emerged as "effectively the pre-eminent force within the political system as a whole."[7] With the indirect parliamentary support of the Agrarians, who had also increased their popular support in the wake of the Depression, the Social Democrats formed a majority government and launched an ambitious reform effort that ultimately transformed Swedish society.

Through the remainder of the decade, the coalition partners introduced Keynesian-style deficit financing, which helped restore growth and reduce unemployment to pre-Depression levels, and a succession of welfare enactments. Among them were unemployment benefits, public works, support for home construction, grants for mothers with children, expanded retirement benefits, and twelve-day paid vacations. The outbreak of World War II forced a temporary suspension of further reform initiatives, but from the early 1950s onward the Social Democrats steadily expanded the scope of welfare provision through legislation providing for a national health-care system, higher basic retirement benefits, supplementary pensions based on individual earnings, government-financed maternity care, and cash subsidies to families with children and others in need. Augmenting these social measures were educational reforms during the 1960s designed to enhance social mobility and greater egalitarianism.

The extension of universal social entitlements to virtually all citizens constitutes the most visible component of a discernible "Swedish model" of advanced industrial society. Empirical measures of welfare-state provision clearly document Sweden's status as one of the world's most comprehensive welfare states, as indicated in table 9.1.

An integral second component of the Swedish model is a largely sustained pattern of economic growth during much of the postwar period, resulting in the attainment of an unprecedented degree of material affluence. Since the early 1960s, Sweden's per capita GDP has ranked among the highest among the industrial democracies.[8] This achievement is based on an overwhelmingly capitalist economy characterized by the production of quality machine goods, transportation equipment, high-grade iron ore and steel, wood and paper products, and a wide variety of consumer products. The Swedish economy is heavily export oriented; the country's principal trading partners include its neighboring Scandinavian states, Germany and other members of the European Union, and North America.

A third component of the Swedish model reflects a distinctive Scandinavian pattern of industrial relations. As the authors of a comprehensive if still preliminary assessment of the Scandinavian pattern observe, labor relations in Sweden (as well as in Denmark, Norway, and Finland) display a number of common features that, in combination, distinguish the Nordic countries from other industrial nations. Among them are unified trade-union movements that embrace most industrial and white-collar workers, a high degree of organization, a deeply rooted tradition of collective agreements between capital and labor, "a largely common labour law regulating conflicts according to the principle of labour peace and the right of collective action," and institutionalized state-capital-labor cooperation "on economic policy and information and consultation. . . ."[9]

The confluence of these social, economic, and institutional components of the Swedish model is intrinsically linked—as Castles argues—with the diffusion of a Social Democratic hegemony of values embracing egalitarianism, social justice, and material affluence. While the Social Democrats can by no means claim a monopoly on the historical origins and contemporary scope of welfare provisions in Sweden, the SAP has indisputably served as the principal driving force behind the expansion of the modern welfare state. Equally important, the Social Democrats have played the crucial political role in overseeing the economy's recovery from the Depression and, subsequently, its postwar economic growth.

In the process, SAP leaders—as government officials—have acted on ideological principles of reformism rather than radical experimentation.

Table 9.1 Measures of Commitment to Public Welfare

Country	General Government Disbursements as a Percentage of GDP[a]	Total Educational Expenditures as a Percentage of GDP[b]	Infant Mortality per 1,000 Live Births[c]
France	50.9	5.9	6
Germany	46.1	4.7	6
Italy	51.0	4.9	7
Sweden	66.4	8.0	4
United Kingdom	42.3	5.5	6
United States	35.8	5.3	8
Canada	46.2	7.3	6
Japan	27.0	3.8	4

Sources: Based on Francis C. Castles, *The Social Democratic Image of Society,* p. 68.

Notes: [a]OECD, "Basic Statistics: International Comparisons," *Economic Surveys 1997* (Paris, 1997).

[b]United Nations Educational, Scientific and Cultural Organization, *Statistical Yearbook 1997* (Paris, 1997). Data are for 1993–1994.

[c]World Bank, *World Development Report 1997* (New York: Oxford University Press, 1997), p. 225.

Eschewing a policy of nationalization of selected industries and services comparable to actions by the Labour party in Britain between 1945 and 1951, and both the Gaullists and Socialists in postwar France, the Social Democrats have facilitated economic expansion through a "coordinated" strategy of macroeconomic management in close cooperation with private capital and organized labor. The principal components of this strategy include orchestrated fiscal, economic, and industrial policies designed to ensure long-term growth (despite recurrent cycles of contraction) while promoting the economic "rationalization" of individual firms and economic sectors in the face of increased international competition and technological change. Accompanying these macroeconomic measures has been the SAP's pursuit of an active labor market strategy whose principal purpose is to promote employment opportunities through job retraining programs and government support for the relocation of workers.

Since the realigning election of 1932, Swedish voters have repeatedly rewarded the Social Democrats for their social and economic performance. Table 9.2 reveals a steady increase in electoral support for the SAP through the 1930s into the early 1940s, followed by fluctuating periods of marginal erosion and recovery through 1968. In four elections (1938, 1940, 1942, and 1968) the Social Democrats won an absolute majority of votes. Only once (1991) has Social Democratic strength fallen below 40 percent.

Social Democratic achievements and the accompanying diffusion of a Social Democratic hegemony of values from the early 1930s onward constitute the crucial ideological and political context for assessing the role played by Sweden's nonsocialist parties as they have sought to maximize their own values and policy priorities through electoral competition and periods of alternative governance. To restate the central questions of this chapter: What difference have the nonsocialist parties made during their own time in office? What have been their contributions to redefining central features of the Swedish model in the face of the Social Democratic value hegemony?

Sweden's Nonsocialist Parties: A Profile of the Liberals, the Center, and the Moderates

Despite long-term Social Democratic political domination, Sweden's three principal nonsocialist parties have maintained their status as representatives of nearly half of the Swedish electorate. When the Social Democrats assumed cabinet office in 1932, the Conservatives, the Agrarians, and the Liberals together claimed 49.3 percent of the popular vote. Their combined share of electoral support declined to 42 percent in 1940, but

Table 9.2 Election Results, 1928–1994[a]

Year	Type[b]	VP	MP	SAP	FP	C	M	KDS	NYD
1928	R	6.4		37.0	12.9	11.2	29.4		
1930	C	4.0		41.4	13.5	12.5	28.4		
1932	R	5.3		41.7	11.7	14.1	23.5		
1934	C	4.0		42.1	12.5	13.3	24.2		
1936	R	7.7		45.9	12.9	14.3	17.6		
1938	C	5.7		50.4	12.2	12.6	17.8		
1940	R	4.2		53.8	12.0	12.0	18.0		
1942	C	6.0		50.3	12.4	13.2	17.6		
1944	R	10.3		46.7	12.9	13.6	15.9		
1946	C	11.2		44.4	15.6	13.6	14.9		
1948	R	6.3		46.2	22.8	12.4	12.3		
1950	C	4.9		48.6	21.7	12.3	12.3		
1952	R	4.3		46.1	24.4	10.7	14.4		
1954	C	4.8		47.4	21.7	10.3	15.7		
1956	R	5.0		44.6	23.8	9.4	17.1		
1958	R	3.4		46.2	18.2	12.7	19.5		
1958	C	4.0		46.8	15.6	13.1	20.4		
1960	R	4.5		47.8	17.5	13.6	16.5		
1962	C	3.8		50.5	17.1	13.1	15.5		
1964	R	5.2		47.3	17.0	13.2	13.7		
1966	C	6.4		42.2	16.7	13.7	14.7		
1968	R	3.0		50.1	14.3	15.7	12.9		
1970	R	4.8		45.3	16.2	19.9	11.5		
1973	R	5.3		43.6	9.4	25.1	14.3		
1976	R	4.8		42.7	11.1	24.1	15.6	1.4	
1979	R	5.6		43.2	10.6	18.1	20.3	1.4	
1982	R	5.6		45.6	5.9	15.5	23.6	1.9	
1985	R	5.4		44.7	14.2	12.4	21.3		
1988	R	5.7	5.5	43.9	12.0	11.9	17.9	2.9	
1991	R	4.5	3.4	37.6	9.2	8.4	21.9	7.0	6.7
1994	R	6.2	5.0	45.4	7.2	7.7	22.3	4.1	1.2

Source: Author's files.

Note: [a]Explanation of party abbreviations:VP = Left party (post-Communists);
MP = Environmentalists-Greens; SAP = Social Democratic party; FP = Peoples' party
(Liberals); C = Center; M = Moderates (Conservatives); KDS = Christian Democrats;
NYD = New Democracy.
[b]Type of election: R refers to Riksdag (parliamentary) elections; C refers to communal
(county and municipal) elections. Social Democrats won an absolute majority of votes. Only
once (1991) has Social Democratic strength fallen below 40 percent.

it has averaged 46.2 percent in Sweden's 16 national elections during the postwar era. The relative strength of the socialist and nonsocialist blocs in national elections since 1948 is depicted in table 9.3. Included in the nonsocialist totals is electoral support for two new parties to the right of the traditional bourgeois bloc: the Christian Democratic Union (*Kristliga Demokratiska Union*) and New Democracy (*Ny Demokrati*), which together amassed 11.1 percent of the vote in 1991 and 7.9 percent in 1994 (see table 9.2). The significance of both of these parties will be discussed below.

The fragmentation of nonsocialist forces among three competing parties has traditionally been a major factor of weakness in center-right efforts to promote an alternative political agenda to that of the Social Democrats. Indeed, Castles attributes long-term Social Democratic political dominance in Sweden (as elsewhere in Scandinavia) in part to the absence of a cohesive conservative party comparable to those in Great Britain and Germany.[10] Bourgeois fragmentation is rooted in the diverse historical origins of each of the parties, their partially overlapping but nonetheless distinctive electoral clientele, and their different ideological priorities over time. Only since the mid-1960s have leaders of the Liberal,

Table 9.3 Aggregate Socialist and Nonsocialist Electoral Support in National Elections, 1948–1994 (percent of vote)

Year	Socialist Bloc	Nonsocialist Bloc
1948	52.5	47.5
1952	50.4	49.5
1956	49.6	50.3
1958	49.6	50.4
1960	52.3	47.6
1964	52.2	43.9
1968	53.1	42.9
1970	50.1	47.6
1973	48.9	48.8
1976	47.5	50.8
1979	48.8	49.0
1982	51.2	45.0
1985	50.1	47.9
1988	49.6	41.8
1991	42.1	53.2
1994	51.6	42.5

Source: Author's files.

Center, and Moderate Unity parties begin a hesitant move toward a common bloc identity in joint opposition to Social Democratic ascendancy.

The Liberals

Swedish liberalism has evolved from a nineteenth-century reform movement inspired by Enlightenment ideals of reason, natural equality, and freedom of association to a solidly middle-class party seeking to achieve an "open and tolerant" society devoid of "dangerous utopianism" (which the Liberals implicitly attribute to Social Democracy). A central theme in the party's contemporary program is the sanctity of the individual: "Liberalism's point-of-departure is the individual. Its goal is individual freedom." To these ends, Sweden's Liberals affirm the equality of citizens (explicitly including gender equality), "a rich network of voluntary and spontaneous communities, [and] a civil society independent of political power." Consistent with their core ideological beliefs, the Liberals oppose "all concentration of power—in the hands of the state, large corporations, and powerful organizations."[11]

With respect to more concrete policy prescriptions, the Liberals distinguish between limited government intervention in economic matters, which they view as necessary to ensure economic growth and to promote maximum employment opportunities, and more encompassing measures to extend greater state control over investments and the direction of general economic development. Consistent with their programmatic principles, Swedish Liberals recognize the necessity of sufficient public expenditures to finance existing welfare services, but they oppose attempts to "socialize" the formulation of capital through taxation policies that might jeopardize personal and corporate savings. In addition, the Liberals have pressed for greater fiscal economies on the part of the government and for minor tax reductions whenever they prove feasible.

The Liberals' advocacy of "social liberal" ideological principles has attracted the support of a highly diverse (but volatile) electoral clientele. Identified in the late nineteenth and early twentieth centuries with the "old middle class" of urban entrepreneurs and intellectuals as well as religious dissidents and prohibitionists, the Liberals currently appeal primarily to civil servants and small-business owners (see table 9.4). Party strength has fluctuated significantly over time, rebounding during the 1940s and 1950s following a long downward spiral—when the Liberals lost many of their traditional supporters to the Social Democrats—and subsequently fluctuating between a high of 14.2 percent in 1985 and lows of 5.9 percent in 1982 and 7.2 percent in 1994.

Table 9.4   **Electoral Support among Occupational Groups (percent of vote) (1994 Election)**

Occupational Groups	Social Democrats	Center	Liberals	Moderates
Industrial workers	73	4	4	6
Other workers	57	9	3	11
Lower-level white-collar workers	51	6	6	19
Middle-level white collar workers	47	7	9	21
Higher-level white collar workers	30	4	17	36
Small business owners	22	13	6	44
Farmers	6	55	3	44
Students	29	7	12	18

Source: Mikael Gilljam and Sören Holmberg, *Väljarenasval* (Stockholm: Fritzes Förlag AB, 1995), p. 101.

The Center Party

The Center claims venerable roots dating from the formation in 1867 of a ruralist parliamentary faction—Sweden's first modern political party—to promote the interests of the nation's farmers in defiance of large landowners and bureaucratic conservatism. The original Ruralist party gradually disintegrated in the course of rapid industrialization and the formation of better organized Social Democratic and Liberal parties, but two successor farmers' parties were established early in the twentieth century. They merged in 1921 as the Agrarian party (*Bondeförbundet*).

Mobilizing an average of 11.3 percent of the popular vote through the remainder of the decade, the Agrarians initially aligned themselves with the Conservatives because of their joint opposition to increased state expenditures. The onset of the Depression, however, prompted party leaders to switch their allegiance to the Social Democrats. Both the Agrarians and the SAP gained support in the realigning election of 1932 and, as previously noted, forged a parliamentary alliance on behalf of an expansionist recovery program. For most of the next 25 years, the Agrarians served as junior coalition partners with the SAP and as co-architects of Sweden's fledgling welfare state.

Conflict with the Social Democrats over proposed legislation to introduce supplementary pensions (discussed below) prompted Agrarian leaders in 1957 once again to change their political alignment and join the other nonsocialist parties as members of the parliamentary opposition. Troubled by a long-term decline in electoral support because of the dwindling number of Sweden's farmers, the Agrarians acted to reinvent themselves as a more broadly based political party. In 1957 the Agrarians adopted the Center party as their current name and redefined their strategic role as a "middle party" representing the interests of the urban middle class in addition to those of farmers.

The Center party endorsed a new program in 1959, stressing the need to improve the economic status of small businessmen, strengthen the home environment through taxation and social policies favorable to families with children, and raise the general level of education. In addition, the Center aimed to counteract what the party viewed as potentially oppressive features of a greater concentration of power on the national level through "a policy that promotes local self-government, a decentralized construction of homes and industry, and a rich provincial and local culture life."[12] Subsequent efforts by party leaders to identify the Center as a champion of environmental issues (including their opposition to a contemplated expansion of nuclear energy plants in the 1970s) have been codified in the Center's current program in terms of "eco-humanism."[13]

As a result of its refurbished political and ideological appeal, the Center party succeeded through the mid-1970s in mobilizing an increasing number of voters. Its share of the popular vote steadily rose from 9.4 percent in 1956 to an historical zenith of 25 .1 percent in 1973. Although farmers still constitute its core clientele, the Center has increasingly attracted the support of civil servants and small-business owners (see table 9.4).

The Moderate Unity Party

Throughout modern Swedish history, the Moderate Unity party (which was known until 1968 as *Högern,* or "The Right") has continually had to redefine the meaning of conservatism in response to continuing processes of economic and sociopolitical modernization. Historically collectivist in the tradition of Burkean and nineteenth-century Continental conservatism, Swedish conservatives emerged in the twentieth century as proponents of classical liberal economic and political individualism. During the postwar decades the Conservatives have come to accept the basic principles of the established welfare state, but they continue to resist radical economic reforms and any increase in collective influences over production and investment. They also remain steadfastly committed to tax cuts and a reduction in the size of the public sector.

With the adoption of a new "humanistic conservative" program in December 1969 (revised in 1978 and 1993), the renamed Moderate Unity party sought to "modernize" its electoral appeal with a greater emphasis on individualism, equality, and social security (the latter defined as a "right of citizenship"). The Moderates also explicitly acknowledge the importance of joint action to achieve "active environmental protection."

At the same time, the Moderates coupled their traditional affirmation of property rights with a defense of democracy: "There is an intimate connection between the political and economic life of society," the program states. "Free and open competition ensures the most effective possible utilization of limited resources. . . . The right of private property provides the basis for a market economy. Mankind's right to dispose of his property is thus a prerequisite for freedom."[14]

To help mitigate the effects of increased bureaucratization in public life, the party advocates more openness and enhanced citizen control in decision-making processes—as well as greater "freedom of choice and competition in those areas in which the public sector is engaged. It is essential to stop further growth of the public sector and the power it exercises."[15]

Ideological renewal—comparable to that undertaken by the Center party a decade earlier—contributed from the early 1970s onward to a resurgence in electoral support for the Moderates. As indicated in table 9.1, the party successively expanded its share of the popular vote from 11.5 percent in 1970 to an average of 19.7 percent in Sweden's 8 subsequent elections. The Moderates continue to draw most of their electoral support from members of the upper and upper middle classes—including industrialists, businessmen, and higher-paid white-collar employees—but they have made inroads among lower-level white-collar workers and even industrial workers as well.

From Splintered Opposition to Bloc Identity

The fragmentation of center-right forces proved conducive to a relatively stable pattern of "competitive-bargaining relations" among nonsocialist leaders and between them and the Social Democrats from 1932 until the late 1950s.[16] Strictly competitive in elections, the nonsocialist parties concentrated on enhancing their capacity to influence government policies principally by maintaining or increasing their relative share of popular support. While especially the Agrarians/Center and the Conservatives/Moderates could count on a loyal core of supporters among farmers and businessmen and higher-level civil servants, respectively, all three parties competed fiercely for support among marginal voters in middle income and more diverse occupational groups (see table 9.4).

Between elections the Center party bargained directly with the Social Democrats as the junior partner in two coalitions (1936–39 and 1951–57), while the Liberals and Conservatives pursued more diffuse bargaining tactics aimed at modifying policy decisions during deliberations in parliamentary committees and extraparliamentary committees of experts that are appointed by the government to consider important initiatives prior to formal legislation. The prevailing "competitive-bargaining" pattern began to change, however, when the SAP introduced legislation to create a compulsory program of supplementary pension benefits in 1957. Center party leaders resigned in protest from cabinet office to join the Liberals and the Conservatives in joint opposition to compulsory features of the Social Democratic proposal. The Center's actions set into motion a gradual convergence of nonsocialist views on important political issues that subsequently transformed Sweden's multiparty system into a bipolar system of socialist and nonsocialist blocs.

At least four factors have contributed to the evolution of a common nonsocialist identity. One is the gradual convergence of nonsocialist ideology.[17] By the late 1950s widespread popular acceptance of the welfare state had significantly mitigated the partisan cleavages that had once separated the nonsocialist parties. Despite the origin of the Center party as an agrarian interest association and historical antagonisms between the Liberals and the Conservatives over democratization and the extension of suffrage rights, the three parties had come to share broadly similar concepts of how society and the economy should be organized.

A second, closely related factor is long-term demographic and social change. As urbanization and economic diversification generated a continued expansion in the number of white-collar workers, traditional socioeconomic sources of electoral support no longer sufficed as a guarantee that the nonsocialist parties could maintain their relative share of popular support. "To the extent that all major parties are permeated by the opinion and attitudes of these groups," Otto Kirchheimer has observed, "one may justifiably say that diminished social polarization and diminished political polarization are going hand in hand."[18] Forced to compete with the Social Democrats and with each other for the same marginal voters, Sweden's nonsocialist leaders resolved that a tactical requisite for challenging Socialist hegemony was to harmonize their policies rather than dissipate energies in self-defeating electoral strife.

A third impetus was the emergence of an outspoken group of youthful reformers within Liberal and Center party ranks during the early 1960s. By emphasizing the need to formulate a common program of sociopolitical transformation based on "progressive, social, and liberal tenets,"[19] leaders of the Liberal and Center youth associations helped prompt an internal debate within both parties on principles of a positive alternative to the policies of the Social Democrats. Their proposals for party and social reform found an appreciable echo among many Conservatives as well, especially within the Conservative Youth Association and in local branches of the Conservative party in southern Sweden.

The specific forms of nonsocialist cooperation proved the object of extended controversy within bourgeois ranks. After their withdrawal from the cabinet in 1957, Center spokesmen initially aligned themselves with the Conservatives in a more outspoken critique of the Social Democratic pension proposal than the compromise position adopted by the Liberals. But once the conflict was settled on SAP terms in 1959, the Center abandoned its informal alliance with the Conservatives and by 1960 joined the Liberals in endorsing the new program of compulsory pensions—thereby paving the way for intensified cooperation between the two middle parties.

During the remainder of the decade and into the 1970s, opposition leaders pursued parallel strategies in their attempt to intensify bloc cohesion. The first of these involved efforts to maximize nonsocialist bargaining leverage within parliament. Since the capacity of the nonsocialist parties to influence pending legislation derived from their combined parliamentary strength, opposition leaders acted increasingly to present a common front in the Riksdag.[20] Simultaneously, nonsocialist officials took preliminary steps to coordinate their parties' electoral strategies as a means to enhance bourgeois competitiveness against the majority Social Democrats. Such efforts were restricted at first to the two middle parties because Liberal and Center leaders remained skeptical about the more negative ideological image projected by the Conservatives. By the mid-1960s, however, the three nonsocialist parties proclaimed a joint moratorium (*Borgfreden*) on intrabourgeois campaign attacks in hopes that an outward display of harmony would enable the nonsocialist bloc ultimately to gain a parliamentary majority.[21] Coordinating specific policy objectives could then await the formation of a nonsocialist cabinet.

A fourth (and decisive) factor that helped translate bourgeois aspirations to forge a joint front against the Social Democrats into a succession of nonsocialist governments was the emergence of new political issues that animated the Swedish public debate from the 1970s through the mid-1990s. Among them were the Social Democrats' own efforts to redefine the Swedish model, recurrent periods of sluggish economic performance, domestic controversy concerning nuclear energy, and the advent of a populist protest movement on the right. Yet another issue subsequently encouraged the formation of a tactical policy alignment between some members of the bourgeois bloc and the Social Democrats: an animated public debate in the early 1990s on Sweden's accession to the European Union.

The Nonsocialists in Office

An incipient decline in SAP electoral support, which began in the 1964 general election,[22] paved the way for the formation of a nonsocialist cabinet a decade later. Bourgeois cohesion had coalesced sufficiently by the beginning of the 1970s to enable Center, Liberal, and Moderate Unity party leaders to present a potentially credible political alternative to an electorate that was increasingly intrigued by the prospect of a change-of-government. Enhancing such a prospect was a growing sense among many Swedish voters that Social Democratic policies had become too radical. Beginning in 1974, the SAP introduced a series of workplace reforms that pointed toward a fundamental redefinition of the established Swedish model in the direction of an unprecedented mixed system of industrial and economic democracy. Among these reforms were the Employment Security Act (which restricted the right of employers to fire workers), the Work Environment Act (which accorded floor-level safety stewards sweeping powers to enforce strict health and safety standards), and the Employee Participation Act (which transformed the traditional right of managers to "direct and allocate work" into an object of collective bargaining).[23] In 1975 the National Federation of Trade Unions (LO) proposed an even more controversial plan to establish a collective system of wage-earner funds with the authority to purchase shares in individual companies (thereby suggesting that the funds could eventually acquire majority ownership of specific firms). Property owners and even many rank-and-file workers viewed the LO plan as potentially threatening to the Swedish economy.

Diffuse apprehension that the SAP-LO reforms would tilt the existing balance of economic and political power in favor of organized labor at the expense of private capital was a principal factor contributing to a shift in the electoral balance between socialist and nonsocialist blocs in the September 1976 election. A second factor was the Center party's success during the campaign in mobilizing widespread voter concerns about a contemplated increase in the number of Sweden's nuclear power plants from 6 to 13 by the mid-1980s. Support for the socialists fell to 47.5 percent, while aggregate nonsocialist strength increased to 50.8. Within the nonsocialist bloc the Center party advanced from 9.4 percent of the vote to 11.1 percent while both the Liberals and the Moderates lost support (see table 9.1). Center chair Thörbjorn Fälldin claimed the prime ministership of a three-party coalition. A bourgeois government thus displaced the Social Democrats in executive office for the first time in 44 years.

Sweden's first experiment in nonsocialist governance since the early 1930s proved inconclusive. Liberal and Moderate endorsement of a modest expansion of Sweden's nuclear power capacity over Center party objections prompted a cabinet crisis in October 1978 when the Center withdrew from the coalition.[24] A minority Liberal government held office until the next election in 1979, when together the nonsocialist parties won 49 percent of the popular vote (compared to 48.8 for the socialists) and a single-seat majority in parliament. The Center, the Liberals, and the Moderates reconstituted a three-party coalition under renewed Center-party leadership but almost immediately confronted yet another policy crisis— this time over tax reform. Center and Liberal leaders negotiated an agreement with the opposition Social Democrats in the spring of 1981 to reduce marginal tax rates in exchange for a simultaneous cut in the amount of deductions allowable for interest paid on home mortgages. In response, Moderate spokesmen—who were opposed to the trade-off on ideological grounds—angrily resigned from the cabinet. Subsequently, the Center and the Liberals formed a two-party minority government that held office until the September 1982 election, when the Social Democrats returned to power with 45.3 percent of the vote.

Overshadowing partisan disagreements over taxation policy was the onset of a sluggish pattern of economic performance accompanied by an increase in both inflation and unemployment. Between 1970 and 1977, Sweden's annual growth rate averaged only 1.8 percent (compared to 3.5 percent in France, 3 percent in the United States, and 2.7 percent in western Germany during the same period). The annual rate of inflation, meanwhile, jumped from 4.3 percent during the 1960s to 9.3 percent in the 1970s, and unemployment rose from an annual average of 1.8 percent in 1956–78 to more than 3 percent by the summer of 1982. In an effort to restore growth and reduce the unemployment rate, the nonsocialist parties outflanked the Social Democrats on the left by socializing much of the nation's ailing shipbuilding industry. Bourgeois cabinets simultaneously sought to encourage private savings for investment purposes by creating new tax-sheltered savings and equity programs. The Center-Liberal cabinet also modified established fiscal and social policies by increasing the value-added tax and reducing health-care benefits.

Once back in office, the Social Democrats restored the nonsocialists' cuts in social services and proceeded to implement a watered-down version of the controversial wage-earner fund system. Their return to cabinet office coincided with the beginning of a general improvement in international economic conditions. An expansion of world trade accompanied by a decline in the world price of oil helped stimulate renewed domestic growth. From a negative rate of -.3 percent in 1981, Sweden experienced a steady increase in its real gross national product (GNP) through 1984 when the annual growth rate peaked at 4.0 percent. By the end of the decade the unemployment rate had declined to less than 2 percent. The electorate honored these positive economic trends by according the Social Democrats another victory in the 1985 election.

In a major departure from its ideological principles, however, the Social Democrats signaled through their actions that the era of reform politics was at an end. The party's leadership was determined to maintain the existing welfare state but, because of severe budgetary constraints, cabinet officials announced stringent restrictions on public expenditures early in 1990. The government's economic policies provoked a short-lived crisis in February when a majority of MPs initially rejected its anti-inflationary package. The cabinet managed to survive the revolt among rank-and-file deputies, but henceforth the Social Democrats were clearly on the defensive.

Parallel with their retreat from reformist politics at home, the Social Democrats initiated a series of moves to embrace the postwar European integration movement. During an initial public debate in the early 1970s on whether or not to follow the Danish lead in applying for membership in the then European Economic Community, party leaders had decided in the face of intense opposition among rank-and-file Social Democrats (as well as members of the Center party) to negotiate a more limited free-trade agreement that would be consistent with Sweden's established foreign policy of neutrality. By the mid-1980s, however, a number of international and regional changes had occurred to prompt a later generation of leaders to reconsider their country's economic and political ties with the Continent. Foremost among them were Mikhail Gorbachev's rise to power in the Soviet Union, which promised an easing of the cold war, and the European Community's firm commitment to attaining an integrated regional market and eventual economic and monetary union during the 1990s.

Recognizing the growing importance of trade with members of the European Community for Sweden's own livelihood in an increasingly globalized economy, the cabinet issued a policy statement in 1987 outlining a strategy to promote closer cooperation between Sweden and the European Community. The proposal entailed extensive coordination of Swedish monetary, fiscal, and industrial policies with those of the EC, the elimination of restrictions on the free flow of investment capital, and the deregulation of agriculture. An unintended consequence of the proclaimed "harmonization" of Sweden's macroeconomic policies with those of the EU was that it set further limits on the government's capacity to pursue an autonomous Social Democratic approach to economic management consistent with the party's historical reformist traditions.

Gorbachev's willingness to sanction liberalization and democratization in Central Europe—culminating in Germany's "rush to unification" in 1990—convinced a growing number of Swedes that neutrality no longer precluded full EC membership. Accordingly, the Social Democratic government submitted a formal application to the European Commission in early 1991. Strongly supporting the cabinet's initiative were the Moderates and the Liberals; in contrast, most farmers (and hence Center party adherents) as well as the postcommunist Left party and a number of younger voters (primarily women) were opposed.

By the time of Sweden's application to the EC, economic indicators were no longer propitious for the Social Democratic government. Inflation surged to an annual rate of 10.5 percent in 1990, and the annual growth rate slowed to −1.1 percent the following year. Thanks to Sweden's active labor-market policy, the unemployment rate of 2.7 percent remained low by international standards but was nonetheless higher than the average annual rate of 1.8 percent from 1986 through 1990. Government efforts to mitigate these trends were severely hampered by externalities over which the Swedish state had no control—including more restrictive macroeconomic policies pursued by Thatcherites in the United Kingdom and the Reagan-Bush administrations in the United States.

Growing LO and rank-and-file worker dissatisfaction with the SAP's austerity policies coincided with an interim electoral realignment in favor of the nonsocialist parties. The principal beneficiaries of the shift were the Moderates and two parties to their right: the Christian Democratic Union, which espouses traditional religious values, and New Democracy, a maverick populist movement that was founded in late 1990, whose programmatic appeal was based on its attacks on bureaucratization and demands to restrict immigration.

The September 1991 election resulted in heavy losses for the Social Democrats and a corresponding increase in votes for a bourgeois alternative. The nonsocialist bloc garnered 55.5 percent of the popular vote, with the Moderates advancing to 21.9 percent from 17.9 percent three years earlier. Both the Liberals and the Center lost support, while the Christian Democrats mobilized 7.0 percent and New Democracy 6.7. In October the Moderates formed a four-party coalition (which included the Liberals, the Center, and the Christian Democrats) under the prime ministership of Carl Bildt.

From the outset, the center-right government confronted formidable challenges to its capacity to enact a coherent policy agenda. One was its minority status in parliament. While the four parties together commanded 170 out of 349 seats in the Riksdag, they lacked 9 votes for a majority in their own right. Hence, the coalition was indirectly dependent on the support of New Democracy's 25 deputies. This dependency not only posed the ever-present risk of a government crisis but also accorded the New Democrats a disproportionate political influence despite strong antipathy among mainstream nonsocialist leaders, especially the Liberals, toward their ideological demands.

An even more daunting obstacle was Sweden's continuing economic malaise. In the face of sluggish growth, increased inflation, and higher unemployment (which rose to 4.8 percent in 1992 and 8.2 percent in 1993), the nonsocialists assigned highest policy priority to reducing taxes and government expenditures in an effort to encourage private investment and curtail Sweden's worsening public deficit. This entailed a succession of budget cuts from early 1992 onward, primarily at the expense of long-established welfare entitlements—including unemployment and retirement benefits, sick pay, and housing subsidies.

Both of these obstacles ultimately thwarted nonsocialist aspirations to achieve fundamental changes in Sweden's political economy and the welfare state. New Democracy repeatedly held the minority government hostage to specific policy demands, even as the founding leaders of the party discredited themselves in the eyes of the electorate through an extended public feud. Economic imperatives loomed even larger. In their efforts to trim public expenditures and welfare entitlements, the nonsocialists confronted Sweden's worse economic crisis since the early 1930s. In tandem with recessionary international economic trends in 1992–93 and an accompanying European currency crisis, which triggered intense pressure on Swedish banks and a de facto devaluation of the krona by 9 percent, the nation's growth rate stagnated. While the annual inflation rate declined substantially (from 10.5 percent in 1990 to 2.3 percent in 1992), Sweden's economic doldrums in combination with a reduction in public revenues caused the public debt to jump from 7.3 percent of the GDP in 1992 to 13.5 percent a year later.

Swedish voters responded to the worsening economic conditions and nonsocialist cuts in social entitlements by restoring the Social Democrats to power in the September 1994 election. The SAP dramatically reversed its earlier decline by mobilizing 45.4 percent of the voters, while combined support for the Moderates, Liberals, and Center plummeted to 41.3 percent. On the right, the Christian Democrats also lost support but managed to retain a reduced number of seats in parliament while New Democracy virtually disappeared from the political landscape with a minuscule 1.2 percent of the vote.

The Social Democrats resumed office in October 1994. Prime Minister Ingvar Carlsson's cabinet introduced an austerity budget of its own that prescribed further reductions in a number of public expenditures but also included an increase in taxes and the reversal of the nonsocialists' curtailment of unemployment and sickness benefits. Carlsson declared that the SAP's principal policy objective would be to reduce the nation's high unemployment rate through economic growth. As a means to that end, the Social Democrats successfully led a campaign to ratify Sweden's accession treaty with the European Union through a popular referendum on November 13, 1994. A narrow majority of 52.2 percent of Swedes endorsed the accession treaty compared to 46.9 percent who voted "no." On January 1, 1995, Sweden joined Austria and Finland as full members of the European Union.

Assessment

The successive phases of nonsocialist governance in Sweden reveal the continued political weakness of a multiparty bourgeois bloc. Despite their best efforts to forge a common bloc identity from the early 1960s onward, nonsocialist leaders proved unable to agree on important policy issues during their first tenure in office. Coalition disputes during the first interregnum of nonsocialist governance from 1976 to 1981, first with the Center party over energy policy, and later with the Moderates over tax reform, caused two government crises and the spectacle of weak minority governments that discredited the nonsocialists' claim that they could sustain a coherent alternative to Social Democracy. Increased fragmentation of bourgeois forces with the advent of the Christian Democrats and New Democracy in the early 1990s seriously undermined the nonsocialists' capacity to govern effectively from 1991 to 1994, even though during the second interregnum the four-party coalition was able to remain intact for the duration of the legislative period. Moreover, division within nonsocialist ranks over prospective Swedish membership in the EU significantly weakened the capacity of the Moderates, Liberals, and Center to present a united electoral front during the 1994 electoral campaign.

Although the center-right parties were able to shift budgetary priorities during their time in office and undertake marginal reductions in the scope of welfare provisions, they were ultimately unable to affect substantial changes in the established Swedish model. This proved virtually impossible for two substantive reasons: macroeconomic imperatives and the return of the Social Democrats to power in defense of the welfare state.

Thus, to address Richard Rose's central question, "Do Parties Make a Difference?," the answer with respect to Sweden's nonsocialist parties is "not very much." Rose's concluding observations about the role of parties in the United Kingdom apply with even greater veracity to the Swedish case: "The differences in office between one party and another are less likely to arise from contrasting intentions than from the exigencies of government. Much of a party's record in office will be stamped upon it by forces outside its control."[25]

This does not mean, however, that Castles' notion of a prevalent Social Democratic image of society in Sweden is impervious to change. Castles' prediction in the late 1970s that the Social Democrats would sustain their ideological commitment to economic and social reform in the face of bourgeois resistance has proved wrong—but not because of any temporary election losses. Instead, the Social Democrats emerged as the principal architects themselves of an ongoing revision of the Swedish model by renouncing their earlier efforts to extend citizen rights and by embracing a neoliberal Continental approach to economic and social management. The party that matters most in Sweden remains the SAP, even in the event of a return of the nonsocialists to power in a future election.

Notes

1. Francis G. Castles, *The Social Democratic Image of Society: A Study of the Achievements and Origins of Scandinavian Social Democracy in Comparative Perspective* (London, Henley, England, and Boston: Routledge & Kegan Paul, 1978).

2. Richard Rose, *Do Parties Make a Difference?* 2nd ed. (Chatham, N.J.: Chatham House Publishers, 1984).

3. Castles, p 96.

4. The principle of cabinet government was introduced in Norway in 1884, in Denmark in 1901, and in Sweden in 1917. Universal suffrage was achieved in Scandinavia through successive reforms spanning 1898 to 1921. See M. Donald Hancock, "Scandinavia," in S. M. Lipset, et al., eds., *Encyclopedia of Democracy* (Washington, D.C.: Congressional Quarterly Press, 1995).

5. During the late 1930s and early 1940s, electoral support for neofascist parties ranged from less than 1 percent in Sweden to 2 percent in Norway and 21 percent in Denmark.

6. These included an increase in the unemployment rate to 8 percent and a drop in the price index for agricultural products to 70 percent of its 1929 level See Dankwart A. Rustow, *The Politics of Compromise: A Study of Parties and Cabinet Government in Sweden* (Princeton, N.J.: Princeton University Press, 1955), p. 103.

7. Castles, p 8.

8. Sweden's estimated per capita gross national product (GNP) in 1995 was $26,096, compared to $26,438 in the United States, $29,542 in Germany, $26,445 in France, and $18,499 in the United Kingdom *OEEC Economic Surveys 1997* (Paris: Organization for Economic Cooperation and Development, 1997).

9. Bernt Schiller, et al, *The Future of the Nordic Model of Labour Relations: Three Reports on Internationlization and Industrial Relations* (Copenhagen: Nordic Council of Ministers, 1993), p. 11.

10. Castles, pp. 77–78.

11. Folkpartiet, *Liberalisms grunder* (http://wwwfolkpartiet, May 23, 1997).

12. Hans Wieslander, ed., *De politiska partiernas program* (Stockholm: Bokförlaget Prisma, 1964), p. 39.

13. Centern, Centerns partiprogram: Grön framtid, Respekt för livet (adopted October 26–27, 1990 in Västerås).

14. http://www.*moderaternas ideprogram,* June 23, 1997.

15. Ibid.

16. The term "competitive-bargaining relations" is derived from Robert Dahl, ed., *Political Oppositions in Western Democracies* (New Haven, Conn.: Yale University Press, 1966), pp. 336–38.

17. This section of my chapter is based on my earlier publication, M. Donald Hancock, *Sweden: The Politics of Postindustrial Change* (Hinsdale, Ill.: The Dryden Press, Inc., 1972), pp. 131–37.

18. Otto Kirchheimer, "The Waning of the Opposition in Parliamentary Regimes," *Social Research* 24 (Summer 1957): 148.

19. Per Ahlmark, et al, *Mitt i 60-talet* (Stockholm: Bonniers, 1966), p. 88.

20. At the urging of the Liberals, nonsocialist MPs initiated informal consultations in 1962 on the preparation of joint opposition motions and the coordination of committee strategies.

21. External events encouraged Sweden's nonsocialist forces to seek three-party cooperation. The nonsocialist parties united on a common "Coalition Parties" program in neighboring Norway to defeat the incumbent Labor party in the September 1965 election to the Storting, and formed the first stable alternative cabinet since 1935.

22. The 1968 election results proved an exception to a gradual downward spiral of Social Democratic strength The SAP's majority of 50.5 percent was primarily an indirect response to the Soviet-led occupation of Czechoslovakia in August.

23. For details of these measures, see M. Donald Hancock and John Logue, "Sweden: The Quest for Economic Democracy," *Polity,* Fall/Winter 1984.

24. The controversy over nuclear energy was tentatively resolved following a popular referendum in March 1980 when a majority of voters endorsed an SAP-Liberal proposal to expand the number of plants to 12 and then eventually phase out all of the plants by early in the twenty-first century.

25. Rose, *Do Parties Make a Difference?,* p 142.

CHAPTER TEN

The Center-Right at the End of the Century

Frank L. Wilson

In most of the countries covered in this volume, the center-right parties are among the oldest and best-entrenched parties. Their age and endurance suggest their ability to adapt to differing political, economic, and social circumstances over the decades. But endurance is also sometimes simply the result of the slow pace of change or the rigid permanence of established political loyalties and institutions. This section examines what our separate country studies suggest about the future ability of center-right parties to transform themselves to meet the demands of a new era.

The Changing Center-Right

Social Bases and Electoral Coalition-Building

In the countries we have examined, the electorates for parties of the center-right remain similar in many ways to the patterns established decades ago. In practice, the Lipset-Rokkan social cleavage structures described over 30 years ago, and noted by them as established in most countries decades before then, usually remain the best explanations for voting coalitions.[1] Center-right parties still find their principal political bastions in the middle and upper classes, among those living in rural and small towns, and from the more religious voters. But these alignments are evolving. The salience of religious voting has diminished due to the overall decline of religiosity, but the religious factor—both different religions and degree of commitment to a religion—continues to be very important in voting decisions in several of our countries, notably France, Germany, and the Netherlands.[2] There are, however, signs of erosion of the social-class basis for voting as class structures and awareness have evolved.[3] The historic prominence of the better-educated, upper-middle-class population remains clear-cut among party members and leaders of the center-right parties in most European countries. But the picture at the mass base is less clear. In broad terms, the traditional alignment of the more privileged sectors of the population with the center-right remains true to a greater or lesser degree in nearly all of our countries. However, overall in Europe the impact of class in structuring the vote is much less significant than in the past. In some countries, such as Greece and Spain, social-class bases for partisan choices seem to have lost nearly all significance. On a broad scale the decline in class impact on party choice is clear. One study demonstrated that class, religion, and other social factors together explain only about 40 percent of the variation in voting support for West European parties.[4] This represents a decline from earlier patterns but by no means the disappearance of the political impact of historic social cleavages. Class is a secondary but important factor in explaining political attitudes and behavior.[5]

Whatever the voting alignments, center-right parties in Europe clearly attempt to extend their appeal beyond the "natural" social categories of the past. It is not surprising that the larger, more successful center-right parties have been most successful in building broad electoral coalitions across class, religion, and regional ties. The British Conservatives have a long tradition of drawing a significant portion of skilled and unskilled working-class voters.[6] In British elections during the 1980s and again in 1992, the Conservatives drew more of the unemployed voters and on several occasions more of the union-member votes than did Labour. In unified Germany, the Christian Democrats have succeeded in implanting themselves among the historically Protestant and nonreligious voters in eastern Germany. The People's party in Spain based its electoral resurgence and ultimate victory on extending its appeal into traditional strongholds of the Socialists: young voters, women, and the urban middle class. But even smaller center-right parties in Scandinavia and the Netherlands have moved beyond traditional bastions to draw in new voters. Otto Kirchheimer's contention that parties of his era no longer could claim "private hunting grounds" is truer than ever in the 1990s.[7] The center-right's loss of religious and upper-class voters is compensated for by gains in areas where it had not polled well in earlier years.

In the past, center-right parties have often sought to deflect the advantage that their left-wing rivals enjoyed from the larger size of the working class by deemphasizing class-based issues and by insisting that the left-right division was irrelevant or outdated. Now, there is new evidence in contemporary social trends to support such center-right denials of the significance of social class. Political and cultural shifts in emphasis from traditional left-right socioeconomic and international security issues to new postmaterial or postmodern issues offer important opportunities for center-right parties to establish new issue bases on which to build new and broader electoral coalitions. Ronald Inglehart and others have noted the greater impact of postmaterialist values on the electoral bases for left-wing parties.[8] Inglehart contends that these shifts in underlying values offer new potential to left-wing parties able to champion the new issues. Others see new "libertarian" and new left parties emerging to challenge the traditional left for the votes of the postmaterialists. Inglehart and others are less clear on the impact of the value shifts on voter support for the center-right parties. Most studies of the impact of postmodern value shifts focus on the impact of these changes on left-wing parties. But the value changes are also affecting center-right parties. Inglehart may be correct when he claims that the "new right" is not the wave of the future,[9] but there are certainly opportunities for the right in the shifting values. In some instances, the center-right parties have been better able to pick up on some postmaterialist issues—notably the environment—than have their leftist rivals. For example, in Sweden, the Center party was the principal opponent of expanding nuclear energy facilities; in Spain, the People's party took more forceful positions on environmental issues than did the social democratic government. More frequently, the center-right parties can benefit from public uncertainty about or outright hostility toward postmaterial issues such as women's equality, legalization of abortion, new morality, minority rights, and so on.[10]

The main opportunity for the center-right parties comes through their opposition to postmodern issues as these issues become incorporated into the left's programs. With economic and security issues crowded off the public agenda for parties of the left, the center-right parties have new issues to address, and must extend their appeal into new parts of the electorate. The parties of the center-right can stand for economic growth and industrialization in ways that might attract not only their usual middle- and upper-class clientele but also votes from working-class voters who are not satisfied with the economic success that fosters the postmaterialism accepted by the left. This often includes large numbers of people with modest incomes who are disadvantaged by changing economies. As left-wing parties adopt more of the postmaterialist agenda, the center-right parties can also become the beneficiaries of new political support from the large number of citizens in western Europe still attached to moral and social positions that conflict with postmodern values of environmentalism, participation, communitarianism, and egalitarianism. It includes also many who are disturbed by the moral issues, immigration, crime, and economic decline and urban blight often linked fairly or more frequently unfairly with the spread of postmodern values. The issues of public order, anti-immigration, and traditional morality may not be "postmodern," but they are new issues that have crept onto the political agendas in modern democracies as much as have the postmodern issues. The challenge for the center-right will be to keep these issues from falling into the domain of far-right parties more willing to engage in demagoguery than are the mainstream parties.

Organizational Dynamics

With a few exceptions, European center-right parties have not been noted for elaborate or well-developed party structures. They were the real-world models for Maurice Duverger's cadre parties: parties with little formal organization and centered around public office-holders and -seekers.[11] Few were able to match the mass-membership, well-structured, and disciplined parties of the left, although several have tried. Center-right parties have generally paid less attention to issues of internal party democracy. They are usually hierarchical organizations with powers over party programs and activities concentrated in the hands of a small group of leaders serving also in the national parliaments and many times in government. It is not surprising that these leaders are often a poor reflection of the party's electorate in that they tend to be more male, older, more urban, and better educated than the overall electorates for their parties. The issue of opening up more opportunities for women has been an important but divisive one in several center-right parties, notably the German CDU, British Conservative party (in spite of Margaret Thatcher), and French RPR and UDF. While the Scandinavian parties have been more open to providing opportunities to women, including top leadership positions, other center-right parties, particularly in the Mediterranean countries, have yet to accept gender equality as an issue, much less take steps to address it.

Most center-right parties have concentrated their organizational efforts at the national level. The result is weak party structures at the grass-roots level, with what organization there is centered around the national and local elected officials in that community. Germany is an exception with its federalism providing strong land-level party units. In Britain, local constituency parties retain key but not exclusive powers of selecting candidates. In general, however, center-right parties, including those in Germany and Britain, tend to be dominated from the top. Many center-right parties expanded their memberships during the 1970s and early 1980s. But at the end of the 1990s, most of the center-right parties covered in this volume are experiencing declining memberships.[12] In addition, those party members who remain are often less active and less in-volved than in earlier periods of membership mobilization.

The "light" organizations of center-right parties are no longer, if they ever were, hindrances to their political success. A variety of political and so-cial changes have made party membership less attractive to both citizens and party elites.[13] In an era when media campaigns are growing in dominance, the need for large numbers of party members has declined. Many party lead-ers now see mass memberships as both too costly in money and leadership time needed to manage, and too limiting on party leaders as they adjust pro-grams and strategies to accord with shifting electoral needs. For their part, citizens are also uninterested in party membership. They are otherwise pre-occupied in leisure activities. If they are looking for political expression, many citizens find social movements or interest groups more effective means of representation than parties. They clearly see less value in joining and be-coming involved in political parties than they did in the past. We have moved beyond mass parties to new party forms at the end of the century.

There are several visions of the postmodern party. Some see the domi-nant pattern as the "cartel party" based on close interaction and sharing between the state and the established, mainstream parties.[14] Cartel parties collude with each other and with the state to protect their hold on poli-tics, fend off challenges from new parties, and help each other survive. They benefit from the state's mandate of free television time on both state and private networks during and outside of campaign times. At the same time that their representative roles are reduced by the blurring of differences be-tween parties, established parties are acquiring greater prestige and privi-leges in their role as public officeholders.[15] An important part of this trend is the expanded state subsidization of party activities including campaign-ing, maintenance of the central party offices, and party research and edu-cation. Over the past two decades, public financing of political parties has become the norm in most European democracies.[16] For example, in 1969 state subsidies to West Germany's CDU amounted to 5.5 million DM (ex-clusive of payments to the party's Bundestag fraktion); in 1989 the subsi-dies had risen to 205.6 million DM.[17] Concerns about corruption and the rapid increases in campaign costs have led states to increase subsidies to po-litical parties and to expand state regulation of their activities. State fund-ing and regulation of party activities usually accord privileged positions to the cartel parties that allow them to thrive without party members' dues or support from associated interests.[18] State subsidies are vital now as par-ties have shifted from labor-intensive mass-membership parties to capital-intensive parties relying on professionals and specialists.

Others describe the new prevalent party type as the "media party," based on the dominance of political parties by professional experts in public relations, marketing and advertising, mass media, opinion surveys, and campaign management.[19] Over time, European parties have become "electoral-professional parties."[20] Party bureaucracies have grown in size but, of greater importance, these bureaucracies have shifted in composition from the part-time political notables of cadre parties and party militants of mass parties to the well-educated, career professionals skilled in organizational management and public relations. Such media parties are strongly hierarchical in their communications and decision-making processes in order to facilitate their leaders' engagement in media-based politics. Discussion of party ideology and doctrine shifts from the ranks of the party's members to professional think-tanks whose advice can be solicited or ignored according to the party leadership's preferences.

While this media-type party is especially important in the United States,[21] it is also spreading widely in Europe. Tony Blair's wildly successful election campaign was certainly not based on the Labour party's organization but rather on Blair's personal campaign team that determined party stands less on the concerns of the party rank and file than on the dictates of focus groups. French presidential elections of all mainstream political families are conducted beyond the traditional party structures through heavy reliance on professional campaign managers. In Italy, *Forza Italia* and the Northern League owed their success not to traditional party campaign tactics but to professional specialists loyal to these parties' leaders or simply "hired guns" selling their services to whomever was interested and able to pay. In Spain, the Popular party's rise to success came without the regional party base usually important in Spanish politics. Similar trends can be seen in both center-right and leftwing parties in smaller European democracies. In short, electoral success in the 1990s depends less on elaborate party organizations than on professionally run campaigns often paid for by state subsidies to the established parties.

Characteristics of both the cartel party and the media party are evident among center-right parties in western Europe. The new party forms may raise important questions about the place of such parties in theories of representative democracy. Can such parties provide the linkage between state and society that we have long counted on parties to do? They no longer need mass memberships and can count almost automatically on a mass electorate while doing little more than finding the lowest common denominator on major policies. Can parties linked to the state remain mediators between the state and its citizens? Some see the cartel parties as less effective in linking people to the state and more adept at brokering between the state and civil society.[22] Should parties lead according to sets of political ideals or should they follow the directions indicated by the latest opinion polls or hunches of campaign strategists? The unwillingness of parties to paint visions of the future and instead their determination to offer photocopies of the present realities may be significant losses in contemporary democracies. Does their dependency on the state reduce their ability to represent their followers against the state? Does the power of the state enable the established parties to rebuff challenges from newer parties perhaps more grounded in the concerns of the citizenry? There is little doubt that "parties with access to state resources and power have a clear advantage in maintaining their own position and denying such power to others."[23] These questions raise basic issues about the ability of contemporary center-right parties to fulfill the representative roles expected in modern democracies. As important as these concerns about their effects on democracy, it is difficult to challenge the fact that these new forms of democratic parties are becoming widespread among west European parties of the center-right.

Party Decline?

Two decades ago, scholars pointed to what seemed the irreversible decline of political parties in western democracies. Undermined by public disillusionment with party politics and the citizens' lack of trust in all parties, challenged by new social movements and "new politics" parties, threatened by weakening electoral alignments, and faced with organizational sclerosis, mainstream parties on both left and right appeared to be in full decline.[24] How surprising it is then that, with the notable exception of Italy, the center-right parties in west European politics at the end of the century are the same ones that seemed on the verge of political extinction 25 years ago. Not only have they survived but today they are more like they were then than they are different.[25] While parties have had their ups and downs—both in terms of their electoral fate and their organizational strength, there is little evidence to indicate a pattern of generalized party decline among the center-right parties in the western European democracies we have examined.

What stands out most clearly is the ability of these parties to endure in spite of scandals, electoral reverses, inept leaders, and the emergence of new parties. Part of the explanation is simple inertia: once established, partisan loyalties are difficult to disrupt. Old parties do not die; they do not even fade away. They continue to hold on to established electorates in spite of changing societies and politics. They have substituted a partnership with the state for earlier dependency on mass memberships. This new collusion of "cartel" parties with the state further helps them maintain their primacy against challengers and cyclical slumps. The result is that the existing patterns have "the look of indestructibility."[26]

If most center-right parties have survived and even thrived, it is important to look at the one big exception: the total collapse of the Christian Democrats in Italy. As Dwayne Woods points out, the DC, whose political
position was based on Italian fears of communism both internally and ex-
ternally, lost its raison d'être when communism collapsed in Eastern Europe
and Italy's own Communist party completed its transformation into a non-
revolutionary, democratic, and no longer threatening participant in national
politics. This occurred simultaneously with public exposure of a vast scandal in party financing, corruption, and diversion of public resources to private uses implicating most of the DC's past and present leadership. Political
scandals, of course, were nothing new to Italy. What made them different
this time was that without the communist fear, citizens could afford to explore other options. And they did: the DC and other center-right parties
virtually disappeared within a few months. New cleavages, especially regional ones, emerged as the new basis of Italian politics. They were not re-
ally "new" since the distribution of resources between north and south had
long been an issue of importance and a source of some tension. Until the
early 1990s, however, these regional cleavages were overwhelmed by the
communist fear issue. Thus the Italian exception to the general pattern of
party durability found elsewhere in Europe. Woods correctly notes that the
current patterns of center-right politics in Italy are still in flux, with some
of the new center-right parties likely to evolve or disappear.

The mainstream parties of the center-right continue to face important
challenges, especially from far-right parties that threaten to cut into their
electorates. But there are no signs of system-wide party decline except for
that already experienced in Italy. There are certainly worries about the future of the British Conservative party after the 1997 debacle, but past experience suggests that the Conservatives will adapt in order to survive and
thrive again. Persistence does not mean the absence of change. To the contrary, center-right parties in Europe may well evolve as the new century begins. The last two decades of the twentieth century have presented new
trials that necessitate change for all parties—right, center, or left. Even as socioeconomic changes seem to have presented new opportunities for center-
right parties, the transformation of these advantages into political gains
depends upon the ability of the leaders and reformers of these parties to
correctly perceive the opportunities and the right directions for change.

The Traditional Center-Right and
the New Challenge of the Far Right

In this volume we have deliberately avoided lengthy discussions of the extreme right parties because they have been covered elsewhere.[27] Here I

want to summarize the problems these extremist parties pose for the moderate parties of the center-right. The far right offers an array of extremist policies that pander to people's worst instincts. Their antidemocratic stances capitalize on public discontent with scandals and the imperfections of our elected officials. This potent but undemocratic populism has appeal to many European voters. In addition, Inglehart suggests that the value changes from materialist to postmaterialist are creating a new axis of political cleavage that is replacing the traditional left/right axis.[28] With environmentalists on the postmaterialist pole, the far right carries the banner of the "fundamentalist" pole. This new cleavage does not mean that the far right will prevail, just as the environmental parties are unlikely to replace the traditional center-left parties. But the far right may gain an advantage as it comes to represent the polar opposite in the new cleavage between traditional values and the new postmodern values.

The political form of right-wing extremism varies widely from the nostalgic fascism of the Italian National Alliance to the populism of the Norwegian Progressive party to the fascist "wannabes" of the French National Front to the skinhead thugs in Britain and Germany. While the far right has grown almost everywhere, its growth has varied from one country to the next for reasons that are not always clear. Even where significant growth of a far-right movement has taken place, the consequences for the traditional center-right have varied between European countries, again for reasons that are not always understood. But in most of Europe, the extreme right poses problems for the mainstream center-right in several areas: competition for voters, framing party agendas and programs, and determining general political strategies in responding to the far right's resurgence.

Electoral Impact of the Far Right

Electoral support for the right-wing extremist parties varies widely in the countries we are studying (see table 10.1). The variance does not appear to be linked with the size of immigrant populations even though racial tensions from large-scale immigration is seen as one of the principal causes of the far right's resurgence. Nor does it appear to be determined by electoral systems. Among countries with proportional representation, which presumably facilitates the entry of new fringe parties, only Norway has seen strong electoral support for the far right.

In some of the countries in our study, the far right's vote is small but volatile. In Germany, for example, far-right parties have often had a stronger presence in land-level elections but failed to break into national politics. These parties sometimes appear to be "flash parties" that suddenly appear as major actors. But they do not always ebb in the way flash parties

Table 10.1   Voting Strength of Far-Right Parties in Parliamentary Elections

Country	Year	Percent of Vote for Far-Right Parties
Britain	1997	nil
France	1997	15.2
Germany	1994	1.9
Greece	1996	2.9
Italy	1996	15.7
The Netherlands	1994	2.5
Norway	1997	15.0
Portugal	1995	nil
Spain	1996	nil
Sweden	1994	1.2

Source: Author's files.

have in the past. The threat of a sudden explosion of support for extremist parties is illustrated by the 1997 Norwegian elections when the far-right Progress party of Carl I. Hagen tripled its vote from the previous election and gained a powerful position to influence cabinet formation and government policies after the election. Even where the far right has not posed an immediate electoral threat, it is a political force to be reckoned with. Its political manifestations may be in separate but sometimes frequent acts of individual violence against immigrants or in street violence by gangs of "skin-heads." It may be reflected in regionalist parties and nationalist movements. It may lurk as small but influential factions in the major parties. There are few center-right parties in Europe that do not face one or more of these versions of the new politics of the far right.

Impact of the Far Right on the Agendas and Programs of the Center-Right

In many ways, the mainstream center-right parties today face the same dilemma that confronted social-democratic parties in the 1950s and 1960s. During these years, social democrats in many European countries competed with communist or other far-left parties for electoral support and political position. Where the communist presence was strongest, moderate center-left parties found that the communists influenced their conduct as they drafted programs, recruited party members, set electoral and coalition strategies, and wooed voters.[29] They could not moderate their policies in response to the emerging bloc of centrist voters without risking that their left-wing supporters would defect to the more doctrinally pure and extreme parties on their left. On the other hand, to join forces with the left was to endanger the moderates' ability to win the votes of the centrists or to govern once in office.

The same plight now confronts the center-right. Like the communists of the past, the far right offers an attractive array of policy promises that its leaders know they will not have to enact into real policies. They can promise the impossible—like expelling immigrants—without worrying that they will be called upon to execute that policy. They can ridicule those in office for their greed and corruption without having their own accounts examined. They can advocate popular but undemocratic political solutions to problems of concern to everyone.

In many western democracies, established parties respond to challenges from new parties by coopting their programs. To some extent that has happened in Europe. The response of the mainstream parties to the resurgence of extreme right parties has often been the incorporation of part of the far right's agenda into their own programs. Over the past decade, many parties—on the left as well as on the center-right—have proposed more restrictive policies on immigration, naturalization, and asylum rights. They have urged more repressive police measures to combat rising crime rates and the decline in the sense of domestic security. Mainstream parties have sought to regain lost terrain by promising stricter enforcement of drug laws and cleaning up of low-cost, crime-ridden public housing. They are more aggressive in finding and prosecuting corruption in their own ranks. As one observer of French politics notes, the cooption of so much of the radical right's agenda by the mainstream parties suggests that the far right has "in fact won an (im)moral victory."[30]

Resistance or Capitulation—Ghettoization of the Far Right and Its Consequences

The moderate center-right has struggled to find the correct response to the challenge of the renewed far right. To ignore the far right and its issues is to allow the extremists to whittle away at the moderates' right-wing supporters; to adopt the far right's issues is to legitimize them and to perhaps alienate other parts of the moderate center-right's normal electoral support; to join forces with the far right brings the risk of governing with an unreliable and undemocratic partner. In most cases now—Italy is an exception—center-right parties have spurned any cooperation with the far right. In most of Europe, the far right finds itself at the end of the century in a political ghetto similar to that in which West European communist parties were consigned during the 1950s and 1960s. But even from their ghetto, right-wing extremists continue to affect the political fate of the center-right.

This dilemma is very real for the center-right parties in countries where the far right has posed the greatest electoral threat. In the aftermath of the 1997 elections in Norway, for example, Carl Hagen's Progressive party holds the balance of power between Labor and the mainstream center-right, neither of which can govern alone. In France, the National Front's support and its presence in run-off elections were the major reasons for the defeat of the center-right.[31] The Gaullists and the UDF are now debating the appropriate course to meet this challenge in future elections. Past experience in France indicates that this will be a difficult task. Tough immigration and naturalization laws, a center-right movement against the Maastricht Treaty, Chirac's populist presidential campaign of 1995, and other attempts by the RPR and UDF to speak to the issues that seem to attract support to the FN have failed to reverse the FN's growing strength in national elections. As one commentator notes, such "attempts to reclaim the FN's mobilizing themes have done nothing to stem the electoral advance of Le Pen and his party—and may arguably have served only to lend them increased legitimacy."[32] As for open cooperation with the far right, that would divide the parties' own supporters. Two-thirds of Gaullist voters and over three-quarters of UDF voters are opposed to such an alliance even after the electoral disaster of 1997.[33]

Those who advocate a strategic alliance between mainstream center-right parties and their far-right rivals often cite the experience of the left in the 1960s and 1970s. Broad alliances of the left and even between communists and centrists contributed to the "domestication" of the communists.[34] This, of course, was a long-term strategy for most center-left parties that faced a strong communist rival. The same is likely to be true now where the mainstream center-right confronts a powerful far-right opponent. Italy offers a current example of an application of this strategy of incorporating the extremes in order to tame the far right. The National Alliance (AN) has become a key partner in the right coalition for the past two national elections, even taking its place in the government of Silvio Berlusconi. But its presence in the government contributed to the majority coalition's instability. The Berlusconi government lasted only seven months, and the Lamberto Dini government of technocrats excluded the National Alliance. The AN later brought about the fall of the Dini government. Nevertheless, by the 1996 elections, the AN's leader, Gianfranco Fini, stood as the most prominent leader of the center-right. As Woods notes, the National Alliance contributes to continued problems of internal divisions and lack of doctrinal coherence that leave the Italian center-right unable to offer a strong alternative to the ruling center-left coalition of Romano Prodi.

In summary, the challenge from the far right is important. In several European countries, it threatens the electability of the mainstream center-right. Center-right parties are struggling to find an appropriate response. In various settings, they have tried isolation, cooption of the far right's issues, or incorporation of the far right into electoral coalitions. So far, none of these strategies appears successful.

Neoliberalism and the Center-Right

By the mid-1970s, the economic crises of that decade brought growing skepticism about the continued utility of the postwar political and social consensus that had dominated politics in most of western Europe. The postwar consensus, built around a mixed economy, Keynesian economics, and a social welfare state, had contributed to Europe's economic recovery and political harmony since the end of the 1940s. In the 1970s, the consensus was challenged by simultaneous economic slump and sky-rocketing inflation. Economic growth slowed or stopped in most west European states and the usual Keynesian remedies did not work. Political clashes grew as economic hardship spread, inflation increased costs of welfare programs, and unions and employers searched for new ways to revive the economy. Political stability was also shaken by the spread of international and domestic terrorism. In short, the old certainties such as belief in the efficacy of Keynsianism, economic planning, and social engineering through welfare programs were all undermined.

In this setting, some politicians, notably those in Britain and the United States, began to give new attention to the writings of intellectuals such as Friedrich von Hayek[35] and Milton Friedman.[36] These scholars and others challenged the old consensus as dangerous to liberty and as antithetical to long-term economic growth. Freedom, for them, came out of the operations of an open and free-market system: capitalism promotes economic freedom and that in turn brings political freedom. They challenged government economic planning and intervention as interfering in the natural and desirable play of market forces. They saw society as too complex to respond to the social engineering of welfare programs. Friedman, especially, argued that the state's primary economic role should be limiting the supply of money in order to control inflation.[37]

While their views remained controversial,[38] the neoliberal intellectuals influenced political key advisors (notably Sir Keith Joseph in Britain) and fostered the growth of right-wing think-tanks (such as Britain's Institute of Economic Affairs and the Centre for Policy Studies) to take the new doctrine to wider audiences. The political impact of neoliberal doctrine was especially important in the United Kingdom, where Margaret Thatcher accepted its tenets and worked for over a decade to enact them.[39] In turn, doctrine-based neoliberalism affected, although to a substantially lesser effect, the United States and Canada[40] and to even less effect continental west European democracies.

In Europe, the popularity of neoliberalism is more than a triumph of political ideas. Neoliberalism has become enshrined as essential in the European Union for practical reasons as much as for doctrinal convictions. Advocates of economic unity have found that the best way to provide fair competition among firms throughout the EU is to eliminate advantages provided by the individual states' regulatory patterns, subsidies, or tax benefits. The easiest approach to "leveling the playing field" or eliminating informal trade barriers posed by different regulatory rules in the separate states is to take the state (even the EU) out of the economy. As a result, European countries which once had elaborate and extensive forms of intervention in their economies have abandoned them—or shifted them to Brussels where they have been reduced or eliminated. State subsidization of enterprises, even those still owned by the state, is discouraged and often requires approval by the EU Commission. Government economic regulations have been reduced in order to avoid obstacles to trade and inequities within the EU.

Yet another practical reason for the shift to neoliberalism has been the rapid growth of international trade. Competition with new trade rivals around the globe requires companies in western Europe to adapt or perish. This necessitates reduction of government economic regulations, more flexible employment policies, strict anti-inflationary policies, and lower taxes. All of these are key elements in neoliberal economics. They are fostered by pragmatic market concerns as much or more than by ideological motivations.

Center-right parties in Europe might be expected to benefit from the apparent shift in the political agenda around the world toward neoliberalism. The electoral successes of neoliberal leaders such as Margaret Thatcher and Ronald Reagan were impressive object lessons to politicians around the world. In addition, social democracy was also tarnished by the failure of state-driven communist economies and fell deeper into decline. Meanwhile, the popularity of neoliberalism as the dominant economic paradigm grew. International economic bodies such as the International Monetary Fund, the World Bank, GATT, and more recently the World Trade Organization took neoliberal practices around the globe. Politicians and pundits use sweeping terms to talk of the change: a sea change, a new era of politics and economics, the death of the social-welfare state, or a shift in paradigms.

The triumph of this neoliberal political agenda is often symbolized by the incorporation of its political doctrines into the practices of even the leftist governments. With origins in conservative Anglo-American regimes, neoliberalism was often spread on the European continent by center-left leaders such as Felipe González, François Mitterrand, and Sweden's Ingvar Carlsson and, more recently, Tony Blair, Romano Prodi, and Lionel Jospin. Governments led by social democrats have implemented much of the neoliberal program or continued its implementation when they have taken over from center-right governments. Indeed, in some cases the center-right parties lagged behind their left-wing rivals in pushing the neoliberal agenda to the fore.

Despite broad dispersion of neoliberal ideas, the question of how widespread is the acceptance of this new agenda is still open. Some European political leaders from all points on the political spectrum have denounced it as an Anglo-American phenomenon—or even aberration. At the elite level, this is well symbolized by the reaction of European politicians to the American triumphalism at the 1997 economic summit in Denver. European leaders from the left and right denounced the American model urged on them by Bill Clinton as inappropriate to their countries and political traditions. Employment flexibility *may* have won out in the United States but it finds far fewer advocates in a Europe plagued with double-digit unemployment. Few European leaders will speak out for low minimum wages as a response to that unemployment; they hope to expand employment with jobs offering fair remuneration.

At the mass level, evidence of a new consensus around neoliberal ideas is scant. While this is not the place for a systematic examination of this, opinion polls in most European countries show that a substantial majority of citizens still favor the social-welfare programs of the old postwar consensus. Europeans value the protection of job security offered not only by unemployment insurance but also by state regulations limiting public and private entrepreneurs' ability to reduce the workforce. While the old debate over government ownership of economic enterprises has lost its vigor at the popular level, the argument seems closed because it is stale rather than resolved in favor of private ownership. Europeans want the advantages that come from government-owned public transportation and complain about the consequences of its privatization in places like Britain. Above all, they are not interested in seeing their costly social-welfare programs reduced in coverage or quality. Governments that ignore that basic fact pay for it at the polls, as seen recently in Britain and France.

In our separate country studies, most of us have found only moderate public support for neoliberalism. In nearly all countries, except perhaps Britain, implementation of neoliberal economic policies, such as reducing the public sector of the economy or state economic regulations, has left the state with much of its power intact and in some cases even enhanced. Almost everywhere, the state has played a much more important role in restructuring the economy than was the case in the United States. In some countries, adoption of neoliberalism by center-right parties produced public reaction against the doctrine and the parties. In Greece, for instance, New Democracy's embrace of neoliberalism at the end of the 1980s resulted in election losses and a reversal of the neoliberal program shortly thereafter. In France, the Gaullists retreated from their neoliberal stances in the build-up to the 1993 and 1995 elections. In other countries, such as Italy, the center-right parties talked of neoliberalism but failed to enact major changes in socioeconomic policies. Even Margaret Thatcher limited her government's attacks on growing costs of the popular National Health Service.

There are also reasons to question whether or not the center-right would benefit politically from the neoliberal agenda. Again, the parallel with the social democratic consensus is useful. While the ideas of social democracy prevailed in western Europe from the late 1940s to the mid-1970s, the center-left was in government for less time than was the center-right. Indeed, in many countries such as France, West Germany, Italy, and even Britain, it was the parties of the center-right that created and implemented the social-welfare state and mixed economy policies that originated in the doctrine and platforms of the left.

That pattern seems to be reemerging in the 1990s with the roles reversed: the public seems readier to see the left implement the neoliberal program than it is to support the center-right parties that built that agenda. Just as voters in many European countries turned to the center-right to temper the economic and social policies of the dominant social democratic agenda after World War II, so many voters in the 1990s and into the next century may turn to the left to moderate and give a human face to the neoliberal agenda. As Jorgen Rasmussen points out, it is often more a question of style than policy content. As a result, cuts in the National Health Service by a Labour government would not immediately be suspect the way exactly the same cuts imposed by a Conservative government would be.

As center-left parties have accepted some of the neoliberal agenda, voters have trusted them to enact those policies. In the Netherlands, Galen Irwin notes that Labor party activists complain that their party is carrying out the program of the rightist VVD. Throughout Europe—Britain, France, Italy, Portugal, Sweden—committed leftists echo that same complaint. And they are correct. In most countries, it has been center-left governments that have reduced state spending on social-welfare policies, cut back on the public sector, and diminished economic regulations. In short, in many settings, the center-right does not benefit from the neoliberal agenda because parties of the left have taken up the same banners. Voters seem more trusting in the ability of these left-wing parties to carry out these changes in a compassionate and fair manner than they are in the center-right's willingness to do so. Voters may be coming to accept the need for sacrificing some of the social benefits and state protections created under the old social democratic consensus. But they want these changes made by parties that seem able to do so without the doctrinal convictions and enthusiasm of the right. A good example is in Britain under Tony Blair's Labour party government: Blair is able to carry out many of the Thatcherite policies of the Conservatives without losing public support because his government is perceived as less tied to the doctrine, more guided by economic necessities, and more caring of the personal costs of their policies than was the Conservative government. The political right may now control the agenda and be the source of policy innovation, but the enactment of these policies "of the right" is more often than not due to the action of center-left governments.

Do Parties Make a Difference?

There is clear evidence in the European democracies we have explored of the spread of a new and common agenda around some but not all neoliberal themes. Differences in the degree of acceptance of the agenda vary more between countries, according to their distinctive historical development and social patterns, than between parties of the left, center, or right within the same country. Party polarization, once a feature of several of these European countries such as France, Italy, and at times Britain, has dropped sharply. The dialogue between parties may often still be intense but the hostilities are generated by personal and historical grudges rather than different and deeply held doctrinal positions.

Party convergence is based on several apparent economic, social, and political "realities." In *Do Parties Make a Difference,* Richard Rose wrote of "something stronger than parties" that limits what changes parties can impose based on their programs and doctrines.[41] Consensus politics is imposed by a variety of forces. Above all, the lack of party differences in conduct comes from the need to respond to a consensual electorate. There are also forces within the parties themselves that limit their ability to impose new doctrines: prudent self-interest that reminds party zealots of what the opposition parties might do in return, internal party divisions, and organizational limitations. Finally, secular forces such as social conditions, shifting public opinion, inertia and bureaucratic procedures, and the effect of events all affect the ability of parties once they are in power to impose their programs, and limit their ability to differentiate themselves from their rivals.

As a result, party differences tend to be subtle. Often the differences are much less evident in party election platforms than they are in actual implementation by different governments. Often the differences in socioeconomic positions are stylistic and symbolic rather than substantive. But style and symbols are important in contemporary politics, not only in election campaigns but in the public's evaluations of government performance. Furthermore, in many but not all of our countries, center-right parties are carving out clear differences on new social issues such as abortion, euthanasia, family issues, immigration and naturalization, law and order, drug use, and so on. They are compelled to do so not only to distinguish themselves from their main rivals on the left but to reply to the challenges from the far right.

Most of our authors, then, maintain that the center-right parties in their countries are different from their left-wing opponents. They claim further that which parties are in office does indeed make a difference in public policy outcomes. Most center-right parties are able to establish clear alternatives, whether substantive or symbolic, at election time even though the consensual nature of their voters places limits on policy differences. These campaign time differences are reflected in differences in public policy. In general, those countries in which clear confrontations occur between government and opposition (Britain, France, Germany, Greece, Portugal, Spain) are more likely to see greater party differences in policy outcomes than those countries in which consensus is traditional (Scandinavia, the Netherlands). Similar conclusions were reached in a recent article by Manfred G. Schmidt, who found that partisan differences were clear in majoritarian democracies but much less clear in consensual democracies.[42]

There is one striking exception to this pattern of subtle but important distinctions between parties of the left and right: policies toward the European Union. As that body grows in importance and power, debates over the EU remain beyond the political parties with only a few exceptions. Divisions on the broad issues of how much unification is desirable cut through parties rather than between them. Divisions over specific EU micro-policies are nearly always buried in the macro-issue of how much integration. For example, the British Conservative party opposed incorporation of the EU social agenda as much on the basis of its opposition to extending the EU's competencies as on ideological grounds. Rarely do such specific issue divisions sort out between parties. The result is that real partisan debate over what the EU is doing is so faulted that this possible means of democratic control over the EU is lost. Almost everything to do with the EU—big decisions on its powers and little decisions on its actual policies—are insulated from partisan politics by the tendency to see the EU as still an aspect of consensual international policy rather than as a domestic political process.

However, with the important exception of European issues, the center-right parties still offer distinctive options to the voters. In an era of converging socioeconomic policies, limitations on government power by growing international considerations, and shifting public opinion, parties remain different and their differences count.

The Future of the Center-Right in Europe

The center-right faces many challenges at the end of the century: changes in socioeconomic structures and cleavages, new party organizational forms, new parties, and in several cases older and or unimaginative leaders. But their principal rivals on the left face similar challenges plus the disadvantage of operating within a possible new consensus unfavorable to the left's traditional values. The center-right parties are among the oldest if not the oldest parties in most of the countries examined. Their durability is a testament to their skills in adjusting to shifting times and needs. Even as the center-right loses in recent major elections in Britain, France, and Italy, it is hard not to be optimistic about their abilities to recover their strength and electoral support.

In most of the countries, except Norway, Sweden, and the newer democracies in Greece and Spain, the parties of the center-right are often successful in conveying the image of being the "natural" or "normal" party of government. Table 10.2 illustrates this governmental predominance of the center-right parties in western Europe. Center-right parties in the Netherlands nearly always are in power. The British Conservative party has governed 75 percent of the time since 1957. It clearly enjoys the distinction of being seen as the natural party of government and it is likely to retain that reputation in spite of its 1997 defeat. The center-right in France, and especially the Gaullists, stand as the "party of order" and "the majority" despite ten years of successful rule under the Socialist François Mitterrand and the Socialists' recent electoral success. In Germany, the CDU/CSU stands predominant, with the SPD at best a part-time alternative when voters see the Christian Democrats as in need of a new leader or a break from governing. Italy's Christian Democrats, long the party of anticommunism with a firm hold on all key ministries, have collapsed, but it is not unlikely that new center-right movements may emerge to reclaim the mantle of the natural party of government. This public standing as the natural governing parties serves well the persistence of the center-right.

266

Table 10.2 Center-Right Presence in Government, 1957–1997

| | | Number of Years Center-Right Held Power | | | |
	Absolute Majority	Center-Right Hegemony	Coalition Including the Center-Right	Total Years	Percentage of Time
Britain	30			30	75
France	22	4	4	30	75
Germany		24	3	27	68
Italy		31	6	37	93
The Netherlands	32		4	36	90
Norway	2		14	16	40
Portugal (since 1974)	8	7	1	16	70
Spain (since 1975)		9	1	10	45
Sweden	5		4	9	23

Notes: Absolute majority: when principal parties of the center-right held a majority on their own.

Hegemony: when principal parties of the center-right held control but shared it with others, e.g., the FDP in Germany or cohabitation in France.

Coalition: when the principal parties of the center-right shared control in a broader coalition including center or left-of-center parties or when the center-right ruled in minority governments.

The neoliberal agenda is certainly a help to the center-right even if it not a guarantee of electoral success. The center-right's ideas set the agenda for politics in most countries, and even when their ideas are rejected, they are discussed seriously by friends and foes alike.

The major threat in most west European countries is the menace posed by the extreme right. Resurgent again after nearly 50 years of postwar eclipse and boosted by their willingness to take extreme positions on new issues, the new radical right threatens the mainstream center-right's electoral base. Its populism even endangers the neoliberal agenda in ways that the traditional center-left cannot. Its nationalism appeals to citizens wary of further entanglement in ever-wider and more intense European integration. In such settings, the center-right now faces its most serious threat since the fascism of the 1920s and 1930s. Even those of us whose political hopes lie to the left must hope that the center-right rises to this challenge and overcomes it.

Notes

1. Seymour M. Lipset and Stein Rokkan, eds., *Party Systems and Voter Alignments: Cross- National Perspectives* (New York: The Free Press, 1967), pp. 1–64.

2. See for example, Russell J. Dalton, *Citizen Politics: Public Opinion and Political Parties in Advanced Western Democracies,* 2nd ed. (Chatham, NJ: Chatham House, 1996), pp. 176–185. See also Jan-Erik Lane and Svante O. Ersson, *Politics and Society in Western Europe,* 2nd ed. (London: Sage, 1991), pp. 64–73.

3. Dalton, *Citizen Politics,* pp. 167–176; Lane and Ersson, *Politics and Society in Western Europe,* pp. 91–96. See also Ronald Inglehart, *Modernization and Postmodernization: Cultural, Economic, and Political Change in 43 Societies* (Princeton, NJ: Princeton University Press, 1997), pp. 252–257.

4. Lane and Ersson, *Politics and Society in Western Europe,* pp. 166–173.

5. Bernadette C. Hayes, "The Impact of Class on Political Attitudes: A Comparative Study of Great Britain, West Germany, Australia, and the United States," *European Journal of Political Research* 29 (January 1995): 69–91.

6. See for example, R. T. McKenzie and A. Silver, *Angels in Marble: Working Class Conservatives in Urban England* (London: Heinemann, 1968).

7. Otto Kirchheimer, "The Transformation of the Western European Party Systems," in Joseph LaPalombara and Myron Weiner, eds., *Political Parties and Political Development* (Princeton, NJ: Princeton University Press, 1966).

8. Ronald Inglehart, *Culture Shift in Advanced Industrial Society* (Princeton, NJ: Princeton University Press, 1990), pp. 248–288; Inglehart, *Modernization and Postmodernization,* pp. 256- 265.

9. Inglehart, *Modernization and Postmodernization,* p. 251.

10. Scott C. Flanagan, "Value Change and Industrial Society," *American Political Science Review* 81 (December 1987): 1303–1319.

11. Maurice Duverger, *Political Parties* (New York: Wiley, 1963).

12. Party membership decline as a percentage of the electorate has affected nearly all parties. See Richard S. Katz and Peter Mair, et al., "The Membership of Political Parties in European Democracies 1960–1990," *European Journal of Political Research* 22 (October 1992): 329–345.

13. Richard S. Katz, "Party as Linkage: A Vestigal Function," *European Journal of Political Research* 18 (January 1990): 143–161.

14. Richard S. Katz and Peter Mair, "Changing Models of Party Organization and Party Democracy," *Party Politics* 1:1 (1995): 5–28. For a critique of the notion of cartel parties, see Ruud Kool, "Cadre, Catch-all or Cartel: A Comment on the Notion of the Cartel Party," *Party Politics* 2:4 (1996): 507–523.

15. Peter Mair, "Popular Legitimacy and Public Privilege," *West European Politics* 18 (July 1995): 40–57.

16. Arthur B. Gunlicks, ed., *Campaign and Party Finances in North America and Western Europe* (Boulder, CO: Westview, 1993); Herbert E. Alexander, ed., *Comparative Political Finance in the 1980s* (Cambridge, England: Cambridge University Press, 1989).

17. Richard S. Katz and Peter Mair, eds., *Party Organizations: A Data Handbook* (London: Sage, 1992), p. 385.

18. See Gordon Smith's argument that the German parties are leaders in developing these features: "The Party System at the Crossroads," in Gordon Smith, William E. Paterson, and Stephen Padgett, eds., *Developments in German Politics 2* (Durham, NC: Duke University Press, 1996), pp. 71–75.

19. Jörg Sesselberg, "Conditions of Success and Political Problems of a Media-Mediated Personality-Party: The Case of Forza Italia," *West European Politics* 19 (October 1996): 715–743.

20. See Angelo Panebianco, *Political Parties: Organization and Power* (Cambridge, England: Cambridge University Press, 1988), pp. 222–235, 262–274.

21. Robert H. Aldrich, *Why Parties? The Origin and Transformation of Party Politics in America* (Chicago: University of Chicago Press, 1995).

22. See especially Katz and Mair, "Changing Models."

23. Paul D. Webb, "Party Organizational Change in Britain: The Iron Law of Centralization?" in *How Parties Organize: Change and Adaptation in Party Organizations in Western Democracies,* Richard S. Katz and Peter Mair, eds. (London: Sage, 1994), p. 129.

24. See Kay Lawson and Peter H. Merkl, eds., *When Parties Fail: Emerging Alternative Organizations* (Princeton: Princeton University Press, 1988; Russell J. Dalton, Scott C. Flanagan, and Paul Allen Beck, eds., *Electoral Change in Advanced Industrial Democracies: Realignment or Dealignment?* (Princeton, NJ: Princeton University Press, 1984); and Russell J. Dalton and Manfred Kuechler, eds., *Challenging the Poltical Order: New Social and Political Movements in Western Democracies* (London: Polity Press, 1990).

25. Thomas Poguntke, "Anti-Party Sentiments—Conceptual Thoughts and Empirical Evidence: Explorations Into a Minefield," *European Journal of Political Research* 30 (April 1996): 319–344.

26. Gordon Smith, "The Party System at the Crossroads," p. 55.

27. See for example Herbert Kitschelt, *The Radical Right in Western Europe: A Comparative Analysis* (Ann Arbor, MI: University of Michigan Press, 1995), and Hans-Georg Betz, *Radical Right-Wing Populism in Western Europe* (New York: St. Martin's, 1994).

28. Inglehart, *Modernization and Postmodernization,* pp. 243–252.

29. Frank L. Wilson, "The Sources of Party Change: The Social Democratic Parties of Britain, France, Germany, and Spain," in *How Political Parties Work: Perspectives From Within,* Kay Lawson, ed., (Westport, CT: Praeger, 1994).

30. Harvey G. Simmons, *The French National Front: The Extremist Challenge to Democracy* (Boulder, CO: Westview Press, 1996), p. 106.

31. James G. Shields, "*La Politique du Pire:* The Front National and the 1997 Legislative Elections," *French Politics and Society* 15 (Summer 1997): 21–36.

32. See Shields, "*La Politique du pire.*"

33. *Le Nouvel Observateur,* July 10–16, 1997.

34. Frank L. Wilson, *The Failure of West European Communism: Implications for the Future* (New York: Paragon, 1993).

35. See for example, Friedrich von Hayek, *The Constitution of Liberty* (London: Routledge and Kegan Paul, 1960), *Law, Legislation and Liberty,* volumes 1, 2, 3 (London: Routledge and Kegan Paul, 1973. 1976, 1979), and *A Tiger by the Tail* (London: Institute of Economic Affairs, 1978).

36. See Milton Friedman, *Capitalism and Freedom* (Chicago: University of Chicago Press, 1960).

37. Milton Friedman and Anna J. Schwartz, *A Monetary History of the United States* (Princeton, NJ: Princeton University Press, 1963).

38. For analytical studies of neoliberal political thought, see Stephen Newman, *Liberalism at Wits' End* (Ithaca, NY: Cornell University Press, 1984), Desmond S. King, *The New Right: Politics, Markets and Citizenship* (Chicago: The Dorsey Press, 1987), and Robert E. Goodin, "Vulnerabilities and Responsibilities: An Ethical Defense of the Welfare State," *American Political Science Review* 79 (September 1985): 775–787. See also a radical left critique in Henk Overbeek, ed., *Restructuring Hegemony in the Global Political Economy: The Rise of Transnational Neo-Liberalism in the 1980s* (London: Routledge, 1993).

39. See Dennis Kavanagh, *Thatcherism and British Politics: The End of Consensus?* (Oxford, England: Oxford University Press, 1987), and Dennis Kavanagh and Anthony Seldon, eds., *The Thatcher Effect: A Decade of Change* (Oxford, England: Oxford University Press, 1989).

40. See Barry Cooper, Allan Kornberg, and William Mishler, eds., *The Resurgence of Conservatism in Anglo-American Democracies* (Durham, NC: Duke University Press, 1988), and Desmond S. King, *The New Right: Politics, Markets, and Citizenship* (Chicago: The Dorsey Press, 1987).

41. Richard Rose, *Do Parties Make a Difference?* 2nd ed. (Chatham, NJ: Chatham House, 1984).

42. Manfred G. Schmidt, "When Parties Matter: A Review of the Possibilities and Limits of Partisan Influence on Public Policy," *European Journal of Political Research* 30 (September 1996): 155–183.

Contributors

William Chandler teaches at the University of California, San Diego. His publications include: *Public Policy and Provincial Politics, Federalism and the Role of the State* and *Challenges to Federalism: Policy-Making in Canada and West Germany,* as well as journal articles and book chapters on party government, Christian democracy, party system change, and immigration politics. Chandler's current research interests focus on the politics of German unification, transitions to democracy, and immigration/citizenship issues. He also has been a visiting professor in Germany at Tuebingen and Oldenburg Universities.

Maria Theresa Frain is currently living in Moscow where she is learning Russian and researching regionalism in the Russian Federation.

M. Donald Hancock received his Ph.D. at Columbia University and is Professor of Political Science and Director of the Center for European Studies at Vanderbilt University. He is the author of *West Germany: The Politics of Democratic Corporatism* (1989) and co- author of *Industrial Renewal and Workplace Democracy in the United States and Western Europe* (1992), *German Unification: Process and Outcomes* (1994), and *Politics in Western Europe,* 2nd ed. (1998).

Galen A. Irwin was educated at the University of Kansas and Florida State University. He taught at the University of Iowa before moving to Leiden University in 1973. He publishes work on political parties and elections, focusing primarily on the Netherlands.

Stathis N. Kalyvas is an Assistant Professor in the Department of Politics at New York University. He is author of *The Rise of Christian Democracy in Europe* (Cornell University Press). His work has appeared in *Politics and Society, Comparative Politics,* and *Comparative Political Studies.*

Jorgen Rasmussen is Distinguished Professor of Political Science at Iowa State University. One of the founders of the British Politics Group, he served as its Executive Secretary for two decades. His books and journal articles have focused on the British Parliament, parties, and land elections. Since 1970, he has co-authored *Major European Governments* (Wadsworth).

Lars Svåsand is Professor of Comparative Politics at the University of Bergen. He has published work on Norwegian and Scandinavian political parties. His latest publication is *Challenges to Political Parties: The Case of Norway* (University of Michigan Press), co-edited with Kaare Strom.

Howard Wiarda is Professor of Political Science and Comparative Labor Relations and the Leonard J. Horwitz Professor of Iberian and Latin American

Studies at the University of Massachusetts, Amherst. He is also Senior Associate at the Center for Strategic and International Studies (CSIS) in Washington, D.C. His most recent books include *American Foreign Policy, Introduction to Comparative Politics, Latin American Politics and Development* 4th edition, *Politics in Iberia: The Political Systems of Spain and Portugal,* and *Corporatism and Comparative Politics.*

Frank L. Wilson is Professor and Head of the Department of Political Science at Purdue University. He is the author of numerous books and articles on French political parties and interest groups. Wilson's most recent book is *Concepts and Issues in Comparative Politics* (Prentice-Hall).

Dwayne Woods is Associate Professor of Political Science at Purdue University. He has published numerous articles on European and African politics, with a particular focus on social movements. His research interests are Western European and Sub-Saharan African politics. Woods is currently working on a book entitled, *The Reconstitution of the Italian Right.*

Index